Human Rights Interventions

Series Editors
Chiseche Mibenge
Stanford University
Stanford, CA, USA

Irene Hadiprayitno
Leiden University
Leiden, Zuid-Holland, The Netherlands

The traditional human rights frame creates a paradigm by which the duty bearer's (state) and rights holder's (civil society organizations) interests collide over the limits of enjoyment and enforcement. The series departs from the paradigm by centering peripheral yet powerful actors that agitate for intervention and influence in the (re)shaping of rights discourse in the midst of grave insecurities. The series privileges a call and response between theoretical inquiry and empirical investigation as contributors critically assess human rights interventions mediated by spatial, temporal, geopolitical and other dimensions. An interdisciplinary dialogue is key as the editors encourage multiple approaches such as law and society, political economy, historiography, legal ethnography, feminist security studies, and multi-media.

More information about this series at
http://www.palgrave.com/gp/series/15595

Moira Lynch

Human Rights Prosecutions in Democracies at War

palgrave
macmillan

Moira Lynch
Department of Political Science
Loyola University Maryland
Baltimore, MD, USA

Human Rights Interventions
ISBN 978-3-030-07268-1 ISBN 978-3-319-96908-4 (eBook)
https://doi.org/10.1007/978-3-319-96908-4

Softcover re-print of the Hardcover 1st edition 2019

Cover design by Fatima Jamadar

This Palgrave Macmillan imprint is published by the registered company Springer Nature Switzerland AG
The registered company address is: Gewerbestrasse 11, 6330 Cham, Switzerland

Acknowledgments

The long journey of this book began when, while studying abroad in Dublin, I took a bus to Northern Ireland to travel on my own. I was enrolled in a Northern Ireland Politics course at University College Dublin and I was enthralled, but I had so many unanswered questions about the conflict and the role of justice in it. Many people in Belfast and Derry generously gave their time to meet with me during that visit and what I thought I knew or understood about the conflict gradually unraveled while I was there. Three years later, I returned and attended a meeting on the Donegal coast, where former combatants and survivors talked about their own conceptions of justice during war. After this, I never looked back.

As my early questions about the role of justice in war evolved into graduate study and this book, I was incredibly fortunate to have the guidance, love, and support from many extraordinary people. First, I wish to thank my PhD advisor, Kathryn Sikkink. Kathryn provided unparalleled mentorship to me in graduate school and served as an incredibly wise and thoughtful guide as I navigated the professional world. Since completing my PhD, there are countless times where I think back on advice and direction that Kathryn provided to me while I was a student, and for all of this, I am incredibly grateful. I also wish to thank Ron Krebs, Lisa Hilbink, Fionnuala Ní Aoláin, and David Samuels, who provided ample feedback, generosity, and support throughout graduate school.

I am equally indebted to a wonderful group of graduate school friends. I was fortunate to be a part of a dissertation writing group whose members brought both sharp editing and a sense of humor to each meeting—many thanks to Ralitsa Donkova, Denis Kennedy, Verónica Michel, Darrah McCracken, and Giovanni Mantilla. I am also grateful to the following dear people for their friendship: Libby Sharrow, Caitlin Dwyer, Caleb Goltz, David Forrest, Matt Hindman, Adriano Udani, Henriet Hendricks, Kjersten Nelson, Eve Ringsmuth, Jonneke Koomen, Brooke Coe, Serena Laws, Isaac Kamola, and to those in Belfast and beyond, Catherine Ross, Elizabeth Super, Catherine O'Rourke, and Aisling Swaine.

I am grateful for the valuable feedback I received on chapters of the book during panels at the Law and Society Association and the International Studies Association conferences. Deep gratitude also goes to those who read my work over the years: Bridget Marchesi, Nadya Nedelsky, Giovanni Mantilla, the members of the Loyola University Maryland Junior Faculty Symposium, Carsten Vala and Janine Holc. Many thanks to my colleague, Doug Harris, for his kind and dedicated mentorship throughout the book writing process. I am also indebted to my editor, Anca Pusca, Katelyn Zingg, and the two anonymous reviewers for their guidance and thoughtful feedback.

The writing of this book was made possible through several institutional grants. I was fortunate to complete field work in Northern Ireland with support from the Transitional Justice Institute Research Fellowship (University of Ulster/University of Minnesota Law School) and I was generously supported by the Oñati International Institute for the Sociology of Law (Gipuzkoa, Spain) to complete my field work in the Basque region. My field work in Sri Lanka was made possible through the University of Minnesota's Scholarly Travel Grants and the Doctoral Dissertation Fellowship. Finally, I am very grateful for the generous research grants I received at Loyola University Maryland. Two summer research grants awarded by the Office of Research and Sponsored Programs enabled me to collect data for the Colombian chapter and to pursue field work there in 2015.

I am inspired and emboldened by a nurturing community of family and friends who continually ground me and remind me of the existence of hope in the midst of so much sorrow. Immeasurable gratitude to the friends who have known me the longest and who I still turn to in times of joy and despair: Carissa Kountantzis, Sarah Flanagan, and Shana Tabak. Thank you to my Minnesota community (both then and now): Holly Hinman, Erik Swenson, Kristen Murray, Bryan Kennedy, Benjamin Roberts, Jessica Minutaglio, Leah Boudreaux, and Lisa Damon. I am also grateful to loved ones in Baltimore for their friendship and support, many of whom have also shared their amazing children with our family: Heather Heiman, Piotr Brzozowski, Stevie Oliver, Tony Oliver, Katie Robinson, Josh Kermond, Whitney Cecil, Jacob Cecil, Meg Smith Aeschliman, Adrien Aeschliman, Erica Wood, Matt Wood, Tim Clark, Lucia Perfetti Clark, Joshua Hendrick, Leah Hendrick, Michelle Gawerc and Melissa Girard. Finally, a tremendous thank you to my students at Loyola University Maryland, who continually inspire and challenge me to reflect on peace and justice issues in new ways every year.

This book is also a product of the deep and constant love I receive from my family, who have shaped me in more ways than I can count. Thank you to my parents, Kate and John Lynch, Tim, Piper, Delaney and Tabitha. I am also grateful to Bill and Edna Bush, Heather Qualy, Bryan Qualy, Alma Qualy-Godinez, Jen and Jack Schneider, Richard Bush and all my nieces and nephews.

Lastly, this book is dedicated to William, Finnian, and Winona. There is nothing sweeter than returning home to you. I love you.

Contents

Abbreviations

AAA	Alianza Apostólica Anticomunista
ALJ	Association for Legal Justice
AUC	Autodefensas Unidas de Colombia
BVE	Batallón Vasco-Español
CAJ	Committee on the Administration of Justice
CAT	Convention Against Torture
CCJ	Colombian Commission of Jurists
CESID	Centro Superior de Información de la Defensa
COI	Commission of Inquiry
CSJ	Consejo Superior de la Judicatura (CSJ)
DPP	Director of Public Prosecutions
ECHR	European Convention on Human Rights
ED	Extrema Derecha
ELN	Ejército de Liberación Nacional
EPA	Emergency Provisions Act (Northern Ireland)
EPL	Ejército Popular de Liberación
ERs	Emergency Regulations
ETA	Euskadi Ta Askatasuna
FARC	Fuerzas Armadas Revolucionarias de Colombia
GAE	Grupos Armados Españoles
GAL	Grupos Antiterroristas Liberación
HET	Historical Enquiries Team
ICCPR	International Covenant on Civil and Political Rights
ICRC	International Committee for the Red Cross
IIGEP	International Independent Group of Eminent Persons
IRA	Irish Republican Army
JPL	Justice and Peace Law

JVP	Janatha Vimukthi Peramuna
LLRC	Lessons Learnt and Reconciliation Commission
LTTE	Liberation Tigers of Tamil Eelam
M-19	Movimiento 19 de Abril
MP	Member of Parliament
NCCL	National Council on Civil Liberties
NGOs	Non-governmental organizations
NICRA	Northern Ireland Civil Rights Association
PA	People's Alliance Party
PNV	Partido Nacionalista Vasco
PP	Partido Popular
PSNI	Police Service Northern Ireland
PSO	Public Security Ordinance
PSOE	Partido Socialista Obrero Español
PTA 1974	Prevention of Terrorism Act (Northern Ireland)
PTA 1979	Prevention of Terrorism (Temporary Provisions) Act (Sri Lanka)
PIICs	Public Interest Immunity Certificates
RUC	Royal Ulster Constabulary
SLFP	Sri Lanka Freedom Party
SPA	1922 Civil Authorities (Special Powers) Act (Northern Ireland)
TULF	Tamil United Liberation Front
UCDP	Uppsala Conflict Data Program
UDR	Ulster Defense Regiment
UK	United Kingdom
UNHRC	United Nations Human Rights Committee
UNP	United National Party
UP	Unión Patriótica

List of Graphs

List of Tables

CHAPTER 1

Introduction

In the summer of 2015, I sat with Padre Alberto Franco in the offices of Comisión Intereclesial de Justicia y Paz to discuss the use of emergency law in Colombia's war. Padre Franco compared the power of the military via emergency decrees in guerilla-controlled regions to a method of *eliminar el agua de los peces*, or removing the water (civil society) from the fish (guerillas). He explained to me that the emergency laws gave legal support to the state's logic by which the internal enemy, suspected guerillas in civil society, was viewed as having no rights.[1] For Padre Franco, the war was fundamentally against civil society and the devastatingly high number of civilian deaths reflects this reality. The picture Padre Franco paints is not uncommon to war zones. Emergency laws foster various forms of rights violations. But Padre Franco also highlighted one of the most significant aspects of these laws: they support a particular logic, one that serves to legitimize actions taken by the state against civilians during conflict. When citizens pursued human rights prosecutions during the Colombian conflict, the state and the military fell back on this logic, using the legitimizing force of law to defend all actions taken in the service of war.

A few years prior to my conversation with Padre Franco, I discovered a similar link between justice efforts and emergency legislation during my field research in Sri Lanka, Northern Ireland, and Spain. My research in these countries focused on how human rights prosecutions were held during armed conflict and why at particular moments. Many of the

M. Lynch, *Human Rights Prosecutions in Democracies at War*,
Human Rights Interventions,
https://doi.org/10.1007/978-3-319-96908-4_1

people I interviewed about human rights prosecutions pointed to the ways in which emergency and anti-terrorism laws restricted investigations of state violence. Certainly, I had expected to find that citizens who sought justice during a war would confront a host of barriers to their efforts. What was most surprising was the extent to which these laws were specifically designed or manipulated to protect state actors from prosecution. Additionally, when I began to trace the origin and evolution of emergency laws across the cases, evidence of resistance emerged. Victims and their families, political actors, human rights attorneys, and members of the judiciary challenged these laws, and the logic of impunity within them, throughout the conflict. The story of human rights prosecutions in democracies at war has not yet been told. This book carefully documents how, within such a highly restrictive environment, citizens sought justice for state violations, and it explains the conditions that made these efforts possible.[2]

The use of justice processes, such as human rights prosecutions and truth commissions, on a global scale is a relatively new phenomenon. A surge in justice mechanisms accompanied the third wave of democratization, and since this time, the burgeoning field of transitional justice has analyzed why some countries pursue justice while others do not. One of the least understood realms of this scholarship involves the pursuit of justice in democracies experiencing internal armed conflict. Though democracies have often been included in large-n studies and comparative case study research that examines the conditions for justice, much of this work employs theories only relevant to post-authoritarian and post-conflict countries.[3] These theories provide explanations for how and why justice is sought *after* a period of violence or repression has largely ended. In democracies at war, in contrast, a number of prosecutions have been held *during* the conflict.

Since human rights prosecutions were held during the conflict in these cases, the level of violence may explain whether and when state actors are investigated for serious abuses. Higher numbers of civilian deaths tend to correlate with fewer domestic prosecutions.[4] Based on this notion, Sri Lanka and Colombia, two countries that endured civilian deaths numbering in the tens of thousands, would be expected to have similar experiences in the realm of justice efforts: few or no prosecutions during the war. Yet, the pattern of prosecutions in these two cases is quite different. First, several prosecutions were held in both cases. Second, the record of prosecutions is actually quite different between the two cases. During Sri

Lanka's armed conflict, 211 state actors, including military personnel, politicians, and police, were prosecuted in 22 separate trials for human rights abuses. During Colombia's civil war, 1073 state actors were prosecuted in 210 separate trials. Colombia prosecuted five times the number of state actors and held close to ten times the number of human rights prosecutions than those in Sri Lanka. Third, prosecutions in both cases do not emerge when the violence begins to wane. In Colombia, for example, prosecutions increase during some of the most violent periods of the war. Thus, the level or scope of violence does not help us to understand patterns of prosecution in these cases.

Alternatively, the timing of prosecutions in democracies at war might be explained by changes in political leadership during the conflict. In other words, it may be possible to predict the timing of human rights prosecutions as government officials assume power and, in order to retain power, attempt to punish their predecessors.[5] Empirical evidence gathered for this book demonstrates, however, that this is not a common thread across the cases. Sri Lanka is an exception, and yet, the small number of prosecutions that are held under President Kumaratunga's administration addresses crimes committed by her predecessor *and* crimes committed during her tenure. In the other three cases, human rights prosecutions are largely implemented by administrations that are responsible for the crimes. For example, in Spain, investigations and prosecutions concerning torture and extra judicial killings conducted during the Partido Socialista Obrero Español (PSOE) administration transpire while the political party is still in power. In Northern Ireland, prosecutions for civilian deaths caused by British armed forces stationed in the region were conducted throughout several years of Conservative Party rule in England. A careful analysis of the political conditions prompting prosecutions reveals that most often prosecutions do not emanate from the will of political officials.

Research on during-conflict justice, which examines the conditions under which justice processes are used as a conflict tactic by governments and rebel groups, has found that democracies are more likely than anocracies and autocracies to enact trials and that this is likely a reflection of domestic audience costs and the fact that international commitments will have a stronger impact on democratic governments. Democratic governments typically respect the rule of law, they are more likely to comply with international law during internal armed conflict, and they tend to have higher rates of judicial independence.[6] Yet, prosecution trends vary across democracies at war, and within individual cases, prosecutions are not a constant throughout the conflict. Explanations that frame justice-seeking efforts as a conflict tactic miss the agency of other key actors who are advocating for justice. Prosecutions are not solely a government or rebel group calculation. On the contrary, prosecutions often emerge and are made possible through the actions of ordinary citizens, civil society organizations, and those working in the legal and judicial sectors.[7]

Human rights prosecutions for serious human rights violations were held in Sri Lanka, Northern Ireland, Spain, and Colombia during their internal armed conflicts. There are currently no theoretical arguments that explain variation in the use of prosecutions in these cases, nor are there explanations for why prosecutions are held at particular moments as opposed to others during the war. Additionally, democracies at war have never been examined on their own in isolation from other cases of conflict.

The Universe of Cases: Democracies at War

Relying on data from the Armed Conflict Dataset (1946–2014)[8] created by the Uppsala Conflict Data Program/Peace Research Institute Oslo (UCDP/PRIO), and Polity IV dataset scores,[9] this book identified eight cases of democracies at war. The book focuses on those conflicts coded by UCDP/PRIO as a "3" (internal armed conflict). The UCDP/PRIO Armed Conflict Dataset defines internal armed conflict as "a contested incompatibility that concerns government and/or territory where the use of armed force between two parties, of which at least one is the government of a state, results in at least 25 battle-related deaths" per year. Polity IV dataset scores (1946–2014)[10] were then matched with the conflict years coded in the Armed Conflict Dataset.[11] The Polity Score assesses regime authority on a 21-point scale ranging from −10 to +10. Polity codes countries with scores between +6 and +10 as "democracies." Eight countries had a Polity rating between +6 and +10 during their conflict years. In order to capture the variability in democratic governance across these cases, they are categorized one step further. Human rights practices employed within a country appear to improve only after democracies reach a certain threshold, equal to 8 on the −10 to 10 Polity scale.[12] Two groups of democracies at war were identified based on this threshold (see Table 1.1): four high-quality democracies at war (Polity Scores = +8 to +10) and four low-quality democracies at war (Polity Scores = +6 to +7).

A few democracies at war have multiple cases of internal armed conflict. For example, the Philippines suffered three different types of intrastate conflict since 1946 that include various factions opposed to the govern-

Table 1.1 Democracies at war

	Conflict years (UCDP/PRIO)	*Polity scores during conflict*
High-quality democracies		
Israel	1949–present	9 and 10
Philippines	1987–present	8
Spain	1978–1991	9 and 10
United Kingdom (Northern Ireland)	1971–1998	10
Low-quality democracies		
Colombia	1964–present	7, 8, and 9
India	1950–present	7, 8, and 9
Sri Lanka	1984–2009	5 and 6
Turkey	1984–present	7, 8, and 9

ment: a Communist insurgent group, a separatist movement in Mindanao, and several military coups.[13] But it was only since 1987 that the Philippines experienced armed conflict under democratic governance. India has also faced several forms of internal conflict since the early years of independence. The conflict years coded in the table only include years in which, according to Polity ratings, democratic governance was consistently held. In this case, consistent means that every conflict year listed in the table was given a score between 6 and 10.

The book examines four democracies at war: Sri Lanka, Northern Ireland, Colombia, and Spain. The four countries were selected for their variation in democratic governance and to test the expectation that high-quality democracies would have stronger justice outcomes compared with low-quality democracies. The four cases represent two high-quality (Spain and Northern Ireland) and two low-quality (Sri Lanka and Colombia) democracies at war. The cases were also selected based on the fact that in each country, one central conflict, as opposed to multiple types of wars (e.g., India and the Philippines), transpired during democratic governance.

Sri Lanka is an interesting case in that its Polity score alternated between 5 and 6 during the conflict years. It is a country that faces enormous challenges, yet never succumbs to full authoritarian governance or state failure, like so many other conflicts. One of the key findings of this book is that low-quality democratic governance does not fully explain rates or patterns of human rights prosecutions. For example, though Sri Lanka and Colombia are categorized as low- quality democracies, Colombia has the strongest record of human rights prosecutions compared to the other three cases. Additionally, though both cases include wars with high levels of violence, increasing or decreasing rates of violence do not explain why, after years of impunity in Sri Lanka, human rights prosecutions are held in the 1990s. Sri Lanka is a case worthy of deeper examination in that, despite a highly constraining emergency institution, there were moments of justice during the war.

The majority of conflict cases in the world occur in non-democratic settings. Out of a total of 92 countries that experienced internal armed conflict in the last three decades, democracies at war comprise only 8% of the total. Why study these cases when they appear to be highly unusual phenomena? Most of the countries in this book have legacies of violence that are familiar, either because of their presence in the news cycle or because they occurred under the leadership of some of the most powerful and influential governments in recent history. There has also been a great deal of external support to both the governments and the non-state armed actors in these wars. In other words, there is an investment from many sectors of the international community in the stakes of these conflicts and their outcomes. Yet, beyond single-case analyses, these countries have never been analyzed together in this manner. This book demonstrates that comparative research on how a democratic state is held to account by its own citizens in the midst of a violent war reveals several important and surprising parallels. Additionally, the book depicts how citizens, that presumably have more resources at their disposal than victims confronting abuse in a dictatorship, face unique and significant barriers to justice. What explains the variable patterns of prosecution across democracies at war?

The Relationship Between Emergency Laws and Human Rights Prosecutions

The enactment of emergency legislation by both non-democratic and democratic governments is incredibly common. When confronting a serious crisis within their own borders, governments typically declare a state of emergency and enact various related measures to control the situation. Human rights law jurisprudence generally defines "emergency" as an exceptional and temporary situation of crisis that constitutes a threat to the state, in which measures taken must be proportionate to the scale of the crisis.[14] The experience of emergencies within states, however, is typically far from temporary; emergency legislation often remains on the books for years or decades. Despite the incongruence between legal definitions of "emergency" and the reality of these situations in many countries, international human rights law establishes certain provisions for how governments can adopt emergency measures during periods of crisis. Under Article 4, paragraph 2, of the International Covenant on Civil and Political Rights (ICCPR), states are permitted to derogate from protecting certain rights, meaning they are able to temporarily place restrictions on citizens' civil rights, normally protected by international law, when they are confronting an internal conflict or emergency.[15]

The effects of emergency legislation on the power and operation of the executive, legislature, and judiciary have been carefully documented,[16] and there is significant scholarly evidence of the ways in which emergency laws weaken human rights protections.[17] In response to the surge in emergency and counter-terrorism measures wielded by states in recent years, legal scholars have examined whether and how these laws can be reconciled with the norms and institutions of democracy and how, when human rights violations are committed by the state, these actors might be held to account. Government accountability could be better ensured if international juridical bodies applied International Humanitarian Law (IHL)[18] more often to situations of internal armed conflict.[19] The European Court of Human Rights, the Inter-American Court of Human Rights, the United Nations Human Rights Committee, and the United Nations Human Rights Council have the power to assess the use of emergency powers by governments. Yet, international human rights bodies tend to avoid applying IHL when assessing situations of internal conflict for fear that it will entail moving beyond their mandated focus on the separate legal regime of international human rights law.[20]

Human rights bodies tend to rely on the government's assessment of the nature and status of the conflict they are experiencing, which further reduces the likelihood that government accountability will be enforced by external actors. State actors are, unsurprisingly, reluctant to apply IHL to their own situation because they are eager to avoid having to commit to extra obligations and they hope to avoid prosecution for human rights violations. But, even if international courts or other human rights bodies did apply IHL, or at least consider it more often in their decisions, pursuing government accountability through the enforcement of IHL remains highly challenging.[21] Common Article 3 is the most likely instrument of IHL to be applied by international bodies, given it has the lowest threshold for determining whether an internal armed conflict exists. In the end, however, identifying what forms of violence qualify as an armed conflict remains extremely difficult for external bodies.[22] This then begs the question, how might government accountability be addressed at the local level?

Legal scholars have debated the merits of several possible models of emergency power as a means to gauge how and whether these laws can be squared with the rule of law in democratic societies and to assess how state actors may be held accountable if they abuse these powers during a crisis. At one end of the spectrum, constitutional relativism promotes the notion that the executive possesses constitutionally based authority to undertake discretionary emergency action. There is no provision within this model for containing the potentially vast authority of the executive during a crisis, and thus the outcome in this scenario is akin to what some refer to as "rule by law" instead of "rule of law."[23] Another model of emergency power, in contrast, supports the existence of extra-legal emergency measures during a crisis as long as they are clearly distinct from and outside the ordinary system of laws. Measures to hold the government accountable for abuses committed during an emergency are developed ex post facto within this model.[24] However, the prospect of holding state actors to account after the conflict has ended may be slim given that following the crisis, the executive could change the rules to ensure immunity from prosecution.[25]

A third model, that of common law emergency oversight, argues that the judiciary should be tasked with subjecting emergency measures to scrutiny and holding state officials accountable where appropriate.[26] Yet, if the executive has applied pressure on the courts, the specific possibilities for judicial scrutiny during conflict are lessened because the courts are no longer functioning as a neutral institution safeguarding the rule of law. Placing the bulk of responsibility for government accountability on the courts, without clear provisions for horizontal accountability, is also fairly shortsighted considering both the legislature and the executive may be uncooperative, or they may try to obstruct judicial proceedings.

Finally, legal formalists argue that accountability can best be ensured if ex ante legal guidelines are established within emergency powers that prevent the blurring of ordinary and emergency laws and operate to contain unilateral power within the executive.[27] Within this model, constitutional provisions are used to determine when and how emergency measures are implemented before a crisis emerges. This model promotes the notion that the potential for unilateral executive action can be better contained if provisions limiting executive power are in place prior to the crisis.

In addition to these models, there is a vast literature that questions the aspiration to hold state actors to account within the context of emergency powers. The suspension of ordinary law often common to a period of emergency is argued to create a "juridical void" in which it is impossible to clearly define the "legal consequences of those acts committed" during the crisis.[28] Accountability is seen as elusive under emergency powers because it is difficult to legally regulate an exceptional time; it is not possible to anticipate future emergencies and determine how best to manage them since they emerge as necessities and necessity has no law.[29]

The argument that pursuing accountability is a considerable challenge during an emergency, if not meaningless altogether, suggests that emergency laws can be powerful tools of avoidance for governments that have committed human rights violations. However, this approach fails to explain the fact that human rights prosecutions were *not* absent in Sri Lanka, Northern Ireland, Spain, and Colombia. State actors were prosecuted for various crimes, including extra-judicial killings, disappearances, and torture, and these prosecutions transpired during the conflict, while emergency laws were in place. Though ordinary law may be subordinated to emergency law during a crisis, prosecution data collected for this book demonstrates that citizens relied on ordinary criminal law (e.g., murder or manslaughter charges) to hold state actors to account. Understanding why and when domestic criminal law operated to support human rights prosecutions is therefore essential for parsing the ways in which emergency law coexists with or dampens ordinary law. International human rights law was also a key tool employed by citizens and their legal representatives for holding state actors accountable domestically and at regional human rights courts. It is not appropriate to simply assume that a legal vacuum will always manifest in the presence of emergency laws. Despite the constraining power of emergency legislation, citizens harnessed domestic and international law to pursue justice in democracies at war.

Emergency and anti-terrorism legislation protects state actors from judicial scrutiny and often liability for human rights abuses. It is not the only institution that has the power to protect state actors. A corrupt judicial system may also prevent victims and their families from obtaining a full investigation of violations committed by the state. This book argues, however, that examining emergency laws is necessary for understanding justice in democracies at war for two important reasons. First, empirical evidence from the four cases in this book demonstrates that governments are more often held to account for human rights abuses when emergency laws are abolished altogether or the laws are altered in such a way that the provisions fostering impunity are weakened or amended. Second, this book documents how emergency legislation can directly produce conditions that promote impunity. For example, the laws may influence or place restrictions on the powers of the judiciary; they may grant a corrupt police force investigation powers during a crisis; or the laws may give military courts control over human rights cases, thereby reducing the impartiality of the proceedings.

Emergency legislation is not static and it does not exist in a vacuum. Emergency laws are challenged, refined, duplicated, or abolished, depending on the political context in which they operate. This book presents an analytical framework to explain how governments use emergency laws to avoid punishment, and how key actors challenge and alter these laws to create openings for justice. Patterns of human rights prosecutions in Sri Lanka, Northern Ireland, Spain, and Colombia reflect changes and continuities in emergency laws. Historical institutionalism provides a useful framework for tracing the origins, evolution, persistence, and disruption of these laws over time and their impact on human rights prosecutions.

Historical Institutionalism and Emergency Law

Historical institutionalism analyzes the origins of institutions and how they change through in-depth examination of historical events, or process-tracing. Institutions are generally understood as "relatively enduring features of political and social life (rules, norms, procedures) that structure behavior and that cannot be changed easily or instantaneously."[30] Central to this approach is the view that institutions are political legacies of concrete historical struggles. A great deal of emphasis is therefore placed on how power relations are reflected in institutional rules and how institutional persistence is a product of increasing returns to power.[31] Very few studies have engaged in historical institutionalist analysis to examine the historical formation and impact of laws *in a cross-national comparative study*. This book makes a novel contribution by highlighting how the specific design, evolution, and regulation of emergency legislation can have profound and variable effects on efforts to hold governments accountable for human rights abuses.

Path dependency analysis promotes the notion that patterns of sequencing and timing matter and that political outcomes are often shaped by critical junctures that can shift institutions onto new paths.[32] Since shifts in emergency legislation reflect patterns of prosecution in these cases, we might expect that critical junctures or exogenous shocks at particular historical moments produced openings for justice. However, what is fascinating about these cases is the extent to which emergency laws undergo incremental changes over time. These changes result from actors who legally challenge the laws, particularly their logic of impunity, and actors that wish to uphold these laws when they are under threat. For example, one could argue that the 1991 Constitution was a critical juncture for human rights prosecutions in Colombia because new regulations and constraints were placed on key aspects of emergency laws that had promoted impunity for decades. Yet, human rights prosecutions did not simply follow this historical moment. Rather, an examination of incremental changes to emergency laws in the years following the 1991 Constitution makes evident that key agents of change and judicial bodies were responsible for the institution's erosion and the opening of space for human rights prosecutions to occur. A process-tracing analysis also reveals that there was considerable pushback on the part of the Colombian military concerning this erosion.

The notion that emergency laws undergo gradual change may at first appear perplexing since these laws are comprised of rules and regulations that are *designed* to be temporary and *intended* to address moments of crisis. Yet, as scholarship on emergency laws has demonstrated, crisis laws are rarely temporary provisions issued by a government.[33] More often, these laws become extended over years or decades, and sometimes beyond a conflict period. Moreover, the four cases in this book illustrate that during the conflict period, emergency laws are contested, revised, reproduced, repealed, and eliminated as a result of actors who wish to challenge or uphold clauses on impunity. Finally, the cases in this book also reveal that governments, specifically in Northern Ireland and Spain, take various steps to normalize emergency laws, by subsuming them in the ordinary legal framework. These, often subtle, iterations are significant moments in which state actors are no longer subject to the same scrutiny required to pass emergency laws. Thus, historical institutionalism is a useful framework for analyzing patterns of human rights prosecution in these cases. Yet, critical juncture and exogenous shock explanations common within historical institutionalist analysis do not suffice. The emergence and timing of prosecutions is only revealed through tracing the gradual evolution of emergency laws over the course of the conflict.

Gradual Institutional Change

Gradual institutional change illuminates precise conditions for when and how an institution can evolve over time through small alterations. Even though institutional changes may be slow or subtle, these changes can signal significant shifts in veto power among interested actors and suggest the presence of influential and resourceful agents of change. An analysis of gradual institutional change also draws attention to the importance of who regulates institutional rules and how oversight is conducted. In essence, as opposed to viewing institutional change as largely exogenous, institutions are argued to be vulnerable to change as a result of their *endogenous* dynamics.[34] Change can result from contestation over the institution's rules. Those who are disadvantaged by the institution may mobilize to alter or remove particular rules, while those who wish to maintain the status quo will mobilize to defend them.[35] This contestation typically produces incremental changes over time and the accumulation of these changes may result in major transformations to the institution.

An examination of institutional change that results from endogenous dynamics also illuminates the variable of compliance: "the need to enforce institutions carries its own dynamic of potential change, emanating not just from the politically contested nature of institutional rules but also, importantly, from a degree of openness in the interpretation and implementation of these rules."[36] Institutions are not merely self-reinforcing. Debates over the application and enforcement of rules by political actors who desire a particular outcome produce important changes to the institution itself. The amount and nature of the resources at the disposal of interested actors can determine the extent to which actors with very little power can produce significant change. For example, when Colombian citizens became armed with a new set of constitutional rights and support from judicial structures to exercise those rights, they were enabled, through litigation, to alter the content and scope of emergency legislation that had previously stood in the way of their justice-seeking efforts. Additionally, actors who are formally charged with enforcing institutional rules, such as members of the judiciary, can be important players in shaping the evolution of an institution over time.[37]

The Emergency Institution

Drawing on historical institutionalism's conceptualization of institutions, this book argues that emergency and anti-terrorism laws put in place during a crisis period can be understood collectively as an institution. Emergency institutions are comprised of the various rules and norms structuring the legal limits of state actor behavior during an internal crisis. They may include provisions for how terrorism is defined and adjudicated; they often include explicit or implicit rules that promote impunity for state violations; and they may include provisions that outline how and whether state actors are legally accountable for their actions while the emergency institution is in place. In essence, while emergency institutions take various forms, a common thread across these institutions is a logic of impunity whereby state actors are afforded protections from judicial scrutiny. The logic of impunity is marked by specific restrictions on the investigation of human rights abuses, such as immunity clauses, controls on the inquest process, expansive arrest and detention powers, or controls over jurisdiction for human rights cases. Because emergency laws have these built-in restrictions, where there is little institutional change over time, there tend to be fewer possibilities for justice. During a crisis period, if the emergency institution undergoes challenges or alterations that weaken government arrest and detention powers, or amend provisions on prosecution, this form of institutional change can create openings for justice. The following discusses the modes of institutional change that are evident in the four empirical cases.

Types of Institutional Change

Three models of institutional change are evident in the cases under study: layering, conversion, and displacement. Layering involves the introduction of new rules on top of or alongside existing rules. As a result of layering, there are changes to how the original rules structure behavior. The very logic of the institution may shift as a result of alterations, particularly if they challenge the institution's original meaning and purpose.[38] Layering was evident in the emergency institution employed during the Northern Ireland conflict (1969–1998). Independent review procedures within the British Parliament produced debate over the emergency institution's logic of impunity, and rulings from the European Court of Human Rights altered key provisions concerning arrest and detention powers. Both conditions produced amendments and revisions to emergency laws over the course of several years.

Conversion is a form of institutional change that occurs when the institution's rules largely stay the same but they are enacted in new ways, often through some form of strategic redeployment by interested parties.[39] Political officials who wish to maintain the status quo of an institution that is under some form of threat may opt to reinterpret or enact the rules of an institution for a new purpose.[40] In both Northern Ireland and Spain, political actors who confronted challenges to these laws converted emergency and anti-terrorism laws from crisis legislation to ordinary laws to avoid judicial scrutiny. The emergency laws continued to restrict human rights prosecutions as they were deployed in a new legal context.

Finally, displacement involves the removal of an old institution and the introduction of new rules and regulations. Displacement of an institution is often abrupt, but it can also transpire gradually. The latter is likely to occur when actors who wish to displace the institution are incapable of creating change as rapidly as they would like.[41] As opposed to layering, new rules are created through gradual displacement. If defenders of the old rules are unable to prevent defection to the new rules, displacement occurs slowly over time.[42] In Colombia, the Constitutional Court issued rulings that challenged military jurisdiction over human rights cases. An accumulation of these rulings eventually pressured the government to create an entirely new military criminal code that incorporated provisions on fair human rights prosecutions in civilian courts.

Emergency institutions underwent gradual change in three of the four cases. Sri Lanka stands apart in that the logic of impunity was largely reproduced over time resulting in institutional continuity and a poor human rights prosecution record. Emergency and anti-terrorism laws in Spain and Northern Ireland experienced two forms of institutional change, conversion and layering, though their experiences of these changes differed in important ways, and Colombia's emergency institution underwent gradual displacement.

The Conditions Shaping Gradual Institutional Change: Political Context (Veto Power), the Characteristics of the Institution (Rule Interpretation and Enforcement), and Change Agents

Gradual institutional change emerges as a result of particular political conditions, characteristics of the institution itself and change agents. A key feature of the political context is veto power. If defenders of the status quo have strong veto possibilities, these actors can protect an existing institution and keep it intact for long periods of time. If defenders of the status quo have weak veto possibilities, the potential for gradual institutional change over time increases. Additionally, characteristics of the institution related to compliance, such as rule interpretation and rule enforcement, contain within them the possibilities for institutional change. Since an institution's rules are often applied or enforced by actors other than the designers of the institution, space is created for change to occur.[43] The more discretion there is in how rules are interpreted and enforced, the greater the likelihood that there will be openings for gradual change in the institution by those who oppose or wish to alter the rules. If there is little room for alternate interpretations of the rules and few oversight mechanisms, the institution is apt to remain static. Discretion tends to vary greatly across institutions and within the same institution it may evolve over time. The agents of change represent the group of actors that cause institutional change. Some change agents aim to reject the status quo while others seek to uphold it. The goals among these actors are not necessarily revolutionary and often, agents of change have multiple incentives for seeking transformation.[44]

Explaining Human Rights Prosecutions in Democracies at War

Building on Mahoney and Thelen's (2010) framework of gradual institutional change, this book provides an explanation for human rights prosecutions in four democracies at war. Emergency institutions contain restrictions on the investigation and prosecution of human rights abuses. Where challenges to these restrictions are successful, resulting in particular forms of institutional change, the higher the rate of human rights prosecutions. Institutional change results from the work of change agents who wish to challenge or preserve the emergency institution and four specific factors shape whether and the extent to which change agents can act: independent oversight of executive emergency powers, judicial review of emergency legislation, judicial independence, and access to a regional human rights court. In essence, both structure and agency play a role in the patterns of institutional change across the four cases (see Table 1.2). For example, parliamentary rules in the United Kingdom concerning oversight of emergency laws enabled members of the opposition party to question and scrutinize executive abuse of these powers. In another exam-

Table 1.2 Explaining human rights prosecutions in democracies at war

Country	*Characteristics of the emergency institution that restrict human rights prosecutions*	*Independent oversight of executive emergency powers*	*Judicial review of emergency laws*	*Positive and negative judicial independence*	*Regional human rights court rulings*[a]	*Change agents*[b]	*Forms of institutional change*	*Prosecution rate (%)*
Sri Lanka	Inquest and immunity clauses	No	No	No	No	None	None	1.6
Northern Ireland	Controls on inquests Juryless courts	Yes	No	No	Yes	Members of the Northern Ireland and British Parliaments Citizens	Conversion and layering	9.6
Spain	Incommunicado detention	Temporary	Temporary	No	No	Members of the Basque Parliament PSOE	Layering and conversion	0.6
Colombia	Military court jurisdiction for human rights violations	No	Yes	Yes	No	Citizens Human rights NGOs Colombian Government and Military	Gradual displacement	22.4

[a]This category refers to regional human rights court rulings on aspects of an emergency institution, not rulings on human rights cases

[b]This category refers to actors that pursued changes to the emergency institution (either to challenge the logic of impunity or to uphold it)

ple, via the 1991 Constitution, Colombian citizens were given the right to petition the Constitutional Court about the unconstitutionality of emergency laws, but petitions may not have had an impact on prosecutions without a high level of judicial independence among Court judges. The following explains how structural factors and change agents shape human rights prosecutions in four democracies at war.

Agents of Change

The empirical chapters make evident that in every country under study, citizens mobilize to pursue human rights prosecutions. This book illuminates an additional form of agency: citizens who attempt to challenge and even abolish emergency laws in order to combat impunity. For example, in Colombia and Northern Ireland, in addition to pursuing human rights prosecutions, citizens attempted to challenge the logic of impunity within the emergency institution via the courts. Citizens in Colombia submitted petitions to the Constitutional Court questioning various aspects of the military criminal code; in Northern Ireland, in the absence of local judicial review mechanisms, citizens brought cases to the European Court of Human Rights that challenged aspects of arrest and detention powers. These citizens contributed to various forms of institutional change. In some cases, agents of change are political actors who directly oppose the normalization of impunity within an emergency institution; in other cases, agents of change are political actors that do not set out to question impunity, but their indirect action or involvement in a formal oversight process leads to amendments (e.g., layering) that alter the emergency institution in important ways. In still other instances, agents of change may be part of a judicial body whose purpose is not necessarily to ensure accountability for human rights violations, but the body's mandate places them in a position where their rulings can increase the likelihood that state actors will be prosecuted. But, institutional change also results from actions taken by those seeking to *preserve* the emergency institution. Agents of change may be the very actors who benefit from the institution's rules, namely, the political party in power. Defenders of the status quo often must mobilize to keep the institution that protects them intact.[45]

The agents of change that emerged in each country became involved as a result of particular structural factors. As Table 1.2 illustrates, various types of change agents became part of the story as a result of the political structures in place and the extent of oversight and review mechanisms available. In essence, the agents of change in each country would not have been able to engage in institutional change without the presence of particular rules that made it possible for them to participate. The empirical chapters trace the motivations of various change agents, the structural factors that enabled or restricted their actions and the resulting forms of institutional change.

Independent Oversight of Executive Emergency Powers

Veto power plays a central role in the executive and the legislative branches regarding the creation and revision of emergency legislation. If the executive has complete control of the emergency institution, unsurprisingly, impunity tends to reign. If a parliamentary body has the ability to create, amend, or abolish emergency laws, there are more opportunities for the institution to change because the opposition may be able to challenge the status quo. However, if the executive has a majority in parliament, challenging the status quo will prove difficult. This is where parliamentary oversight mechanisms can prove useful. In the Northern Ireland case, for example, an independent review of emergency legislation initiated by parliamentary actors afforded opportunities for the opposition to lobby for reforms. Members of civil society were also able to voice concerns about the emergency institution through the independent review process.

Judicial Review of Emergency Laws

In addition to oversight mechanisms, enforcement of the institution and its rules matter. In the realm of criminal law, human rights law, and emergency powers, judicial bodies are important enforcement actors that can challenge or uphold the emergency institution. Legal scholars advocating for common law emergency oversight advocate for strong judicial review powers in order to ensure accountability. For example, in Colombia, the Constitutional Court became a central site of contestation involving citizens, the human rights advocacy community, government actors, and military personnel, concerning whether and how human rights cases should be prosecuted in military courts. This struggle over the meaning and enforcement of military jurisdiction had deep and lasting impacts on the pattern of human rights prosecutions during Colombia's civil war.

Judicial Independence

Judicial interpretation and enforcement of an emergency institution's rules raises the matter of judicial independence. Judicial independence can both promote human rights and be an avenue for accountability. If judicial independence exists, the power of the courts is protected and judges have the ability to review the actions of other government agencies without the fear of losing their jobs. Though the defining elements of judicial independence are contested, it is typically secured through constitutional provisions that guarantee terms of office for judges and restrict haphazard removal of personnel; prohibit the prosecution of civilians in military courts; employ selection criteria for judicial posts based on merit qualifications; stipulate the courts are a separate branch of government from the executive and the legislature; and ensure that courts are fiscally autonomous.[46] Judicial independence comprises two key components: negative judicial independence, which includes the provisions described above, and positive judicial independence, which refers to what judges actually do in cases where political actors are involved.[47] The latter involves an evaluation of whether judges regularly challenge powerful government officials in their rulings or tend to defer to the executive.

Positive judicial independence is particularly relevant to the question of human rights prosecutions in democracies at war because citizens are requesting the courts engage in two potentially difficult and dangerous tasks: prosecute active members of the military and government for human rights violations and challenge or strike down the incumbent administration's emergency powers. Moments of institutional change and human rights prosecutions emerge when, within a volatile environment, judicial actors refrain from protecting the executive. Judicial independence is not, of course, necessarily a constant across judicial bodies within a country. In Spain, for example, while judges were willing to investigate and prosecute state actors for extra-judicial killings, they were far less willing to investigate torture claims made by detainees. As the chapter on Spain demonstrates, this disparity can be explained by the fact that anti-terrorism laws legitimized and facilitated incommunicado detention.

Regional Human Rights Courts

The value of international human rights treaties to social mobilization has been found to be greatest in countries that are undergoing transition, or that have some semblance of democracy, but whose institutions are largely in flux.[48] During the bulk of the conflict years, citizens in Northern Ireland did not have local political representation because the Northern Ireland parliament was not functioning. Additionally, citizens did not have access to a local judicial review mechanism tasked with scrutinizing emergency laws. In this climate, citizens attempted to challenge the emergency institution through submissions to the European Court of Human Rights. Particular rulings from this Court altered emergency laws and shaped the prosecution of human rights cases in Northern Ireland. Though both Spain and Colombia had access to regional human rights courts, citizens did not pursue challenges to emergency laws in this venue because local judicial review mechanisms were in place to perform this task. Chapter 6 provides further discussion on the comparative use of regional courts by these three countries.

The Argument of the Book

This book argues that the possibility for state actors to be held accountable through human rights prosecutions in democracies at war is shaped by the extent to which agents of change, including citizens, human rights NGOs and political actors, were able to challenge, alter, or eliminate the emergency institution. Challenges to the emergency institution were made possible through four specific political and judicial factors: independent oversight of executive emergency powers, judicial review of emergency laws, judicial independence, and access to regional human rights courts. Table 1.2 illustrates how in conjunction these conditions produced particular types of institutional change that resulted in various rates of human rights prosecutions. In Sri Lanka, the absence of both independent oversight and an effective judicial review mechanism resulted in institutional continuity because there were no avenues for citizens or other actors to challenge the logic of impunity in emergency laws. Low levels of judicial independence and the absence of a regional human rights court further constrained the possibilities for justice. The small number of prosecutions resulted from the temporary political will of one politician, President Kumaratunga, which is discussed further in Chap. 2.

In the Northern Ireland case, conversion conducted prior to the conflict period permanently transferred controls on the inquest process from emergency laws to ordinary law. Investigations of human rights violations suffered tremendously as a result. During the conflict, independent oversight of executive emergency powers within the British Parliament produced layering, or revisions, to particular clauses within the emergency institution. In the absence of a local judicial review mechanism, citizens challenged the emergency institution at the European Court of Human Rights, which also produced layering of key amendments. In the end, while layering opened up some space for human rights prosecutions, conversion prevented a number of cases from reaching the courts altogether. The combination of the two forms of institutional change resulted in only a slightly higher rate than the number of prosecutions in Sri Lanka.

The emergency institution in Spain also underwent conversion and layering though in a manner distinct from Northern Ireland. In the early years of Spanish democracy, during the creation of interim anti-terrorism laws, Basque politicians challenged provisions that facilitated the use of torture on detainees. A short period of layering resulted in which revisions were made to the laws. By the late 1980s, however, the Spanish government had transferred all the crisis legislation into ordinary law and then permanently into the Penal Code. This act of conversion shielded the anti-terrorism provisions from independent oversight originally mandated in the Constitution and from the review powers enshrined in the Constitutional Court. Conversion of the entire emergency institution by the late 1980s shaped the low number of torture prosecutions in the ensuing years. Thus, while openings for justice were created over a lengthy period of layering in the Northern Ireland case, in Spain, layering was conducted over only a few short years. Since the democratic transition, Spanish democracy has largely been characterized by a normalization of anti-terrorism measures in ordinary law. Conversion significantly limited the number of torture allegations investigated by the courts.

Finally, in Colombia, gradual displacement of the emergency institution resulted from a strong judicial review mechanism, the Constitutional Court, and high levels of judicial independence within the Court. Incremental changes to the military criminal code, resulting from Court rulings, pressured the government to create an entirely new code reflective of human rights standards. Prosecutions increased dramatically after gradual displacement was initiated. Though still remarkably low, Colombia's rate of human rights prosecutions is higher than the other cases as a result of this particular form of institutional change.

Data and Methodology

The book focuses solely on human rights violations committed by the state during internal armed conflict, not with the intention to minimize or ignore the serious abuses committed by non-state actors in these conflicts. Since the research concerns democracies at war as unique phenomena, the book investigates a largely unexplored tension at the heart of these cases. On the one hand, prosecutions may be easier for victims of state violence in these cases given there is an array of democratic norms and institutions in place. On the other hand, given their central and quite visible role in a violent conflict, democratic governments may go to great lengths to design "legitimate" protection mechanisms in the law to avoid judicial scrutiny. The book finds that state actors do utilize emergency and anti-terrorism legislation to secure protection from criminal prosecution, and yet the data gathered for the book shows that a number of state actors were tried in criminal courts for committing serious human rights abuses. This book documents what enabled both scenarios to be present simultaneously and it details how various agents of change challenged the notion that security of the state trumps all.

This book investigates the extent to which state actors were held accountable for human rights abuses through criminal prosecutions. Criminal prosecutions are of course only one means of measuring government accountability. The pattern of prosecutions in these cases was selected as the most appropriate measure of accountability because it has direct links to the logic of impunity embedded in emergency legislation. Constraints on accountability within emergency legislation largely relate to the ways in which state actors may be held to account (or not) in a court of law. For example, some of the clauses in emergency laws under study in this book refer directly to state immunity from prosecution, while other clauses place constraints on the criminal investigation process.

Table 1.3 includes summary statistics and the comparative prosecution record across the four cases. The prosecution record is calculated by dividing the number of civilian deaths investigated in a prosecution by the estimated total number of civilians killed by state actors in the conflict. The data on the incidence of torture and disappearance is quite limited in some of the cases and reports often vary, even among local organizations. In Sri Lanka and Northern Ireland, torture was often prosecuted in civil courts (e.g., habeas corpus cases) as opposed to criminal courts, and civil court prosecution data was not collected for this book. Thus, for compara-

Table 1.3 Comparative human rights prosecutions

Country	*Number of victims in prosecutions*	*Total number of victims*	*Prosecution record (%)*	*Number of state actors prosecuted*	*Convictions*	*Acquittals*
Sri Lanka	261	16,745	1.6	211	123 (58%)	88 (42%)
Northern Ireland	35	363	9.6	57	20 (35%)	37 (65%)
Spain	22	70	31	32	30 (94%)	2 (6%)
	32 (torture)	5500 (torture)	0.6	119	95 (80%)	24 (20%)
Colombia	4358	19,437	22.4	1073	1009 (94%)	64 (6%)

tive purposes, in order to capture a consistent and accurate portrayal of human rights prosecutions, the prosecution record employs data on extra-judicial killings by the state and the prosecutions for these crimes.

The Spanish case is distinctive in a few key ways. Clauses permitting incommunicado detention in Spain's anti-terrorism laws provided cover to police who engaged in torture on suspected Euskadi Ta Askatasuna (ETA) detainees. Thus, the logic of impunity in Spain's emergency institution involves one particular type of crime. Empirical evidence from the case demonstrates that while prosecutions for state-sanctioned killings were not in any way restricted by anti-terrorism laws, hundreds of torture investigations were either never conducted or never made it to the courts as a result of provisions in these laws. Thus, two sets of prosecution data are presented under Spain in Table 1.3 in order to signify that while, at first blush, Spain appears to have a high level of prosecutions compared with the other cases, when prosecutions for torture are added, the picture shifts considerably. The disparity in rates of prosecution within Spain illustrates the importance of closely analyzing emergency laws in order to understand prosecutorial outcomes.

To code human rights prosecutions, I analyzed the Annual Human Rights Reports Submitted to Congress by the U.S. State Department for each of the four countries between the years 1976 and 2014. I counted prosecutions by coding criminal prosecutorial activity where state actors were accused of extra-judicial killing, torture, rape, or disappearance. In order to avoid over-counting or including inaccurate information, I only coded trials that actually commenced and concluded. Thus, if a report mentions an investigation or an initial charge, I did not code the trial until the proceedings started. The prosecution data includes initial criminal trials as well as the results of appeals. If, for example, a local court convicts four soldiers, and a higher court upholds their convictions during an appeal, I counted both sets of convictions in their respective years. Prosecutions in regional human rights courts, such as the European Court of Human Rights, are discussed in the book but they are not included in the prosecution data because my focus is on what conditions prompted local prosecutions. Finally, I only coded prosecutions that involved state violence related to the conflict. Thus, I did not count, for example, the handful of torture prosecutions in the mid-late 2000s of Spanish police officials accused of torturing members of immigrant communities after the Madrid bombing.

I created four original datasets of human rights prosecutions based on this coding scheme. The datasets include the years of the trial, the number of state actors prosecuted, the type of criminal charge, the outcome of the trial, the type of court (e.g., military, civilian, local, appeals), the number of deaths investigated in the trial (an individual murder versus a massacre) or the number of victims, and details on the victims and the locations of the crimes. The state actors that are investigated in each case include government officials and members of the police and security forces. In some cases, prosecutions of paramilitary members are also included in the data if evidence in the trial points to extensive collaboration between paramilitary members and state actors.

A total of 304 prosecutions are coded across the four cases involving 1492 state actors. In each empirical chapter, the prosecution data is depicted in graphs to demonstrate chronological patterns in human rights prosecutions. All of the graphs in the book display trends in the number of state actors prosecuted per year between 1976 and 2014. Trends in the number of actors prosecuted are more useful visually than a display of the number of prosecutions per year. Often, several defendants are prosecuted in one trial. Only presenting the number of trials per year would prevent an understanding of the actual growth in prosecutions over time.

Table 1.3 also includes summary statistics on convictions and acquittals to demonstrate an additional measure of accountability. Prosecution data alone does not provide a complete picture of the extent to which state actors are found responsible for human rights abuses. Notably, the country with the highest prosecution record, Colombia, also has one of the highest overall rates of convictions. One of the main explanations for this outcome is found in the relationship between emergency law and prosecutions. When emergency laws in Colombia were amended so that human rights cases were increasingly transferred from military courts to civilian courts, the rates of conviction increased. As the empirical chapters demonstrate in detail, varying levels of judicial independence also matter greatly for the verdicts across the four cases.

I conducted field research in Sri Lanka, Northern Ireland, and Spain between 2009 and 2011 and in Colombia in 2015. During this time, I conducted a total of 44 interviews with attorneys who had worked on domestic prosecutions and trials at regional human rights courts; journalists who covered human rights trials; staff at Public Prosecutor's offices; members of the police force; judges; leaders of government-led human rights institutions; staff from local human rights organizations; politicians and legal scholars. Through these interviews, I obtained valuable information on specific elements of the investigation and trial process, the design and implementation of emergency and anti-terrorism legislation and a view into the experiences of victims and their families at multiple stages of judicial inquiries. These interviews also provided enormous guidance on the political conditions immediately surrounding pivotal moments in the prosecution data. Many of these conversations prompted me to examine relationships and factors I had not yet explored and I am deeply indebted to each and every person who graciously agreed to meet me. I am acutely aware that several of the people I spoke to were facing intimidation from their own governments and, in some cases, threats and harassment. The generosity they showed me by giving their time and sharing their knowledge, when it may have been safer not to, I will not forget.

During field research I also conducted archival research to obtain documents not readily available, including several Commission of Inquiry reports in Sri Lanka, reports of victim testimony on torture in Spain, and victim *denuncias* (claims) of state violence gathered by non-governmental organizations (NGOs) in Colombia. In addition to field research, I also analyzed several types of other primary and secondary documents to identify the conditions prompting human rights prosecutions. I assessed annual human rights reports on each country, produced by both domestic and international organizations; the transcripts of domestic trials and the judgments at the European Court of Human Rights and the Inter-American Court of Human Rights; the Commission of Inquiry mandates and reports; the transcripts of inquiry proceedings; and domestic and international media coverage of trials. Through careful study of each country's constitutions, emergency, and anti-terrorism laws, I established the origins of the emergency institution and the extent to which it underwent change. I also examined emergency provisions that were rolled into ordinary laws (e.g., inquest laws and criminal codes) and the transcripts from parliamentary session debates on emergency and anti-terrorism legislation. Finally, I consulted several secondary sources for detailed histories of each country.

Implications of the Research

Comparative analysis of how emergency measures shape human rights prosecutions points to a few key implications. First, despite the powerful grip emergency laws can have on societies in crisis, accountability for state human rights violations is not necessarily impossible. *Ex ante* constitutional provisions that limit executive abuse of emergency powers can play an important role in enabling human rights prosecutions. The extent to which emergency laws impact prosecutions may often be dependent on the level of veto power within the executive, the degree to which these laws are monitored, contested, and reformed within the parliament and reviewed by a judicial body. Tracing the origins, emergence, and maintenance of these laws matters greatly for understanding their impact and persistence.

Additionally, the book's findings on the precise ways in which emergency laws have direct implications for how and whether state actors are held accountable for human rights abuses has potential relevance for other cases where democracies are confronting internal war. Both Israel and India, for example, have legal models and institutional structures that are remnants from the British colonial period, and both countries have experienced emergency institutions for decades. Scholarship on the Israeli government's adherence to the rule of law and international human rights norms is vast, but little work has been done to examine the ways in which legal models and institutional structures established during the state's creation have potentially shaped the possibilities for and the limitations on government accountability. Similarly, while India has confronted a variety of internal conflicts since independence from Britain, no research has examined the diversity of prosecution outcomes across Indian states and their potential relevance to existing emergency legislation.

Emergency legislation is not on the decline, nor does it necessarily cease at the end of violent conflict. Understanding the relationship between these laws and human rights prosecutions will continue to be central to analyses of democracies at war.

Overview of the Book

The core of the book comprises four chapters on human rights prosecutions during the conflicts in Sri Lanka, Northern Ireland, Spain, and Colombia. Each empirical chapter includes the following components: a historical background to the conflict; the origin and evolution of the emergency institution; the conditions that prompted institutional change and created openings for prosecutions; and a discussion of the human rights prosecution data, including emblematic cases. Chapter 2 details the highly constraining power of emergency laws in Sri Lanka and the conditions that produced a handful of human rights prosecutions midway through the conflict. Emergency and anti-terrorism laws in Sri Lanka include explicit immunity and inquest clauses that encourage and facilitate impunity regarding state violations. Very few prosecutions were held in Sri Lanka as a result, and the handful of prosecutions that occurred largely emerged through the temporary political will of one political leader.

Chapter 3 demonstrates how aspects of the design and implementation of emergency laws in Northern Ireland produced constraints on the ability for investigations to move forward in state violence cases and for the courts to issue fair judgments. Controls on the inquest process originally placed within emergency provisions were shielded from oversight and judicial scrutiny after they were folded into ordinary criminal law. Additionally, state violence cases were determined by a largely biased community of judges in juryless courts, a feature of emergency laws created at the start of the conflict. Patterns of human rights prosecutions reflect these conditions as well as amendments made to emergency laws, brought about through independent oversight of executive emergency powers and rulings by a regional human rights court.

Chapter 4 examines the violence between ETA and the Spanish government during the early years of Spanish democracy. Protections for state actors who engaged in torture were built into anti-terrorism laws through the legalization of lengthy, unmonitored detention periods, known as incommunicado detention. While legal reforms established during Spain's democratic transition helped to facilitate prosecutions for state-sponsored killings during the 1980s and early 1990s, investigations and prosecutions of torture allegations were crippled by anti-terrorism laws that normalized and legitimized ill-treatment at the hands of the state.

Chapter 5 discusses the origin of Colombia's military criminal code in emergency decrees and the decades-long military jurisdiction over human rights cases that followed. This chapter traces a shift from prior years of government impunity to a period in the mid-late 1990s when human rights prosecutions emerged and steadily increased over time. As a result of two key factors, judicial review of emergency legislation and judicial independence among judges on the Constitutional Court, the military criminal code was altered, prosecutions were steadily transferred from military courts to ordinary courts and the number of prosecutions increased. Chapter 6 puts the four empirical cases into comparative perspective and it provides an analysis of the theoretical and substantive implications of the book's central findings.

Notes

1. Interview with Padre Alberto Franco, Bogotá, Colombia, May 2015.
2. Some of the arguments set forth in this chapter were first published as an article. See Moira Katherine Lynch. "A Theory of Human Rights Prosecutions and Emergency Law: Bringing in Historical Institutionalism," *Journal of Human Rights* 14(4) (2015): 504–524.
3. Olsen, Tricia D, Leigh A. Payne, and Andrew G. Reiter. *Transitional Justice in Balance: Comparing Processes, Weighing Efficacy.* Washington DC: United States Institute of Peace Press, 2010; Binningsbø, Helga Malmin, Jon Elster, and Scott Gates. 2005. Civil War and Transitional Justice: 1946–2003, A Dataset, Paper prepared for presentation at the "Transitional Justice and Civil War Settlements" workshop in Bogotá, Colombia, October 18–19, 2005; Backer, David. Cross-National Comparative Analysis, in Audrey Chapman, Hugo van der Merwe, and Victoria Baxter, eds., *Assessing the Impact of Transitional Justice: Challenges for Empirical Research.* Washington DC: United States Institute of Peace Press, 2009.
4. Olsen, Payne and Reiter, 126.
5. Grodsky, Brian. *The Costs of Justice: How New Leaders Respond to Previous Rights Abuses.* Notre Dame, IN: University of Notre Dame Press, 2010; Nalepa, Monika. *Skeletons in the Closet: Transitional Justice in Post-Communist Europe.* New York: Cambridge University Press, 2010; Loyle, C. E., and C. Davenport. Transitional injustice: Subverting justice in transition and post-conflict societies. *Journal of Human Rights* 15(1) (2016): 126–149.
6. Loyle, C. E., and H. M. Binningsbø. Justice during armed conflict: A new dataset on government and rebel strategies. *Journal of Conflict Resolution* 49(5) (2016): 12.

7. Zalaquett, Jose. Confronting Human Rights Violations Committed by Former Governments: Principles Applicable and Political Constraints in Neil Kritz, ed., *Transitional Justice: How Emerging Democracies Reckon with Former Regimes*. Washington DC: United States Institute of Peace, 1995; Sikkink, Kathryn. *The Justice Cascade: How Human Rights Prosecutions Are Changing World Politics*. New York: W.W. Norton and Company, Inc., 2011.
8. Pettersson, Therése, and Peter Wallensteen. Armed Conflicts, 1946–2014. *Journal of Peace Research* 52(4) (2015).
9. Marshall, Monty G., Ted Gurr, and Keith Jaggers. Polity IV Project. Political Regime Characteristics and Transitions, 1800–2016. Dataset Users' Manuel, 2016.
10. The Polity conceptual scheme examines concomitant qualities of democratic and autocratic authority in governing institutions, rather than discreet and mutually exclusive forms of governance. This perspective envisions a spectrum of governing authority that spans from fully institutionalized autocracies through mixed, or incoherent, authority regimes (termed "anocracies") to fully institutionalized democracies. The "Polity Score" captures this regime authority spectrum on a 21-point scale ranging from −10 (hereditary monarchy) to +10 (consolidated democracy). The Polity "scheme consists of six component measures that record key qualities of executive recruitment, constraints on executive authority, and political competition. It also records changes in the institutionalized qualities of governing authority. The Polity data include information only on the institutions of the central government and on political groups acting, or reacting, within the scope of that authority. It does not include consideration of groups and territories that are actively removed from that authority (i.e., separatists or "fragments"; these are considered separate, though not independent, polities) or segments of the population that are not yet effectively politicized in relation to central state politics" (Marshall et al. 2016).
11. Polity IV was identified by the author as the most appropriate measure of democracy given the timing of the armed conflicts under study. Freedom House Scores, for example, begin in 1973. Within the universe of cases, some of the conflicts predate this year. However, for the years following 1973, Freedom House scores the four cases in this book in a manner consistent with Polity IV ratings.
12. Bueno De Mesquita, Bruce, George W. Downs, Alastair Smith, and Feryal Marie Cherif. Thinking Inside the Box: A Closer Look at Democracy and Human Rights. *International Studies Quarterly* 49(3) (September 1, 2005): 439–457.

13. Uppsala Conflict Data Program. 2014. UCDP Conflict Encyclopedia. Uppsala University Department of Peace and Conflict Research. www.ucdp.uu.se/database
14. Gross, Oren and Fionnuala Ní Aoláin. *Law in Times of Crisis: Emergency Powers in Theory and Practice.* New York: Cambridge University Press, 2006.
15. States are not permitted to derogate from Article 6 (right to life), Article 7 (prohibition of torture or cruel, inhuman or degrading punishment), Article 8, paragraphs 1 and 2 (prohibition of slavery), Article 11 (prohibition of imprisonment because of inability to fulfill a contractual obligation), Article 15 (the principle of legality in the field of criminal law), Article 16 (the recognition of everyone as a person before the law), and Article 18 (freedom of thought, conscience and religion) (ICCPR Art. 4, Para 2).
16. Rossiter, Clinton. *Constitutional Dictatorship: Crisis Government in the Modern Democracies.* Princeton: Princeton University Press, 1948.
17. Questiaux, N. Study of the Implications for Human Rights of Recent Developments Concerning Situations Known as States of Siege or Emergency. Commission on Human Rights, Sub-Commission on Prevention of Discrimination and Protection of Minorities. E/CN.4/Sub.2/1982/15, 1982; Fitzpatrick, Joan. *Human Rights in Crisis: The International System for Protecting Rights During States of Emergency.* Procedural Aspects of International Law Institute, 1994.
18. International Humanitarian Law (IHL) includes two main legal instruments that regulate internal armed conflicts: Common Article 3 to the 1949 Geneva Conventions and the 1977 Additional Protocol II to the Geneva Conventions. For more information about IHL, see Frits Kalshoven and Liesbeth Zegveld. 2001. *Constraints on the Waging of War: An Introduction to International Humanitarian Law.* International Committee for the Red Cross. Geneva, Switzerland.
19. Gross and Ní Aoláin (2006); See also Fitzpatrick (1994).
20. Gross and Ní Aoláin, 349.
21. Gross and Ní Aoláin, 353.
22. Gross and Ní Aoláin, 358.
23. Scheuerman, William E. Emergency Powers. *Annual Review of Law and Social Science* 2 (2006): 262.
24. Gross, Oren. Chaos and Rules: Should Responses to Violent Crises Always Be Constitutional? *Yale Law Review* 112 (2003): 1011–134.
25. Krebs, Ronald R. In the Shadow of War: The Effects of Conflict on Liberal Democracy. *International Organization* 63 (Winter 2009): 177–210.
26. Scheuerman (2006).
27. Scheuerman (2006).

28. Agamben, Giorgio. *State of Exception*. Chicago: The University of Chicago Press (2005), 49–50.
29. Schmitt, Carl. *Political Theology*. Translated by George Schwab. Cambridge: MIT Press (1985); Agamben (2005).
30. Mahoney, James and Kathleen Thelen. A Theory of Gradual Institutional Change, in James Mahoney and Kathleen Thelen, eds., *Explaining Institutional Change: Ambiguity, Agency, and Power*. New York, New York: Cambridge University Press (2010): 4.
31. Mahoney and Thelen, 4.
32. Pierson, Paul. "The Path to European Integration: A Historical Institutionalist Approach," *Comparative Political Studies* 29(2) (1996): 123–63; Capoccia, Giovanni and R. Daniel Keleman. The Study of Critical Junctures: Theory, Narrative and Counterfactuals in Historical Institutionalism. *World Politics* 59(3) (2007): 341–369.
33. Gross and Ní Aoláin (2006).
34. Mahoney and Thelen, 8.
35. Jacobs, Alan M. "Policymaking as Political Constraint: Institutional Development in the U.S. Social Security Program," in James Mahoney and Kathleen Thelen, eds., *Explaining Institutional Change: Ambiguity, Agency, and Power*. New York, New York: Cambridge University Press (2010), 97.
36. Mahoney and Thelen, 10.
37. Mahoney and Thelen, 14.
38. Mahoney and Thelen, 16–17.
39. Mahoney and Thelen, 16.
40. Slater, Dan. Altering Authoritarianism: Institutional Complexity and Autocratic Agency in Indonesia, in James Mahoney and Kathleen Thelen, eds., *Explaining Institutional Change: Ambiguity, Agency, and Power*. New York, New York: Cambridge University Press (2010), 140.
41. Mahoney and Thelen, 24.
42. Mahoney and Thelen, 16.
43. Mahoney and Thelen, 13
44. Mahoney and Thelen, 22.
45. Jacobs, 97.
46. Domingo, Pilar. Judicial Independence and Judicial Reform in Latin America, in Andreas Schedler, Larry Diamond and Marc F. Plattner, eds., *The Self-Restraining State: Power and Accountability in New Democracies*. Boulder, CO: Lynne Rienner Publishers (1999); Apodaca, Clair. The Rule of Law and Human Rights, *Judicature* 87(6) (2004): 292–299; Camp Keith, Linda, C. Neal Tate and Steven C. Poe. Is the Law a Mere Parchment Barrier to Human Rights Abuse? *The Journal of Politics* 71(2) (2009): 644–660.

47. Russell, Peter. Toward a General Theory of Judicial Independence, in Peter Russell and David O'Brien, eds., *Judicial Independence in the Age of Democracy: Critical Perspectives from Around the World.* Charlottesville: University Press of Virginia (2001); Hilbink, Lisa. The Origins of Positive Judicial Independence, *World Politics* 64(4) (2012): 587–621.
48. Simmons, Beth. *Mobilizing for Human Rights: International Law in Domestic Politics.* New York: Cambridge University Press (2009), 13–15.

Bibliography

Agamben, Giorgio. 2005. *State of Exception.* Chicago: The University of Chicago Press.

Apodaca, Clair. 2004. The Rule of Law and Human Rights. *Judicature* 87 (6): 292–299.

Backer, David. 2009. Cross-National Comparative Analysis. In *Assessing the Impact of Transitional Justice: Challenges for Empirical Research*, ed. Audrey Chapman, Hugo van der Merwe, and Victoria Baxter. Washington, DC: United States Institute of Peace Press.

Binningsbø, Helga Malmin, Jon Elster, and Scott Gates. 2005. Civil War and Transitional Justice: 1946–2003, A Dataset. Paper Prepared for Presentation at the 'Transitional Justice and Civil War Settlements' Workshop in Bogotá, Colombia, October 18–19.

Capoccia, Giovanni, and R. Daniel Keleman. 2007. The Study of Critical Junctures: Theory, Narrative and Counterfactuals in Historical Institutionalism. *World Politics* 59 (3): 341–369.

De Mesquita, Bueno, George W. Downs Bruce, Alastair Smith, and Feryal Marie Cherif. 2005. Thinking Inside the Box: A Closer Look at Democracy and Human Rights. *International Studies Quarterly* 49 (3): 439–457.

Domingo, Pilar. 1999. Judicial Independence and Judicial Reform in Latin America. In *The Self-Restraining State: Power and Accountability in New Democracies*, ed. Andreas Schedler, Larry Diamond, and Marc F. Plattner. Boulder: Lynne Rienner Publishers.

Fitzpatrick, Joan. 1994. *Human Rights in Crisis: The International System for Protecting Rights During States of Emergency*, Procedural Aspects of International Law Institute. Philadelphia: University of Philadelphia Press.

Grodsky, Brian. 2010. *The Costs of Justice: How New Leaders Respond to Previous Rights Abuses.* Notre Dame: University of Notre Dame Press.

Gross, O. 2003. Chaos and Rules: Should Responses to Violent Crises Always Be Constitutional? *Yale Law Review* 112: 1011–1134.

Gross, Oren, and Fionnuala Ní Aoláin. 2006. *Law in Times of Crisis: Emergency Powers in Theory and Practice.* New York: Cambridge University Press.

Hilbink, Lisa. 2012. The Origins of Positive Judicial Independence. *World Politics* 64 (4): 587–621.

International Covenant on Civil and Political Rights (ICCPR). 1966. 999 U.N.T.S. 171 and 1057 U.N.T.S. 407, New York, December 16, 1966, Entered into Force March 23, 1976 [the Provisions of Article 41 (Human Rights Committee) Entered into Force March 28, 1979]. Available: www.ohchr.org. 17 June 2015.

Interview with Padre Alberto Franco, Bogotá, Colombia, May 2015.

Jacobs, Alan M. 2010. Policymaking as Political Constraint: Institutional Development in the U.S. Social Security Program. In *Explaining Institutional Change: Ambiguity, Agency, and Power*, ed. James Mahoney and Kathleen Thelen. New York: Cambridge University Press.

Kalshoven, Frits, and Liesbeth Zegveld. 2001. *Constraints on the Waging of War: An Introduction to International Humanitarian Law*. Geneva: International Committee for the Red Cross.

Keith, Camp, C. Neal Tate Linda, and Steven C. Poe. 2009. Is the Law a Mere Parchment Barrier to Human Rights Abuse? *The Journal of Politics* 71 (2): 644–660.

Krebs, Ronald R. 2009. In the Shadow of War: The Effects of Conflict on Liberal Democracy. *International Organization* 63: 177–210.

Loyle, C.E., and H.M. Binningsbø. 2016. Justice During Armed Conflict: A New Dataset on Government and Rebel Strategies. *Journal of Conflict Resolution* 49 (5): 1–25.

Loyle, C.E., and C. Davenport. 2016. Transitional Injustice: Subverting Justice in Transition and Post-conflict Societies. *Journal of Human Rights* 15 (1): 126–149.

Lynch, Moira Katherine. 2015. A Theory of Human Rights Prosecutions and Emergency Law: Bringing in Historical Institutionalism. *Journal of Human Rights* 14 (4): 504–524.

Mahoney, James, and Kathleen Thelen. 2010. A Theory of Gradual Institutional Change. In *Explaining Institutional Change: Ambiguity, Agency, and Power*, ed. James Mahoney and Kathleen Thelen. New York: Cambridge University Press.

Marshall, Monty G., Ted Gurr, and Keith Jaggers. 2016. *Polity IV Project. Political Regime Characteristics and Transitions, 1800–2016. Dataset Users' Manuel*. Retrieved February 10, 2016. http://www.systemicpeace.org/inscrdata.html

Nalepa, Monika. 2010. *Skeletons in the Closet: Transitional Justice in Post-communist Europe*. New York: Cambridge University Press.

Olsen, Tricia D., Leigh A. Payne, and Andrew G. Reiter. 2010. *Transitional Justice in Balance: Comparing Processes, Weighing Efficacy*. Washington, DC: United States Institute of Peace Press.

Pettersson, Therése, and Peter Wallensteen. 2015. Armed Conflicts. *Journal of Peace Research* 52 (4): 1946–2014.

Pierson, Paul. 1996. The Path to European Integration: A Historical Institutionalist Approach. *Comparative Political Studies* 29 (2): 123–163.

Questiaux, N. 1982. Study of the Implications for Human Rights of Recent Developments Concerning Situations Known as States of Siege or Emergency. Commission on Human Rights, Sub-Commission on Prevention of Discrimination and Protection of Minorities. E/CN.4/Sub.2/1982/15.

Rossiter, Clinton. 1948. *Constitutional Dictatorship: Crisis Government in the Modern Democracies*. Princeton: Princeton University Press.

Russell, Peter. 2001. Toward a General Theory of Judicial Independence. In *Judicial Independence in the Age of Democracy: Critical Perspectives from Around the World*, ed. Peter Russell and David O'Brien. Charlottesville: University Press of Virginia.

Scheuerman, William E. 2006. Emergency Powers. *Annual Review of Law and Social Science* 2: 257–277.

Sikkink, Kathryn. 2011. *The Justice Cascade: How Human Rights Prosecutions Are Changing World Politics*. New York: W.W. Norton and Company, Inc.

Simmons, Beth. 2009. *Mobilizing for Human Rights: International Law in Domestic Politics*. New York: Cambridge University Press.

Slater, Dan. 2010. Altering Authoritarianism: Institutional Complexity and Autocratic Agency in Indonesia. In *Explaining Institutional Change: Ambiguity, Agency, and Power*, ed. James Mahoney and Kathleen Thelen. New York: Cambridge University Press.

Uppsala Conflict Data Program. 2014. UCDP Conflict Encyclopedia. Uppsala University Department of Peace and Conflict Research. www.ucdp.uu.se/database

Zalaquett, Jose. 1995. Confronting Human Rights Violations Committed by Former Governments: Principles Applicable and Political Constraints. In *Transitional Justice: How Emerging Democracies Reckon with Former Regimes*, ed. Neil Kritz. Washington, DC: United States Institute of Peace.

CHAPTER 2

Human Rights Prosecutions and Institutional Continuity in Sri Lanka

The historical legacy of emergency and anti-terrorism laws in Sri Lanka dates back to its colonial history in the early twentieth century, just prior to the country's independence from Britain. The very notion of protecting government actors from judicial scrutiny as part and parcel of emergency decrees was established during this time, and today, almost a century later, the language of impunity and adherence to it, persists. The emergency institution underwent virtually no change throughout the conflict period. At moments, Parliament introduced amendments to existing emergency laws. However, the provisions that maintained the core logic of impunity within the emergency institution, specifically immunity and inquest clauses, were simply reproduced over time. The lack of transformational change within the emergency institution resulted in a very low number of human rights prosecutions. Tracing institutional continuity in this case reveals that change was stymied as a result of a lack of independent oversight to check executive emergency powers, the absence of judicial review, the lack of access to a regional human rights court, and consistently low levels of judicial independence.

Despite this landscape, a small number of prosecutions were held in Sri Lanka, catalyzed not by changes to the emergency institution itself but rather by a shift in political leadership

In the mid-1990s, a candidate who ran on a human rights platform assumed the presidency. Once elected, President Chandrika Kumaratunga

M. Lynch, *Human Rights Prosecutions in Democracies at War*, Human Rights Interventions,
https://doi.org/10.1007/978-3-319-96908-4_2

pushed forward one key human rights prosecution, and she initiated three Commissions of Inquiry that helped to propel criminal investigations of disappearances and massacres committed by government actors. The handful of human rights prosecutions enabled her to appear to be delivering on her campaign promises, and her creation of Commissions of Inquiry tended to expose abuses committed by former regimes, though not exclusively. Two successful prosecutions involved crimes that transpired during her tenure. Sri Lanka's emergency institution serves as an important example of how restrictions on accountability within an emergency institution create a stranglehold on human rights prosecutions, particularly when certain conditions are absent.

The chapter is organized as follows: the second section presents historical background to the Sri Lankan conflict; the third section discusses the creation and evolution of the emergency institution, and the specific ways in which it promulgated impunity; the fourth section provides an overview of the human rights prosecution data; the fifth section discusses how and why President Kumaratunga initiated a small number of human rights prosecutions; the chapter concludes with remarks on the landscape of accountability in Sri Lanka since the end of the war in 2009.

Historical Background to the Conflict in Sri Lanka

Sri Lanka is a multi-party democracy and the current form of government is a mix of presidential and parliamentary systems. Prior to the 1978 Constitution, the prime minister was the head of state and the president was mainly a figurehead. The 1978 Constitution then created the first office of the Executive President, modeled after the American system, while retaining a parliamentary system of government. The president is now elected directly by the people, members of parliament are elected by a modified form of proportional representation, and the prime minister and other Cabinet members are appointed by the president from a party or coalition that commands a majority in parliament.[1] Of the 21 million people living on the island, approximately 74% are Sinhalese, 18% are Tamil, 7% are Muslim, and 1% comprise smaller ethnic communities, including the Burghers and Veddahs.

After the country's independence from Britain in 1948, politics in Sri Lanka (known as Ceylon until 1972) was dominated by two largely Sinhalese parties, the right-wing United National Party (UNP) and the left of center Sri Lanka Freedom Party (see Table 2.1). The first party representing the minority Tamil community, the Federal Party, was formed

Table 2.1 Political parties in power during the Sri Lankan conflict

Years	*Political party*	*President*
1978–1989	United National Party (UNP)	Junius Richard (J. R.) Jayewardene
1989–1993	United National Party (UNP)	Ranasinghe Premadasa (assassinated in 1993)
1993–1994	United National Party (UNP)	Dingiri Banda Wijetunge
1994–2005	People's Alliance (PA) (formerly Sri Lanka Freedom Party)	Chandrika Kumaratunga
2005–2015	United People's Freedom Alliance (coalition of several parties)	Mahinda Rajapaksa
2015–	Sri Lanka Freedom Party	Mathripala Sirisena

in 1949 in response to citizenship restrictions placed on Indian Tamil estate workers. Later, in 1972, members of the Federal Party and the Muslim United Front formed the Tamil United Front party, in protest to the anti-minority provisions of the 1972 Constitution. A few years later, the main Tamil parties joined together to form the Tamil United Liberation Front (TULF), which remained the central Tamil political party throughout the war. As communal tensions grew between Sinhalese and Tamils in the early 1980s, the minority Muslim community formed their own party, the Sri Lanka Muslim Congress.

The presidency was held by the UNP from 1978 to 1994. The Janatha Vimukthi Peramuna (JVP), or People's Liberation Front, which formed as a party from a radical, leftist, Sinhalese faction, first fielded candidates in local elections as a political party in 1981 (Sri Lanka Sessional Paper 2000). The party became a main contender with the UNP and the Sri Lanka Freedom Party by the late 1990s. The People's Alliance (PA) party, which formed ahead of the 1994 presidential election, was comprised of the Sri Lanka Freedom Party and other coalition partners. The PA held the presidency from 1994 to 2005. Before the 2004 elections, a coalition of several parties, including the Sri Lanka Freedom Party and the JVP, formed the United People's Freedom Alliance. The Alliance put forth Mahinda Rajapaksa, who narrowly won in the 2005 presidential election, defeating the prime minister and UNP candidate Ranil Wickremasinghe. Rajapaksa was re-elected for a second term in 2010. Then, after governance became increasingly authoritarian under Rajapaksa, Mathripala Sirisena, a former minister in Rajapaksa's administration, won the presidential election in January 2015.

The Sri Lankan legal system is built on a combination of indigenous and colonial (Dutch and British) laws; however, the current system most closely resembles English law (common law). At the time of Sri Lanka's independence from Britain in 1948, the Governor-General, on the advice of the prime minister, appointed members of the Supreme Court.[2] The Governor-General was a position that led the country in partnership with the Sri Lankan Parliament during the transition to independence. Appointments to the lower courts, including the district and magistrate courts, were made by the Judicial Service Commission, which was comprised of the Chief Justice and two additional judges of the Supreme Court. Between 1948 and 1974, the Supreme Court handled serious criminal offense cases and the District Court managed the majority of civil suits (Redden and Schlueter 1990). The Court of Criminal Appeal, established before independence in 1938, heard appeals from the decisions of the Supreme Court. Strict separation of powers was established by the 1948 Constitution. However, the 1972 Constitution altered this and several other aspects of the legal system.

The 1972 Constitution made Sri Lanka a Republic, and though the initial motivation for its creation stemmed from years of demands for constitutional reform, the Constitution essentially abandoned the separation of powers enshrined in the former constitution.[3] For example, it abolished the Judicial Service Commission, granting the executive complete control over judicial appointments and dismissals. In addition, judicial review was abolished and a non-elected president was granted the power to appoint members of the Constitutional Court, which was established to decide the constitutionality of bills presented to Parliament. The 1972 Constitution also altered the structure of the judicial system through the creation of the High Court, which took over from the Supreme Court on all criminal matters. A High Court resides in each of the 16 judicial zones throughout the country.[4]

The 1978 Constitution, still in effect today, further reformed the legal system in Sri Lanka. While it included the first constitutional section on fundamental rights, including freedom from torture, and attempted to restore the independence of the judiciary through the reinstatement of judicial review and provisions securing judges' tenure, the executive was simultaneously granted wide swaths of power. This was used by various subsequent administrations to intimidate members of the judiciary. The president became an elected post through the 1978 Constitution and this position retained its power to appoint judges of the Supreme Court and the Court of Appeal.

In contrast to civil law legal systems, where an investigating judge plays a key role in determining the possibility of an indictment, most of the evidence gathering and investigation in criminal cases within Sri Lanka is conducted by police officers. Thus, when the security forces are responsible for committing a violent crime against a citizen, virtual colleagues of the offender are responsible for investigating the details of the incident and the offender's potential culpability. The Attorney General in Sri Lanka, the chief legal officer of the state, is responsible for making decisions on whether or not to file an indictment in state violence cases. The government in power traditionally appoints this post.[5]

During the Sri Lankan conflict, the Department of the Attorney General came under fire in several instances over the paradox of its position in state violence cases. Victims of extra-judicial execution, for example, were legally represented by the same entity responsible for the violation. An office of a Director of Public Prosecutions was briefly established between 1973 and 1977 to remedy this matter, but it was subsequently abolished. Calls for an independent prosecutor's office by human rights advocates and Commissions of Inquiry reports persisted in the 1980s and 1990s, however, the government failed to establish such a body. Though reforms to the Attorney General appointment process were developed in 2001 through the 17th Amendment, President Rajapaksa nullified the provisions years later. President Rajapaksa often made direct appointments to public offices, including the Attorney General and the appellate courts.[6]

In the last several decades, the Sri Lankan government faced violent insurgencies from both Sinhalese and Tamil opposition groups. Serious internal conflict within the country first emerged after the JVP, prior to becoming a political party, conducted an insurgency in the South of the country in 1971, which was largely based on the economic marginalization of Sinhalese rural youth. Shortly afterward, discriminatory government policies against the minority Tamil community, concerning use of the Tamil language and access to higher education, grew. In 1977, the main Tamil party, TULF, called for a separate homeland for Tamils. When anti Tamil riots followed, Tamil militancy increased, particularly in the north and east, where many Tamils resided. The Liberation Tigers of Tamil Eelam (LTTE) emerged as the dominant Tamil politico-militant group, espousing a separatist agenda. In addition to an increase in the centralization of power within the executive via the 1978 Constitution, the party in power during this time, the UNP, also expanded its authority via emergency and counter-terrorism measures.

Anti-Tamil violence increased significantly in 1983, when thousands of Tamils were attacked and killed by Sinhalese mobs, following the LTTE killing of 13 Sri Lankan soldiers in Jaffna. This escalation in violence prompted the Indian government to push for peace negotiations, particularly out of concern for spillover effects on its southernmost state of Tamil Nadu. The eventual agreement that was reached between the Indian and Sri Lankan governments, the Indo-Lanka Accord, provided an Indian peacekeeping force in the region and plans for the devolution of regional power to the Tamil community. The LTTE rejected this pact and the peacekeeping presence ended in failure after the Indian forces engaged in battle with local rebels, often wielding excessive force against civilians. The JVP then launched a second insurgency in 1987 against government politicians and public sector workers, in apparent protest to the Indo-Lanka Accord.[7]

By 1990, however, the opposing factions of the conflict mainly involved the Sri Lankan government and the LTTE. Violence decreased somewhat under the Kumaratunga administration (1994–2005) as it attempted negotiations with the LTTE and secured a short-lived ceasefire in the mid-1990s. In early 2002 a second ceasefire agreement was reached, facilitated by the Norwegian government. Ultimately, the ceasefire broke down after the LTTE suspended its involvement a year later and the Sri Lankan government formally withdrew from participation in the ceasefire in 2008. Rajapaksa's rise to power in 2005 resulted in a more powerful, centralized executive, and the continued enactment of repressive emergency and counter-terrorism measures. Splintering within the LTTE followed and violence began to escalate in the north and east regions of the country. In the last few years of the war, the government, aided by a LTTE splinter group the pro-state paramilitary Karuna faction, moved into a dominant position in the war, regaining territory in the northern and eastern regions and dismantling the LTTE leadership. After almost 30 years of civil war, in which tens of thousands of lives were lost, the conflict in Sri Lanka concluded in May 2009 when the government armed forces defeated the LTTE. Thousands of civilians perished in the final few months of the war and hundreds of thousands were internally displaced. Violence has not resumed on a large scale since 2009; however, the recovery process in terms of rebuilding infrastructure, the reintegration of combatants, and the pursuit of accountability has been slow.

Though I largely draw on international human rights law and domestic criminal law to analyze human rights violations in the Sri Lankan conflict, international humanitarian law is a relevant, overlapping framework in situations of internal armed conflict. Sri Lanka ratified the 1949 Geneva

Conventions in 1959 but failed to sign or ratify the 1977 Protocols. Common Article 3 of the Geneva Conventions is therefore the only international humanitarian law, or law of war, that can be applicable to this case. The International Committee of the Red Cross consistently made visits to Sri Lanka throughout the civil conflict in order to protect and aid victims, monitor violations, and train parties to the conflict in international humanitarian law. However, neither the Sri Lankan government nor the LTTE formally recognized international humanitarian law as applicable to the internal war. In response, third parties not associated with the conflict, including various NGOs and the UN, made statements concerning the government's violation of the Geneva Conventions. One of the most important moves made by the UN regarding the violations of international humanitarian law (as well as international human rights law) involved its report issued in March 2011, which followed the work of a special panel investigation of the war crimes committed in the final months of the conflict in 2009. Within this report, the UN finds the Sri Lankan government to have violated international humanitarian law, specifically Common Article 3 of the Geneva Conventions, regarding requirements of distinctions between combatants and civilians, the ban on attacks on civilians or civilian objects; the ban on indiscriminate or disproportionate attacks against civilians; the requirement of precautions before and during attacks; the requirement of special protection to medical and humanitarian personnel and objects; the ban on starvation of the civilian population and denial of humanitarian relief; the ban on enforced disappearances; requirements of minimal level of treatment for those deprived of liberty; and requirements regarding the dead and missing.[8]

When a conflict ends as a result of a victory by one party over another, the likelihood of prosecuting the victors is very low.[9] It is likely that it will continue to be difficult to pursue government accountability in Sri Lanka, never mind the mounting international pressure and the UN call in 2015 for a hybrid court to prosecute those responsible for the worst abuses during the war. The following discusses how during the conflict years a highly restrictive emergency institution in Sri Lanka narrowed the scope for human rights prosecutions.

The Emergency Institution in Sri Lanka

Emergency and counter-terrorism laws can influence how security force members, political actors, and police are held to account for human rights violations. They do so in three specific ways: the laws often contain immunity clauses for actions performed by security forces and police during a crisis; the laws can include provisions concerning inquests (the investigation of wrongful deaths by a coroner) that remove state actors from scrutiny, grant more power to the state over the inquest process or abolish the right to an inquest entirely; and they often contain clauses on expansive powers of arrest and detention, which can grant legitimacy and cover to state actors who are participating in disappearances, torture, and extrajudicial killings. In the Sri Lankan case, immunity and inquest clauses in particular, narrowed the possibilities for holding state actors to account.[10] In the following, I discuss the history of emergency and counter-terrorism laws in Sri Lanka and demonstrate how the design and regulation of these laws shaped human rights prosecutions in this case.[11]

As discussed in Chap. 1, four factors shape whether the restrictions on human rights prosecutions in emergency laws will be altered or upheld: independent oversight of executive emergency powers, judicial review powers, judicial independence, and regional human rights court rulings. In Sri Lanka, the executive maintained a tight grip on the creation and promulgation of emergency laws and there were virtually no independent oversight mechanisms to check the laws' effects on human rights prosecutions. Additionally, though judicial bodies can be key in monitoring government abuse of emergency legislation (aka the common law emergency oversight model), with a few exceptions, judicial review was highly limited in this case. The executive's power to appoint Supreme Court judges greatly reduced the level of judicial independence across the conflict period, and citizens had no access to a regional human rights body for making claims against the government. As a result, the emergency institution, and its provisions on government immunity and controls over inquests, remained largely intact.

The History of Emergency Laws in Sri Lanka

Emergency laws in Sri Lanka originate in the British colonial period. The 1947 Public Security Act (now known as the Public Security Ordinance or PSO) was the last piece of legislation enacted by the British before independence and it was designed to quell agitation from striking leftist trade union members.[12] Prior to the terms of the PSO, the Governor of Sri Lanka, appointed by King George VI, had the power to declare a state of emergency and assume control of any government department.[13] The PSO gave powers to the Governor-General, who was also appointed by the King to run the island in partnership with Sri Lankan members of

Parliament, as part of the transition to autonomy. The 1947 PSO deemed certain government departments, such as food distribution and transportation, essential to the survival of the nation, and it determined that it was legitimate to infringe on civil liberties in order to protect these sectors.[14] Later, in the 1970s, instead of designing new regulations to address the onset of political violence, successive administrations relied on the emergency provisions outlined in the PSO to declare states of emergency and issue regulations. The PSO was amended in 1949, 1953, 1959, 1978, and 1988. It continues to be used today.[15]

Emergency regulations were developed in 1971 to respond to violence instigated by the JVP. Increasing riots and violence between the Sinhalese and Tamil populations prompted subsequent regulations. Then, in 1979, former President Jayawardena issued the Prevention of Terrorism (Temporary Provisions) Act (PTA) in response to escalating violence in the North. The PTA is not an emergency regulation but its powers are similar to emergency laws in several ways. The PTA primarily defines some terrorism offenses, outlines penalties, and confers certain powers on the Executive. Though it was initially created to be temporary, the 1979 PTA was amended to become permanent in 1982. Aspects of the law were modeled on the PTA developed in 1974 by the British government to address the conflict in Northern Ireland, though there are important distinctions between the two.[16] For example, the definition used for acts of terrorism is more narrowly defined in the UK law than the Sri Lankan PTA. The UK law defines terrorism as "the use of violence for political ends, and includes any use of violence for the purpose of putting the public or any section of the public in fear,"[17] while the Sri Lankan 1979 PTA defines terrorism broadly as "unlawful activities."[18] It is noteworthy that within the preamble of the Sri Lankan PTA, justification for the law is sought by referencing actions taken by other democracies at war: "And whereas other democratic countries have enacted special legislation to deal with acts of terrorism."[19] Crisis law is portrayed here as but one set of tools employed by a legitimate state to confront internal violence. Yet, the claims of legitimacy are expansive; explicit clauses protecting state actors from prosecution were built into emergency legislation early on.

Emergency regulations were in force within Sri Lanka continuously from 1983 to 2001, with the exception of five months in 1989.[20] Under the terms of the Ceasefire Agreement of February 2002, certain provisions of the PTA were suspended. Specifically, search operations and arrests under the PTA by government forces were to cease and future arrests were to be conducted in accordance with the Criminal Procedure Code.[21] There was a lapse in emergency regulations between 2001 and 2005, during the Kumaratunga administration, due to a loss of a majority in Parliament for the ruling party; however, remaining provisions of the PTA and sections of the PSO were utilized by the president during this time to effectively continue emergency rule.[22] Following the assassination of Foreign Minister Lakshman Kadirgamar in 2005, the Sri Lankan government initiated the Emergency (Miscellaneous Provisions and Powers) Regulations, and after an assassination attempt in December 2006 on Defense Secretary Gotabhaya Rajapaksa (the president's brother), the government announced that provisions of the PTA would be reintroduced through a new set of Emergency Regulations (ERs).[23] The reinstatement of the PTA, in conjunction with increasing violence between the LTTE and government security forces during this time, signaled the unraveling of the 2002 Ceasefire Agreement.

More recently, emergency regulations were promulgated on May 2, 2010, one year after the end of the war. Several provisions outlined in the 2005 Emergency (Miscellaneous Provisions and Powers) Regulations were repealed at this time, *with the exception of the immunity clauses.*[24] In August 2011, the state of emergency was not renewed by Parliament and accompanying emergency regulations were no longer in force. However, at the same moment, President Rajapaksa ordered new regulations under Section 27 of the PTA, which essentially mirrored executive powers in the lapsed emergency regulations.[25] When President Sirisena took office in January 2015, there were no immediate efforts to dismantle the emergency institution in Sri Lanka and it is therefore unclear to what extent government accountability is possible under the current administration.

The Sri Lankan government has had a spotty record in reporting its use of emergency laws and, in line with research that has found international monitoring bodies to be fairly powerless to effect change in emergency institutions, there have been few repercussions from international organizations. Under Article 4 of the ICCPR, states are to report their derogations to the UN Human Rights Committee once an emergency is declared. Several states, including Sri Lanka, do not notify the Human Rights Committee of the derogations in a timely manner, if at all. For example, the Sri Lankan government did not report the 2005 ERs to the Human Rights Committee until June 2010. In addition, though Article 4 mandates that reasons for an emergency be given when notifying the Committee, the Sri Lankan government has not always obliged. The government notified the Human Rights Committee of Emergency Regulations (ERs) in May 2000 but it did not provide reasons. In its notification of derogation to the UN Human Rights Committee on June 9, 2010, the Sri Lankan government explains the changes within the 2010 ERs as reflective of the military defeat of the LTTE a year prior, coupled with the "need for vigilance to ensure the complete recovery of arms caches secreted by the LTTE and the reintegration back into society of LTTE cadres, after successfully completing programmes of rehabilitation and of vocational training."[26] No justification is provided for why crisis measures are required in the post-conflict period.

Immunity Clauses in Emergency Legislation

One of the most direct ways in which emergency laws impact efforts to hold state actors to account in Sri Lanka is through the inclusion of immunity provisions. Both the emergency regulations and the PTA contain clauses explicitly protecting state actors from investigation and prosecution. The ICCPR requires states to ensure an effective remedy for victims whose rights are violated.[27] Though Sri Lanka ratified the ICCPR in 1980, ERs and the PTA disregard elements of this treaty by incorporating immunity clauses for security force members and police officers. Even before Sri Lanka ratified the ICCPR, the government sought to shield state actors from prosecution through Sections 9 and 23 of the 1947 PSO. Section 23 stipulates,

> No prosecution or other criminal proceeding against any person for any act purporting to be done under any provision of this Part or of any Order made thereunder shall be instituted in any court except by, or with the written sanction of, the Attorney-General; and no such suit, prosecution or other proceeding, civil or criminal, shall lie against any person for any act in good faith done in pursuance or supposed pursuance of any such provision.[28]

Section 26 of the PTA, passed in 1979, includes the same immunity clause.[29] After the PTA was passed, the Supreme Court could not review the law's constitutionality because Article 80 of Sri Lanka's 1978 Constitution prevents judicial review of any legislation enacted after 1978.[30] The immunity clause within the PTA remains in effect today. During human rights prosecutions, defense counsel rarely invoked the immunity clauses. The "good faith" clause was briefly introduced in one successful prosecution, the Krishanthi Kumaraswamy case, but it was then quickly dismissed.[31] Instead, the immunity clauses in emergency legislation act largely to prevent the indictments of state actors.

A few years after the PTA was passed, the Jayawardene administration created the Indemnity Act 1982, which was extended through 1988 only, and provided similar protections for government officials, security force members, and police, acting while on duty to enforce law or acting "in the public interest."[32] ER 71 stipulated similar protections, until it was repealed in June 1993.[33]

Though immunity provisions for state actors were in effect throughout the conflict via the PTA, the Rajapaksa administration, which began in 2005, enacted additional clauses within Emergency (Miscellaneous Provisions and Powers) Regulation No. 73 of 2005 and Emergency (Prevention and Prohibition of Terrorism and Specified Terrorist Activities) Regulation 19 of 2006. Both regulations provide protection to persons authorized by the government who have "acted in good faith" in pursuance of the emergency laws.[34]

Clauses on Inquests and Post-mortems in Emergency Legislation

In addition to clauses that provide immunity for state officials acting under the emergency regulations or the PTA, successive administrations in Sri Lanka have also promulgated impunity through regulations on inquests and post-mortems.[35] A forensic autopsy performed at a coroner's inquest can be an important tool for human rights advocacy. For example, government culpability may be ascertained scientifically by "matching the circumstances under which a person was last seen with identification of his or her body and signs of ill treatment."[36] The UN *Manual on Effective Prevention and Investigation of Extra-legal, Arbitrary and Summary Executions* codifies such investigative procedures.[37]

Similar to the continued enactment of immunity clauses, governments tended to simply reformulate inquest clauses over time to ensure the investigation of a civilian death largely lay in the hands of the perpetrators themselves or their colleagues; or, to ensure that a family's right to an inquiry into the death of their loved one was eliminated altogether.

Ordinary law in Sri Lanka mandates an inquest when a person dies in custody of the police or military, or when a person dies at the hands of police or military in the line of duty.[38] In 1983, ER 15A was created by the government, allowing security force members to dispose of bodies without a post-mortem or inquest. During July of that year, the regulation complicated efforts to determine whether people who disappeared during communal violence were dead or missing.[39] The regulation also acted to effectively destroy physical evidence in possible disappearance, extra-judicial or torture cases, making it enormously difficult to bring charges against the perpetrators.[40] In February 1990, the provision authorizing security force members to dispose bodies without inquest was rescinded by the Premadasa administration. However, ER 55(B-F), which placed limits on complete, public inquiries into the causes and circumstances of deaths, remained in force. In 1993, Regulations 45 and 46, concerning inquest procedures and post-mortems, were rephrased to permit police to bypass ordinary law only when police or a member of the armed forces had reason to believe that the death took place in the course of an "armed confrontation," and that the victim was waging war against the state.[41]

In May 2000, ER 55FF, a regulation on inquests, was briefly introduced by the Kumaratunga administration then reportedly removed from the newly issued ERs (Miscellaneous Provisions and Powers). ER 55D(1), which remained in force during this time, mandated that when a person dies at the hands of the armed forces or police or in their custody, the police must notify a magistrate, who will order a post-mortem examination.[42] After the exam is performed, however, the police could return the body to relatives or, in the interest of national security and maintenance of public order, bury or cremate the body. In addition, if the Inspector General of Police applied for a High Court inquiry into the death under the emergency procedures, no other inquiry could be initiated, closing off attempts to investigate the death through normal procedures.[43]

In 2005, Regulations 54 to 57 of the Emergency (Miscellaneous Provisions and Powers) Regulations, reproduced the provisions found in Regulation 55FF, which had been revoked in May 2000 by Kumaratunga, by allowing a police officer or security force member to deviate from normal criminal law if the officer "has reason to believe that the death may have been as a result of any action taken in the course of duty either by him or by an officer subordinate to him, or where any person dies in police custody or military custody."[44] Regulation 56 dictates that the magistrate cannot order a post-mortem nor determine the manner of the disposal of the body without receiving information from the Inspector General of Police. This regulation effectively provides space for possible interference by the Inspector General of Police, particularly in cases where the deceased person has been subjected to torture.[45] Regulations 54 to 57 were repealed shortly after enactment on October 13, 2005; however, they were brought back in through the 2006 emergency regulations.[46] The regulations on inquests and post-mortems were in force during the final years of the war in Sri Lanka, from 2007 to 2009.

The commissioners leading the 1994 Commission of Inquiry into disappearances in the northern and eastern provinces issued a strong critique of emergency regulations on inquests in their final report. The report states, the inquest regulations "encouraged a section of the Army to cross the invisible line between the legitimate Security Operation and large scale senseless arrests and killings."[47] The consistent inclusion of inquest provisions in emergency regulations resulted in a virtual lockdown on a citizen's right to an inquiry where the police or security personnel were involved in a civilian's death. Since the prosecutorial process emanates from the inquest, it is not surprising that only a small number of state actors were tried throughout the war.

The general inaccessibility of emergency regulations to the public further compounds the problem of immunity and inquest clauses. Inconsistencies among the Sinhala, Tamil, and English versions of emergency regulations are a recurring issue. Additionally, emergency regulations go into effect before they are actually published in the government gazette and they are usually published along with a myriad of other notifications. Emergency regulations are rarely announced publicly, therefore, reformulations or the continuation of provisions that promote impunity, often go unnoticed by those who are most affected.

The previous discussion on the historical evolution of emergency laws and immunity and inquest clauses illustrates that the emergency institution in Sri Lanka did not undergo any real substantive change. Various provisions that protected state actors from judicial scrutiny were repealed followed by immediate reintroduction. Unlike the other cases in this book, in which layering or gradual displacement altered the logic of impunity within the emergency institution, human rights prosecutions remained highly circumscribed by inquest and immunity clauses.

The Absence of Independent Oversight of Executive Emergency Powers

Gradual institutional change is often possible only if those defending the status quo have weak veto power and if there are opportunities for different levels of discretion in the interpretation and enforcement of the institution's rules. Independent and consistent review of the institution's rules via a parliament or other monitoring body can act as a check on executive power and strong veto power if the executive has a majority in parliament. The power of immunity and inquest clauses to limit human rights prosecutions in Sri Lanka during the war was strengthened as a result of the executive's strong veto power. Additionally, no independent oversight body existed to review emergency and counter-terrorism laws and check executive abuse of power.

The 1972 Constitution, the first constitution of an independent Sri Lanka, is one of the main tools that severely weakened democracy in the country. Rule of law and judicial independence declined after 1972 and there were virtually no checks on the emergency regime.[48] The 1978 Constitution sought to curb this trend somewhat by including provisions for legislative oversight of emergency powers, strengthening judicial independence, and creating a remedy for violations of fundamental rights. The 1978 Constitution contains provisions allowing for emergency powers and limitations on certain rights during a crisis period.[49] The PSO enables the president, as opposed to Parliament, to declare a state of emergency and to create emergency regulations under Section 5 as necessary.[50] There is no established definition of a state of emergency nor is there a set threshold of violence; thus, the president possesses the sole authority in determining what constitutes a crisis and, in turn, what necessitates the expansion of executive power. Articles 155 (5) and (6) of the Constitution restrict a state of emergency to a period of one month and requires the proclamation to be approved by parliament within 14 days. Chapter XVIII of the constitution on public security initially proposed that a two-thirds majority be required to approve emergency proclamations in Parliament after a state of emergency had been in force for 90 days; in the end, however, the 10th Amendment to the Constitution, added in 1986, requires only a simple majority.[51] These legislative oversight provisions included in the 1978 Constitution (and the 1978 amendments to the PSO) were intended to curb abuse of emergency power by the executive. However, presidents' political parties tended to command a majority in Parliament throughout most of the conflict (1983–2009) with the exception of a few years in the early 2000s.[52] Because parliament tended not to scrutinize the president's declarations, it was commonplace for states of emergency to be renewed after one month.

After a state of emergency is declared by the president and approved by Parliament, emergency regulations can then be adopted granting various powers to the executive. Additionally, the president can add on new regulations to existing ones when he/she sees fit.[53] A limited degree of parliamentary control over emergency regulations is given by Section 5(3) of the PSO, which provides that a regulation may be added to, altered, or revoked by resolution of Parliament. Though Parliament is given the opportunity to scrutinize emergency laws through this provision, at no time during the war did it exercise this right.[54]

The creation and maintenance of the emergency regime during the war in Sri Lanka was largely at the discretion of the executive. Both the 1978 Constitution and the PSO grant extensive legislative power to the president and the simple majority requirements for parliamentary approval result in rubberstamping of emergency regulations. There was no regular, *independent* oversight mechanism in place to check executive authority during the war.

Judicial Review Powers

Strong executive power can be buttressed by constitutional provisions for judicial review of emergency powers, as reflected in the common law emergency oversight model. Sections of the 1978 Constitution did in fact create openings for some judicial challenges in the late 1980s and 1990s. The PSO initially restricted the possibility for judicial review through a clause which states that neither the existence of an emergency or an emergency regulation, nor an order, rule, or direction made under such a regulation, may be called in question in any court.[55] However, Article 155 of the 1978 Constitution provides that no emergency regulation can be in contravention of the constitution. Thus, if emergency regulations were seen to be in violation of fundamental rights enshrined in the constitution, judicial challenges to these laws could be brought to the Supreme Court, which holds jurisdiction for constitutional remedies of rights violations.[56] For example, an emergency regulation that banned circulating any posters or fliers without permission from the police was ruled to be in violation of the constitutional right to freedom of expression and the right to equality and it was therefore struck down as unconstitutional in the *Joseph Perera v. Attorney General* (1987) case.[57] Additionally, in the *Channa Peiris v. Attorney General* (1994) and *Sunila Rodrigo v. de Silva* (1997) cases, among others, the Supreme Court upheld the constitutional rights of freedom from arbitrary arrest and detention under emergency rule.[58] In the 1999 ruling on *Karunatiaka v. Dayananda Dissanayake*, the Supreme

Court found that the state had failed to establish evidence that there was a threat to public security in its issuance of an emergency regulation and it was therefore struck down.[59]

These cases are significant in that, for a time, judges in the Supreme Court shifted from a prior course of deference to the executive to one in which executive action under emergency powers was scrutinized and citizens' rights were upheld in order to curb abuse of power. In the end, however, the emergency institution and its dire effects on human rights prosecutions remained largely intact. None of the judicial challenges concerned immunity or inquest clauses, nor did they directly confront the issue of government accountability for human rights violations. The court was willing to strike down regulations that infringed on citizens' constitutional rights, but its activism during these years did not include consideration of cases that directly examined the commission of serious human rights abuses by the state. In essence, the ability for the Supreme Court to challenge the emergency institution was circumscribed by what are enshrined as fundamental rights in the constitution. The right to life is not included in the list of rights, nor is a right to a judicial remedy.[60]

Judicial Independence

Judicial review in Sri Lanka was also largely restricted due to low levels of judicial independence. The fact that the executive had the power to appoint Supreme Court judges meant the trend of judicial activism was temporary. Presidents often stacked the Supreme Court with political allies, and from 1999 to 2009, Chief Justice Sarath Silva, notorious for shutting down dissent on the bench, repeatedly sought to ensure that judges with independent views, such as Mark Fernando and Justice C. V. Wigneswaran, did not sit on significant constitutional cases.[61] The legal challenges at the Supreme Court did not fundamentally alter the emergency institution in Sri Lanka, and, as a result, they failed to pave a path for human rights cases to be heard.

The Absence of a Regional Human Rights Court

Unlike other cases in this book, Sri Lanka is not a member of a regional human rights court so there have been no judicial challenges to emergency laws at the international level. There has been critique from various domestic and international bodies. The UN Human Rights Committee and the

UN Working Group on Enforced or Involuntary Disappearances has criticized Sri Lanka's emergency regulations as incompatible with international standards and recommended their reform or elimination.[62] Domestic organizations and bodies have also called for reforms. For example, the final report of the 1998 Commission of Inquiry recommended, "the utilization of the powers under the Emergency Regulations be minimized" and it urged "parliament to scrutinize each Regulation before promulgation and Human rights Groups (sic) be given the opportunity to make submissions" each time a regulation is under review.[63] There is no evidence of a government response to these recommendations.

While in theory judicial review may have been a key condition for challenging provisions within Sri Lankan emergency laws, the parameters for review were quite limited. Additionally, the opportunities for judges to act independently and scrutinize executive action were minimal.

The rate of human rights prosecutions was abysmally low during the conflict. The remainder of the chapter provides detail on how, in the absence of conditions required to transform the emergency institution, one political leader's rise to power created a short-lived and shallow opening for justice in Sri Lanka's civil war.

Human Rights Prosecution Data

In Sri Lanka, approximately 16,745 civilians lost their lives at the hands of government actors between 1976 and 2008.[64] Original data collected for this book illustrates a rise in human rights prosecutions between 1997 and 2005. Twenty-two prosecutions of state actors for human rights violations were held. Within these trials, 211 state actors were prosecuted, 88 defendants were acquitted, and 123 defendants were convicted. Approximately half of the prosecutions involved army personnel, while the other half involved members of the police force. The majority of prosecutions involved murder charges (e.g., massacres, individual extra-judicial killings, and murder during detention) or abduction (e.g., disappearance) charges.[65] Though a few state actors were prosecuted for torture in criminal trials, the majority of torture charges were filed in civil cases. In civil cases, citizens can either file a case at the Supreme Court, which has fundamental rights jurisdiction (e.g., rights, such as freedom from torture, that are enshrined in the Sri Lankan Constitution), or file an application for a writ of habeas corpus in the Court of Appeal.[66] In civil cases, victims are awarded compensation and the accused does not receive a prison sentence. The prosecution data on Sri Lanka includes only criminal trials.

Of the 16,745 civilians killed by the state, 261 of the deaths were investigated and prosecuted in criminal trials, a rate of 1.6%. Though the war escalated after 1983, prosecutions of state actors did not commence until the early 1990s. By this time, Sri Lanka had weathered two insurgencies by the JVP. In addition, Tamil separatist militancy had evolved into a serious, organized threat. Reports of extra-judicial killings and disappearances were also at an historical high. Between 1983 and 1994, an estimated 14,062 civilians were killed.[67] Additionally, 25,061 disappearances were reported.[68] Though there was significant evidence linking government security forces and police to a large portion of these violations,[69] little had been achieved up to this point in the way of holding specific individuals to account.

Graph 2.1 illustrates that the increase in the number of state actors prosecuted largely occurs during President Kumaratunga's two administrations (1994–2005). A few prosecutions transpired before the steady rise that began in 1997. For example, though three police officers were convicted in 1991 for the murder of a human rights lawyer, Wijedasa Liyanarachchi, the initial charge of murder was dropped to conspiracy and wrongful confinement.[70] One year later, 20 members of the military were tried for the massacre of 67 civilians in Kokkadicholai. However, despite strong evidence gathered by a Commission of Inquiry into the incident, 19 of the 20 military officers were acquitted.[71] The landscape noticeably shifts after Kumaratunga is in office in that in addition to the rise in state actors who are tried, there is an increase in the number of convictions. While Kumaratunga was in office (1994–2005), the courts handed down 108 convictions and 47 acquittals in human rights cases. In addition, during this time, investigations covered the largest number of civilian deaths. Seven separate massacres involving the deaths of 180 civilians were investigated under Kumaratunga.[72] In 2000 alone, 88 members of the security forces were convicted in the case of 4 disappearances after massive amounts of evidence were produced in Commissions of Inquiry created by Kumaratunga. Not all of the prosecutions can be described as success stories. On the contrary, even in the case of conviction, sentences were often not proportionate given the fact that, for example, enforced disappearance was not a crime in the Penal Code. Issuing

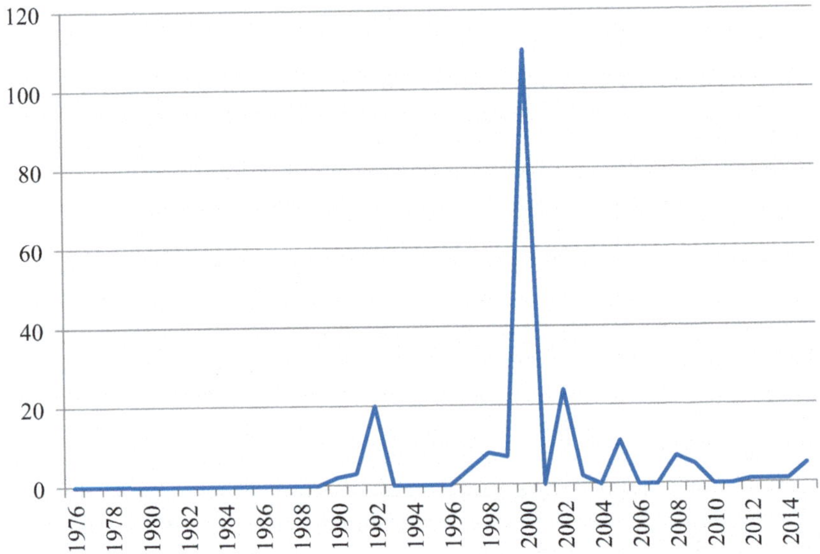

Graph 2.1 The number of state actors prosecuted per year in Sri Lanka

a charge of abduction with intent to murder was a serious failing in disappearance cases since thousands of civilians never reappeared, nor were their remains ever located. Abduction with intent to murder also carried a lighter sentence than enforced disappearance, a crime now enshrined in international law as a serious human rights violation.[73]

The overall picture of accountability shifts again after Mahinda Rajapaksa is elected in 2005. The political will to encourage accountability, even in a handful of cases, does not continue under this administration. In fact, no human rights prosecutions are initiated under Rajapaksa; the data illustrate that a few trials that are drawn out from the mid-1990s conclude during his term. The prosecutions that transpire between 2012 and 2014 involve state actors but the crimes are wholly unrelated to the conflict and more a symptom of Rajapaksa's highly authoritarian governance. The entrenchment of impunity in Sri Lanka is evident in the prosecution data and it is intimately tied to an emergency institution whose logic is to shield state actors from judicial accountability. What then prompted the prosecutions under Kumaratunga?

Prosecutions During the Kumaratunga Administration

In Sri Lanka, a rise in human rights prosecutions can be traced to one political leader's time in office. Once elected in 1994, President Chandrika Kumaratunga broke a prior trend of government impunity through four specific actions: direct involvement in one human rights trial and the creation of three Commissions of Inquiry that helped to prompt prosecutions of military and police officials. The commissions include the Commission of Inquiry into Involuntary Removal or Disappearance of Persons in the Western, Southern, and Sabaragamuwa Provinces (1994), the Batalanda Commission (1995), and the Pinto-Jayawardena (2010).

During the 1980s, when violence had reached an all-time high in Sri Lanka, civil society groups, particularly those critical of the government, largely operated under a climate of fear. Despite this, by the early 1990s, the number of non-governmental organizations in the country had grown to 3000. In response, the government sought to reduce the influence of these groups by developing emergency measures that regulated and monitored NGO actions. For example, on December 22, 1993, the government issued an emergency regulation making registration with the government mandatory for NGOs whose yearly receipts exceeded 50,000 rupees ($454 US dollars).[74] If receipts exceeded 100,000 rupees ($909 US dollars), a government official was assigned to the organization to monitor all receipts and disbursements. Some NGOs refused to register while others complied. When a provincial councilor was abducted, allegedly by the incumbent UNP, around the same time the emergency law on NGOs was issued, several organizations responded by publicly demanding protection for civil liberties and "clean government."[75] The public outcry for regime change during this time was more tangible than it had ever been, and it was at this moment that the PA party saw an opportunity.

The PA, which formed from a coalition of the Sri Lanka Freedom Party and other smaller parties, initiated a political campaign focused on government transparency, a society free from fear and corruption, and an end to a powerful executive. The PA had support from the Sri Lankan Muslim Congress and the TULF; as a result of its commitment to initiate a peace process with the LTTE and enact devolution of power, it also gained widespread support from constituents in the North and East and former militant Tamil groups.[76] The party manifesto promised to investigate "murder, disappearances, unresolved crimes and political victimization which occurred in the recent past" and stated, "within three months of coming into power we will take immediate steps to provide to families information about the disappeared."[77] The most widely distributed party poster displayed a picture of the party's presidential candidate, Chandrika Kumaratunga, with the tag-line, "To end a period of murder, vote for People's Alliance."[78] Massive popular support for these ideals contributed to the party's victory at the parliamentary elections in August 1994 and Kumaratunga's win in the presidential election in November. In the latter, she won all electoral districts with the exception of one. In addition to strong support from the Tamil population and civil society groups demanding government accountability, the PA won a clear majority among Sinhalese voters.[79]

Following on her promise of a negotiated peace, Kumaratunga initiated a ceasefire between the government and the LTTE in January 1995. However, the process broke down within only a few months and violence continued, primarily in the northern and eastern regions of the country. In the aftermath of one major pillar of her election campaign failing, Kumaratunga pursued an additional pillar, government accountability for human rights abuses. One of the first cases that benefited from Kumaratunga's rise to power in the mid-1990s involved a crime that had become relatively common by this point in the war. Seventeen-year-old Krishanthi Kumaraswamy, a young Tamil woman, was abducted at a Chemmani checkpoint in 1996, then raped and murdered by several army personnel. This tragedy was compounded when her mother, brother, and friend disappeared after inquiring about her at a police station. Because the incident involved a young, innocent person, there was substantial public outcry.[80] Once in power, there was clear political will from the Kumaratunga administration to punish the perpetrators. In 1997, the Chief Justice, with input from President Kumaratunga, initiated a trial-at-bar. A trial-at-bar is headed by a panel of judges as opposed to a trial by jury and is argued to be particularly useful in human rights cases because it expedites the proceedings and gives witnesses an opportunity to tell their story in a timely manner, as opposed to years or even decades later.[81] The swift pace of judicial proceedings on this case was highly unusual for the time. In the end, six soldiers were convicted for rape and murder and two soldiers were acquitted.[82]

The second human rights case that benefited from Kumaratunga's actions concerned the abduction, torture, and murder of more than 50 high school students in Embilipitiya in 1989. The victims' families and local politicians agitated for a judicial response to the crime, which fueled public outrage and support from various local organizations.[83] Though the Human Rights Task Force, a government-sponsored monitoring body, had filed a report on the case and made complaints about the delays in bringing the case to trial, charges were not brought against the accused until 1994.[84] The Embilipitiya case received significant attention after a Commission of Inquiry on disappearances shed light on government and security officials' responsibility for the crime. This non-judicial inquiry, and others created by Kumaratunga, was the first to document, publicize, and acknowledge the immense scale of disappearances in the country since the war commenced in 1983. The impact of the commissions' findings on disappearances was staggering and it illuminated a clear path for further criminal investigation and prosecution. Kumaratunga's creation of the three 1994 Commissions of Inquiry on disappearances as well as the later 1998 All-Island Commission of Inquiry resulted in the indictment of 262 security personnel, a major shift from a prior pattern of inaction on this issue.[85] In the end, however, only a handful of cases covered by the commissions proceeded to trial. The reason for this disparity is intimately tied to the fact that Kumaratunga largely pursued these cases in order to reap political gains.

Kumaratunga created seven Commissions of Inquiry during her administration. In 1994, only a few months into her tenure, President Kumaratunga appointed three regional Commissions of Inquiry to investigate the disappearances that had transpired throughout the country after January 1, 1988. Later, in 1998, she established a commission to tackle the disappearance cases that the 1994 commissions failed to consider due to time constraints. Its mandate was expanded to the entire island, which included 10,316 files. It was considered to be a great improvement from its predecessor and the commission sought to recommend legal proceedings to be issued against persons identified as responsible for enforced disappearances.[86] The 1998 commission's final report implicated agents of the state and paramilitaries acting in collaboration with the government in 4473 cases. The final report also included some of the most thorough and responsive recommendations to date, including: tasking the Sri Lankan Human Rights Commission with identified torture cases; the creation of an independent human rights prosecutor to handle disappearance cases; that "the utilization of the powers under the Emergency Regulations be minimized" and that "human rights groups be given the opportunity to make submissions" each time an emergency law is under review; the creation of a crime of enforced disappearance; and inclusion of the concept of command responsibility in the Penal Code.[87] None of these recommendations were implemented.

The work of one of the three regional commissions created in 1994, the Commission of Inquiry into Involuntary Removal or Disappearance of Persons in the Western, Southern and Sabaragamuwa Provinces, was particularly helpful to the Embilipitiya case.[88] The commission received complaints on the disappearance of 53 schoolboys from Embilipitiya, and in its final report, within a chapter on impunity, the commission challenged the army's claims that a long-term detention facility, in which the schoolboys were likely held, did not exist at the Sevana army camp.[89] The commission also submitted a special report on the Embilipitiya incident to President Kumaratunga.

In addition to creating a commission that helped to launch the Embilipitiya trial, President Kumaratunga took a somewhat unexpected stance by declining an army officer's promotion after he was acquitted in the Embilipitiya trial. The 1999 Embilipitiya trial convicted six soldiers and one high school principal for abduction with intent to murder, wrongful confinement, torture, and murder.[90] Many activists and victims' families considered the sentence, ten years of imprisonment, to be insufficient. Because the crime of enforced disappearance is not enshrined in the Penal Code, the accused were subject to a far less serious charge of "abduction."[91] A senior army officer, Lt. Col. Parry Liyanage, acquitted in the case for lack of evidence, filed a fundamental rights petition in the Supreme Court claiming he was due a promotion to Brigadier General. The Supreme Court ruled in favor of Liyanage. However, given his involvement in the Embilipitiya case, and the commission's findings that he was directly involved in the disappearance of the schoolboys, President Kumaratunga refused to award the promotion.[92] The Embilipitiya case is significant because though the rate of disappearances in Sri Lanka was one of the highest in the world by the mid-1990s, there had been no prosecutions, let alone convictions, that acknowledged this crime (abduction and murder) as part of a widespread pattern of violence.

In addition to the commissions on disappearances, Kumaratunga created a Commission of Inquiry on the Batalanda Housing torture case in 1995. A housing complex was used to torture, detain, and disappear dissidents during the late 1980s and early 1990s. The final report of the commission, issued in 2000, implicated senior politicians from the UNP, which had held power in the former administration, and high-ranking police officers. One of the most important findings of the commission involved evidence that a Senior Superintendent of Police, Douglas Peiris, was directly responsible for the design and function of the torture and detention operations at Batalanda, including the abduction and detention of police colleagues that were investigating the disappearances.[93] Peiris fled the country soon after the Commission of Inquiry was created. Therefore, the possibility of an immediate prosecution that built on the commission's work was seriously delayed. It was not until 2009 that Peiris and four other policemen were convicted for abduction and unlawful detention with intent to murder three individuals.[94]

Finally, in 2001, President Kumaratunga convened the Bindunuwewa Commission[95] to inquire into the deaths of 28 Tamil youth at a detention center. Detainees within the detention center were violently attacked by a mob of Sinhalese civilians while the police officers on duty looked on. The commission report, which was not published, identified two senior police officers as responsible for not preventing the killings and junior officers for direct involvement in the deaths. Two police officers were convicted on the charge of murder by the High Court in 2003, however, the Supreme Court overturned the convictions in 2005.[96] Though the commission's findings were not used as evidence directly in the trial proceedings, the information from the commission prompted Kumaratunga to initiate an investigation into the incident.

Kumaratunga's actions during her tenure (1994–2005) were significant in altering the human rights record in Sri Lanka for a time. Her efforts to shed light on the devastating pattern of disappearances, which reached the tens of thousands, are often heralded and it is noteworthy that two of the cases that benefited from her actions (the Kumaraswamy and Bindunuwewa cases) concerned crimes that transpired on her watch. Yet, Kumaratunga is not widely regarded by the human rights community as a crusader for justice. Members of civil society organizations that aligned themselves with Kumaratunga during her first campaign for the presidency commented to me in interviews that the PA saw an opportunity to go after its political rivals by capitalizing on the popular demand for government accountability.[97] One interviewee commented that the high-profile trials and the 1994 Commissions of Inquiry were simply a means to "demonize the previous regime."[98] With the exception of the Kumaraswamy and Bindunuwewa cases, this is largely true. Much of Kumaratunga's focus was on crimes committed during previous administrations, and though extra-judicial killings decreased dramatically during her tenure (see Graph 2.2[99]), the majority of human rights abuses were not investigated. Disappearances also continued at a rapid rate.

In 2001, in an attempt to regain a majority in Parliament, Kumaratunga worked with the JVP to develop the 17th Amendment to the Constitution. The amendment was important in that it removed power from the executive to appoint judges and other key positions, including the Attorney General, and it placed power in the hands of a Constitutional Council. Given the importance of judicial challenges to emergency laws and the necessity for judicial independence in this regard, the amendment may have led to significant changes to the emergency institution. However, the election in 2005 of Mahinda Rajapaksa, his disregard for the 17th Amendment, and the introduction of the 18th Amendment in 2010 nullified any hope of transformation within the emergency institution.[100]

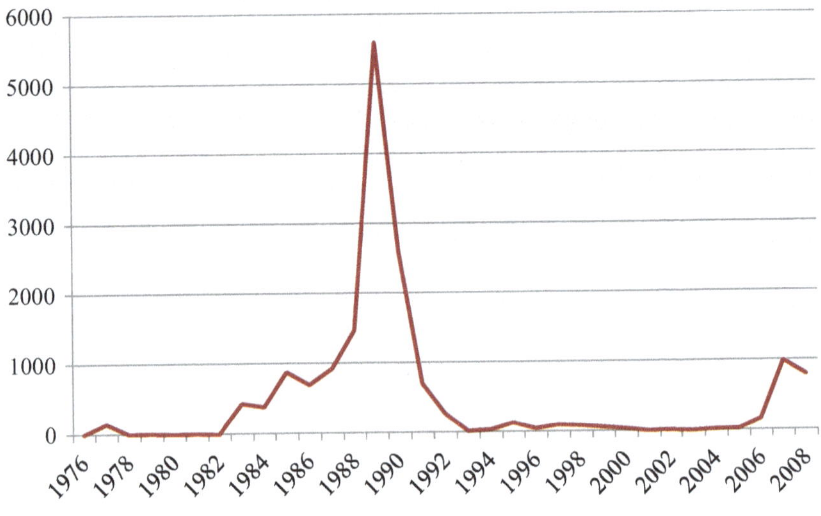

Graph 2.2 Extra-judicial killings of civilians by the Sri Lankan state, 1976–2008

The Final Years of the War: "Talking About Rights Is Irrelevant at Best"[101]

After Rajapaksa took office in 2005, any hope for accountability declined. Emergency laws that had lapsed between 2001 and 2005 (with the exception of the PTA) were resurrected and executive power increased dramatically. In the face of continued government impunity, some citizens took complaints to the United Nations Human Rights Committee (UNHRC). Victims of state human rights violations in Sri Lanka lack the option to bring their case to a regional human rights court, however, after exhausting domestic remedies, victims or their counsel, can file a claim with the UNHRC, per the First Optional Protocol to the International Covenant on Civil and Political Rights (ICCPR), which Sri Lanka acceded to in October 1997. If the UNHRC deems the claim valid, it will issue a communication to the Sri Lankan government, urging specific actions. Unlike European Court of Human Rights rulings, the UNHRC communications are not binding. Between 2005 and 2009, 12 communications, which found violations of various ICCPR provisions, were issued to the Sri Lankan government by the UNHRC.[102] The government failed to implement any of the recommendations laid out by the UNHRC.

In a particularly alarming ruling in 2006, commonly known as the Singarasa case, the Sri Lankan Supreme Court responded to the UNHRC's recommendation to provide the complainant with an effective remedy of retrial or release and compensation, by deciding that the Sri Lankan state's accession to the Optional Protocol was an unconstitutional exercise of legislative power and an unconstitutional conferment of judicial power on the Human Rights Committee.[103] The Supreme Court declared the State's accession to the Covenant constitutional. However, given Sri Lanka's dualist system, which requires the creation of domestic law in order to enforce international treaties the government has ratified, the Covenant does not have domestic force. Singarasa's application to the UNHRC and its subsequent recommendations were therefore found to be without legal basis. This ruling was widely criticized for its complete disregard of the State's obligations under ICCPR and its manipulation of constitutional provisions to make a false claim concerning the UNHRC's "judicial power."[104] One human rights attorney commented to me that after the Singarasa ruling in 2006, he encouraged complainants to bypass the Supreme Court and instead go straight to the UNHRC because judgments like those in the Singarasa case provide precedent and serve to legitimize arguments made by "extremists" that the international community is trying to violate Sri Lanka's sovereignty.[105]

The increase in authoritarian rule under Rajapaksa is further illustrated by the president's failure to respond to complaints by a major international donor. The Generalized System of Preferences Plus (GSP+) is a European Union trade concession whose eligibility is based on compliance with international human rights treaties. Sri Lanka had access to this concession for their apparel exports. In June 2010, after temporarily withdrawing the concession in February due to human rights concerns, and offering an extension to the Sri Lankan government to which there was no reply, the European Union fully withdrew the GSP+ concession.[106] This and the prior examples of the government flagrantly disregarding its human rights obligations indicates, as one director of a civil society organization in Colombo described, that in the final years of the war the country moved further away from democratic institutions enshrined in the India model toward an East Asian model in which economic development is the priority and "talking about rights is irrelevant at best."[107]

Future Accountability and the Emergency Institution

Following the end of the war in May 2009, there was intense debate over the role of the government in the deaths of thousands of civilians in the war's final months. Almost two years after the war ended, a UN panel issued a report in which it found credible allegations that the government of Sri Lanka was responsible for most of the civilian deaths in the final months of the conflict.[108] The report recommended the UN Secretary-General promptly establish an independent international mechanism to monitor domestic accountability processes and investigate alleged violations. In March 2014, the UN Human Rights Council voted to open investigations into the violence during the years 2002–2011, and a report of findings was issued in September 2015. This report strongly recommends the creation of a hybrid special court that integrates domestic and international judges, prosecutors, and investigators in order to address what it documents as several instances of war crimes committed by both the government and the LTTE. In a 2016 visit to Sri Lanka, the High Commissioner for Human Rights Zeid Ra'ad Al Hussein, recognized that Sri Lanka's new political context under President Sirisena may assist the country in finally confronting decades of impunity.[109] The possibilities for accountability under Sirisena, however, are largely unclear. Though emergency regulations lapsed in 2011, several similar provisions have remained in the PTA. This is noteworthy not only because modes of arbitrary arrest and detention and immunity clauses remain lawful but also because the PTA is not subject to the same, albeit limited, parliamentary oversight as the PSO and the Constitution.[110] The logic of impunity within the emergency institution therefore continues unabated. In order for the emergency institution to be subject to rigorous and consistent challenge, certain conditions are required: independent oversight of executive emergency powers, judicial review of emergency laws, and a strong record of judicial independence. The following chapters illuminate how these conditions can loosen the restrictions on human rights prosecutions that are embedded in emergency institutions.

Notes

1. Manoharan, N. *Democratic Dilemma: Ethnic Violence and Human Rights in Sri Lanka*. New Delhi: Samskriti (2008).
2. Redden, Kenneth Robert and Linda L. Schlueter, eds. *Modern Legal Systems Cyclopedia, Volume 9A, Part II, Country Studies*. Buffalo, NY: William S. Hein and Company Law Publisher (1990).
3. Redden and Schlueter (1990).
4. Pinto-Jayawardena, Kishali. 2010. Post-War Justice in Sri Lanka: Rule of Law, the Criminal Justice System and Commissions of Inquiry, International Commission of Jurists.
5. Redden and Schlueter (1990).
6. Pinto-Jayawardena (2010).
7. Sriram, Chandra Lekha. Dilemmas of Accountability: Politics, the Military and Commissions of Inquiry during an Ongoing Civil War – The Sri Lankan Case, *Civil Wars* 5(2) (2002): 96–121.
8. United Nations. Report of the Secretary-General's Panel of Experts on Accountability in Sri Lanka. New York: United Nations (2011, March 31).
9. Olsen, Tricia D, Leigh A. Payne, and Andrew G. Reiter. *Transitional Justice in Balance: Comparing Processes, Weighing Efficacy*. Washington DC: United States Institute of Peace Press (2010).
10. Immunity clauses and inquest provisions within emergency laws are not to be confused with formal amnesty laws, which prohibit prosecution of certain actors and are typically created by governments to halt violent conflict or assist a negotiated transition process (Mallinder 2009).

11. Some of the arguments set forth in this chapter were first published as an article. See Moira Katherine Lynch. 2015. "A Theory of Human Rights Prosecutions and Emergency Law: Bringing in Historical Institutionalism," *Journal of Human Rights* 14(4): 504–524.
12. Pinto-Jayawardena (2010).
13. Ceylon Yearbook (1948).
14. Coomaraswamy, Radhika and Charmaine de los Reyes. Rule by Emergency: Sri Lanka's Post-Colonial Constitutional Experience. *International Journal of Constitutional Law* 2(2) (2004): 272–295.
15. See Udagama (2015) for a useful discussion on how the PSO was not entirely a product of British colonialism but rather was pushed by local political elites from the independence movement.
16. Sieghart, Paul. 1984. Sri Lanka: A Mounting Tragedy of Errors. Report of a Mission to Sri Lanka in January 1984 on behalf of the International Commission of Jurists and its British Section, JUSTICE.
17. Prevention of Terrorism Act (1974).
18. Prevention of Terrorism (Temporary Provisions) Act No. 48. (1979). (Colombo, Sri Lanka: Gazette of the Democratic Socialist Republic of Sri Lanka).
19. Prevention of Terrorism Act No. 48, 1979.
20. Coomaraswamy and de los Reyes (2004).
21. Law and Society Trust (LST). 2003 Report. *Sri Lanka: State of Human Rights.* Colombo, Sri Lanka.
22. Udagama, Deepika. An Eager Embrace: Emergency Rule and Authoritarianism in Republican Sri Lanka, in Asanga Welikala, ed., *Reforming Sri Lankan Presidentialism: Provenance, Problems and Prospects.* Centre for Policy Alternatives (2015), 290. http://srilankan-presidentialism.org/ (accessed September 20, 2015).
23. Centre for Policy Alternatives. Statement on the Introduction of the Emergency Regulations 2006. Colombo, Sri Lanka; Law and Society Trust (LST). 2007 Report. *Sri Lanka: State of Human Rights.* Colombo, Sri Lanka.
24. The Gazette of the Democratic Socialist Republic of Sri Lanka, Extraordinary. (2010) No. 1651/24, May 2, restructuring of 2005 Emergency (Miscellaneous Provisions and Powers) Regulations; United Nations, 2011.
25. Udagama, 313–314.
26. United Nations Human Rights Committee. Notifications Under Article 4(3) of the Covenant (Derogations). Sri Lanka. Retrieved August 18, 2010. http://treaties.un.org/Pages/ViewDetails.aspx?src=TREATY&mtdsg_no=IV4&chapter=4&lang=en
27. See ICCPR (1966) Art. 2, Para 3.

28. Public Security Ordinance. (1947) (Colombo, Sri Lanka: Gazette of the Government of Ceylon).
29. Prevention of Terrorism Act Sec. 26, 1979.
30. Coomaraswamy and de los Reyes (2004).
31. Interview 24, Colombo, Sri Lanka, January 2011; Interview 25, Colombo, Sri Lanka, January 2011.
32. Indemnity Act of 1982. Sri Lanka.
33. Amnesty International. Sri Lanka: When Will Justice Be Done? (ASA 37/15/94) July 1994.
34. EMERGENCY (MISCELLANEOUS PROVISIONS AND POWERS) REGULATIONS. (2005) No. 1 of 2005, Regulation No. 73, published in The Gazette of the Democratic Socialist Republic of Sri Lanka, Extraordinary; EMERGENCY (PREVENTION AND PROHIBITION OF TERRORISM AND SPECIFIED TERRORIST ACTIVITIES) (2006). Regulation 19, The Gazette of the Democratic Socialist Republic of Sri Lanka, Extraordinary No. 1474/5, December 6, 2006.
35. The provisions on inquests in emergency legislation have been in force and rescinded at different times throughout the conflict under various regulation numbers, including Regulation 15A, Regulation 55FF, Regulations 45 and 46 and later, Regulations 54–57.
36. Clark, Ann Marie. *Diplomacy of Conscience: Amnesty International and Changing Human Rights Norms*. Princeton: Princeton University Press (2001), 115.
37. See also the purpose and creation of the "Minnesota Protocol" in Clark (2001).
38. See the Code of Criminal Procedure Act No. 15 (1979).
39. Annual Human Rights Reports Submitted to Congress by the U.S. Department of State: Sri Lanka. 1983.
40. Sieghart (1984); Law and Society Trust (LST). 1994 Report. *Sri Lanka: State of Human Rights*. Colombo, Sri Lanka; Law and Society Trust (LST). 2001 Report. *Sri Lanka: State of Human Rights*. Colombo, Sri Lanka.
41. Law and Society Trust (LST). 1993 Report. *Sri Lanka: State of Human Rights*. Colombo, Sri Lanka.
42. Amnesty International. Sri Lanka: New Emergency Regulations – Erosion of Human Rights Protection. July 2000.
43. Amnesty International (2000)
44. Regulation 54, No. 3 2005 Emergency (Miscellaneous Provisions and Powers) Regulations; Law and Society Trust (LST). 2006 Report. *Sri Lanka: State of Human Rights*. Colombo, Sri Lanka.
45. Civil Rights Movement Note. Inquests and the Disposal of Dead Bodies. 09/03/2005.

46. Law and Society Trust (2006, 2007).
47. Final Report of the Commission of Inquiry into the Involuntary Removal or Disappearance of Persons in the Northern and Eastern Provinces, Sessional Paper No. VII (1997), 5.
48. Udagama, 301.
49. See the Constitution of the Democratic Socialist Republic of Sri Lanka (1978), Art. 155 (2 and 3).
50. Coomaraswamy and de los Reyes (2004).
51. Udagama, 304–305.
52. Udagama, 309.
53. Udagama, 310.
54. Coomaraswamy and de los Reyes, 27; Welikala, Asanga. 2008. *A State of Permanent Crisis: Constitutional Government, Fundamental Rights and States of Emergency in Sri Lanka*. Colombo, Sri Lanka: Centre for Policy Alternatives, 203.
55. See Public Security Ordinance No. 25, Sec. 3, 8 (1947).
56. Udagama, 315.
57. Udagama, 322.
58. Welikala (2008) and Pinto-Jayawardena (2010).
59. Udagama, 322.
60. Even though Sri Lanka has ratified the ICCPR, which includes the right to life (Article 2) and a right to remedy after violations (Article 6), under its dualist legal system, in order for the ICCPR to be applicable domestically, international law has to be transformed into domestic law by Parliament.
61. International Crisis Group. Sri Lanka's Judiciary: Politicized Courts, Compromised Rights. Asia Report No. 172, June 30, 2009.
62. Amnesty International (2000).
63. Final Report of the Commission of Inquiry into Involuntary Removal and Disappearance of Certain Persons (All Island), Sessional Paper No. I, 2001, 85.
64. I calculated this total through my research of U.S. State Department reports and local non-governmental organization human rights reports. The total excludes civilian deaths resulting from crossfire between LTTE and security forces and thus focuses on targeted killings of civilians by security force members and police through extra-judicial executions or massacres. This count omits the tens of thousands of civilians who died in the final months of the war (January–May 2009). These deaths are omitted in order to ascertain an appropriate comparison between the number of conflict-related deaths that were investigated and prosecuted and the total number of deaths during the conflict. Though the 2011 UN report on the final stages of the war concluded the government was responsible

for the majority of deaths, the Sri Lankan government disputes this finding. Neither a truth-seeking body nor a judicial process has confirmed the number of civilian deaths in the final months of the war or those responsible. Thus, any inclusion of data from January to May 2009 in the total of civilian deaths at the hands of the state risks misrepresentation. As of the writing of this book, no human rights prosecutions have been held regarding civilians killed in the final months of the war.

65. Abduction was typically the charge in cases where victims were disappeared because the crime of enforced disappearance does not exist in Sri Lankan criminal law.
66. Udagama, Deepika. Taming of the Beast: Judicial Responses to State Violence in Sri Lanka, *Harvard Human Rights Journal* 11 (1998): 269–294.
67. U.S. Department of State (1983–1994); Law and Society Trust (1993, 1994).
68. Association for Families of the Disappeared (2009).
69. Amnesty International Country Reports, Sri Lanka. 1985–1988.
70. U.S. State Department 1991.
71. U.S. State Department 1992.
72. The prosecutions for the Wavulkelle, Bolgoda Lake, Kumarapuram, Embilipitiya, Mylanthanai, and Bindunuwewa massacres were all completed during Kumaratunga's administration. The Mirusuvil massacre trial began in 2002 and was completed in 2015
73. Pinto-Jayawardena (2010, 127).
74. Law and Society Trust (1993).
75. Law and Society Trust (1994, 17).
76. Wickramaratne, J. 2015. "Executive Presidency: A Left Perspective," in Asanga Welikala, ed., *Reforming Sri Lankan Presidentialism: Provenance, Problems and Prospects*. Centre for Policy Alternatives. http://srilankan-presidentialism.org/ (accessed September 20, 2015).
77. Law and Society Trust (1994).
78. Asian Human Rights Commission. December 1994. "Sri Lanka: Will the New Government Dismantle the Machinery of Terror?" http://www.hrsolidarity.net/mainfile.php/1994vol01no01/1923/(accessed July 1, 2011).
79. Sriram (2002).
80. Interview 20, Colombo, Sri Lanka, January 2011; Interview 22, Colombo, Sri Lanka, January 2011.
81. Interview 23, Colombo, Sri Lanka, January 2011; Interview 24, Colombo, Sri Lanka, January 2011.
82. Punyasena, Wasana. "The Façade of Accountability: Disappearances in Sri Lanka," *Boston College Third World Law Journal* 3(1) (2003):115–158;

International Crisis Group. "Sri Lanka's Human Rights Crisis," Asia Report, No. 135, June 14, 2007.

83. International Crisis Group (2007).
84. Law and Society Trust (1994) and Pinto-Jayawardena (2010).
85. U.S. State Department (2003).
86. Final Report of the Commission of Inquiry into Involuntary Removal and Disappearance of Certain Persons (All Island), Sessional Paper No. I, 2001.
87. Final Report, Sessional Paper No. 1, 2001.
88. Interview 22, Colombo, Sri Lanka, January 2011.
89. Final Report of the Commission of Inquiry into the Involuntary Removal or Disappearance of Persons in the Western, Southern and Sabaragamuwa Provinces, Sessional Paper No. V, 1997.
90. Punyasena (2003) and Pinto-Jayawardena (2010).
91. Amnesty International (2009); Int. 22, 2011; Pinto-Jayawardena (2010).
92. Pinto-Jayawardena (2010).
93. Pinto-Jayawardena, 96.
94. U.S. State Department (2009).
95. Pinto-Jayawardena (2010)
96. Law and Society Trust (2004).
97. Interview 21, Colombo, Sri Lanka, January 2011; Int. 20, 2011; Int. 22, 2011; Int. 25, 2011; Law and Society Trust (1994) and Law and Society Trust (1995).
98. Int. 20, 2011.
99. Data on extra-judicial killings from 1976 to 2008 is based on U.S. Department of State Annual Human Rights Reports, the Law and Society Trust's Annual State of Human Rights Reports (Colombo, Sri Lanka), Amnesty International reports and data gathered by the Association for Families of the Disappeared (Colombo, Sri Lanka).
100. Centre for Policy Alternatives. Statement on the Eighteenth Amendment. 2010. Colombo, Sri Lanka.
101. Int. 25, 2011.
102. Law and Society Trust (2007) and Pinto-Jayawardena (2010).
103. Law and Society Trust (2007).
104. Bastiampillai, Bertram, Rohan Edirisinghe, and N. Kandasamy, eds. 2010. *Sri Lanka Prevention of Terrorism Act: A Critical Analysis*. Centre for Human Rights and Development (CHRD), Colombo, Sri Lanka.
105. Int. 23, 2011.
106. "Sri Lanka Loses GSP+," *The Sunday Leader*. July 5, 2010, retrieved February 28, 2011.
107. Int. 25, 2011.
108. United Nations (2011).

109. Al Hussein, Zeid Ra'ad. Statement by the United Nations High Commissioner for Human Rights at the End of His Mission to Sri Lanka. February 9, 2016.
110. Centre for Policy Alternatives. The Need to Repeal and Replace the Prevention of Terrorism Act. May 9, 2013. Colombo, Sri Lanka. http://www.cpalanka.org/the-need-to-repeal-and-replace-the-prevention-of-terrorism-act-pta/ (Accessed October 6, 2015).

Bibliography

Al Hussein, Zeid Ra'ad. 2016. Statement by the United Nations High Commissioner for Human Rights at the End of His Mission to Sri Lanka, February 9.

Amnesty International. Sri Lanka: When Will Justice Be Done? (ASA 37/15/94) July 1994.

———. Sri Lanka: New Emergency Regulations – Erosion of Human Rights Protection. July 2000.

Amnesty International Country Reports, Sri Lanka. 1985–1988.

Annual Human Rights Reports Submitted to Congress by the U.S. Department of State: Sri Lanka. 1983–1994.

Annual Human Rights Reports Submitted to Congress by the U.S. Department of State: Sri Lanka. 1991.

Annual Human Rights Reports Submitted to Congress by the U.S. Department of State: Sri Lanka. 1992.

Annual Human Rights Reports Submitted to Congress by the U.S. Department of State: Sri Lanka. 2003.

Annual Human Rights Reports Submitted to Congress by the U.S. Department of State: Sri Lanka. 2009.

Asian Human Rights Commission. 1994. Sri Lanka: Will the New Government Dismantle the Machinery of Terror? December. http://www.hrsolidarity.net/mainfile.php/1994vol01no01/1923/. Accessed 1 July 2011.

Association for Families of the Disappeared. 2009. Statistics on Enforced Disappearances, 1988–2009. Colombo, Sri Lanka.

Centre for Policy Alternatives. Statement on the Introduction of the Emergency Regulations. 2006. Colombo, Sri Lanka.

Centre for Policy Alternatives. Statement on the Eighteenth Amendment. 2010. Colombo, Sri Lanka.

Centre for Policy Alternatives. The Need to Repeal and Replace the Prevention of Terrorism Act. 2013. Colombo, Sri Lanka, May 9. http://www.cpalanka.org/the-need-to-repeal-and-replace-the-prevention-of-terrorism-act-pta/. Accessed 6 Oct 2015.

Ceylon Yearbook. 1948.

Civil Rights Movement Note. Inquests and the Disposal of Dead Bodies. 09/03/2005.
Clark, Ann Marie. 2001. *Diplomacy of Conscience: Amnesty International and Changing Human Rights Norms*. Princeton: Princeton University Press.
Coomaraswamy, Radhika, and Charmaine de los Reyes. 2004. Rule by Emergency: Sri Lanka's Post-colonial Constitutional Experience. *International Journal of Constitutional Law* 2: 272.
Final Report of the Commission of Inquiry into Involuntary Removal and Disappearance of Certain Persons (All Island), Sessional Paper No. I, 2001.
Final Report of the Commission of Inquiry into the Involuntary Removal or Disappearance of Persons in the Northern and Eastern Provinces, Sessional Paper No. VII, 1997.
Final Report of the Commission of Inquiry into the Involuntary Removal or Disappearance of Persons in the Western, Southern and Sabaragamuwa Provinces, Sessional Paper No. V, 1997.
Indemnity Act. 1982. Sri Lanka.
International Crisis Group. Sri Lanka's Human Rights Crisis. Asia Report, No. 135, 14 June 2007.
———. Sri Lanka's Judiciary: Politicized Courts, Compromised Rights. Asia Report, No. 172, 30 June 2009.
Interview 20, Colombo, Sri Lanka, January 2011.
Interview 21, Colombo, Sri Lanka, January 2011.
Interview 22, Colombo, Sri Lanka, January 2011.
Interview 23, Colombo, Sri Lanka, January 2011.
Interview 24, Colombo, Sri Lanka, January 2011.
Interview 25, Colombo, Sri Lanka, January 2011.
Law and Society Trust (LST). 1993. Report. *Sri Lanka: State of Human Rights*. Colombo, Sri Lanka.
———. 1994. Report. *Sri Lanka: State of Human Rights*. Colombo, Sri Lanka.
———. 1995. Report. Sri Lanka: State of Human Rights. Colombo, Sri Lanka.
———. 2001. Report. *Sri Lanka: State of Human Rights*. Colombo, Sri Lanka.
———. 2003. Report. *Sri Lanka: State of Human Rights*. Colombo, Sri Lanka.
———. 2006. Report. *Sri Lanka: State of Human Rights*. Colombo, Sri Lanka.
———. 2007. Report. *Sri Lanka: State of Human Rights*. Colombo, Sri Lanka.
Manoharan, N. 2008. *Democratic Dilemma: Ethnic Violence and Human Rights in Sri Lanka*. New Delhi: Samskriti.
Olsen, Tricia D., Leigh A. Payne, and Andrew G. Reiter. 2010. *Transitional Justice in Balance: Comparing Processes, Weighing Efficacy*. Washington, DC: United States Institute of Peace Press.
Pinto-Jayawardena, Kishali. 2010. Post-war Justice in Sri Lanka: Rule of Law, The Criminal Justice System and Commissions of Inquiry. International Commission of Jurists.

Prevention of Terrorism Act. 1974. United Kingdom.

Prevention of Terrorism (Temporary Provisions) Act No. 48. (1979). (Colombo, Sri Lanka: Gazette of the Democratic Socialist Republic of Sri Lanka).

Public Security Ordinance. (1947). (Colombo, Sri Lanka: Gazette of the Government of Ceylon).

Punyasena, Wasana. 2003. The Façade of Accountability: Disappearances in Sri Lanka. *Boston College Third World Law Journal* 3 (1): 115–158.

Redden, Kenneth Robert, and Linda L. Schlueter, eds. 1990. *Modern Legal Systems Cyclopedia, Volume 9A, Part II, Country Studies*. Buffalo: William S. Hein and Company Law Publisher.

Report of the Commission of Inquiry into the Batalanda Housing Scheme. Sri Lanka Sessional Papers, 2000.

Sieghart, Paul. 1984. Sri Lanka: A Mounting Tragedy of Errors. Report of a Mission to Sri Lanka in January 1984 on Behalf of the International Commission of Jurists and its British Section, JUSTICE.

"Sri Lanka Loses GSP+," *The Sunday Leader*. July 5, 2010. Retrieved February 28, 2011. http://www.thesundayleader.lk/2010/07/05/sri-lanka-loses-gsp/

Sriram, Chandra Lekha. 2002. Dilemmas of Accountability: Politics, the Military and Commissions of Inquiry During an Ongoing Civil War – The Sri Lankan Case. *Civil Wars* 5 (2): 96–121.

The Gazette of the Democratic Socialist Republic of Sri Lanka, Extraordinary. 2010. No. 1651/24, May 2, Restructuring of 2005 Emergency (Miscellaneous Provisions and Powers) Regulations.

Udagama, Deepika. 1998. Taming of the Beast: Judicial Responses to State Violence in Sri Lanka. *Harvard Human Rights Journal* 11: 269–294.

———. 2015. An Eager Embrace: Emergency Rule and Authoritarianism in Republican Sri Lanka. In *Reforming Sri Lankan Presidentialism: Provenance, Problems and Prospects*, ed. Asanga Welikala. Centre for Policy Alternatives. http://srilankanpresidentialism.org/. Accessed 20 Sept 2015.

United Nations. 2011. *Report of the Secretary-General's Panel of Experts on Accountability in Sri Lanka*. New York: United Nations.

United Nations Human Rights Committee. Notifications Under Article 4(3) of the Covenant (Derogations). Sri Lanka. Retrieved August 18, 2010. http://treaties.un.org/Pages/ViewDetails.aspx?src=TREATY&mtdsg_no=IV4&chapter=4&lang=en

Welikala, Asanga. 2008. *A State of Permanent Crisis: Constitutional Government, Fundamental Rights and States of Emergency in Sri Lanka*. Colombo: Centre for Policy Alternatives.

Wickramaratne, J. 2015. Executive Presidency: A Left Perspective. In *Reforming Sri Lankan Presidentialism: Provenance, Problems and Prospects*, ed. Asanga Welikala. Centre for Policy Alternatives. http://srilankanpresidentialism.org/. Accessed 20 Sept 2015.

CHAPTER 3

Conversion, Layering, and Human Rights Prosecutions in Northern Ireland

During the conflict in Northern Ireland, the emergency laws contained fewer explicit protections for state actors compared with legislation in Sri Lanka. However, key aspects of the design and implementation of the emergency institution produced serious constraints on the ability for investigations to move forward in state violence cases and for the courts to issue fair judgments. Controls on the inquest process originally placed within emergency provisions were shielded from oversight and judicial scrutiny after they were folded into ordinary criminal law. This form of conversion prevented the investigation of the majority of state violence cases during the conflict. Additionally, state violence cases were determined by a largely biased community of judges in juryless courts, a feature of emergency laws created at the start of the conflict. The emergency institution was not entirely static, however. As a result of two key factors, independent oversight of executive emergency powers and access to a regional human rights court, revisions were made to amendments concerning human rights prosecutions. Ultimately, the processes of conversion and layering within the emergency institution did not erode the powerful logic of impunity. This chapter provides detail on why, and it discusses the effects of these conditions on human rights prosecutions.

The chapter is organized as follows: the first section presents historical background to the Northern Ireland conflict; the second section describes the creation of the emergency institution in Northern Ireland and the use

M. Lynch, *Human Rights Prosecutions in Democracies at War*, Human Rights Interventions,
https://doi.org/10.1007/978-3-319-96908-4_3

of conversion; the third section explains how independent oversight of executive powers and rulings from the European Court of Human Rights produced layering; the fourth section presents prosecution data and detailed cases of human rights prosecutions; and the fifth section concludes by explaining the impact of conversion and layering on human rights prosecutions.

Historical Background to the Conflict in Northern Ireland

The conflict in Northern Ireland (1969–1998) emerged out of centuries of British dominance throughout the island. The British colonized the region as early as the twelfth and thirteenth centuries, and by the seventeenth and eighteenth centuries, the majority Catholic population in Ireland was largely overpowered by the military strength of the British government and their Protestant allies. Though Catholic communities engaged in some resistant efforts during this time, particularly concerning land rights, a fully formed opposition movement did not emerge until the early twentieth century. Irish nationalists mounted a political and militant struggle for independence from Britain and the Irish Republican Army (IRA) pursued various tactics of guerilla violence. In response, the British government created the Government of Ireland Act in 1920, which established a parliament in Belfast to rule over the six counties in the north of the island, often referred to as Ulster. Through a partition process, the remaining 26 counties in the south of the island became the independent nation of Ireland. Northern Ireland was defined since its inception by a stark division between two communities: Nationalists, mainly Catholic, who supported the unification of all the counties in Ireland independent from British rule, and Unionists, mainly Protestant, who supported the northern counties' union with Britain.

From 1922 until the 1960s, the largely Protestant Ulster Unionist Party held power in the Northern Ireland Parliament and many Catholics living in the region refused to recognize the Northern Ireland state. The few nationalist politicians elected to Parliament vacillated between abstention and participation in government affairs during this time.[1] The security forces and police in Northern Ireland emerged out of pre-partition Protestant defense organizations and thus were predominantly comprised of Protestants and those who supported unionism. The majority of the judiciary was also largely Protestant. In this milieu, discrimination against Catholics in housing and public sector employment grew.

In the mid-1960s, a civil rights movement modeled after the movement in the United States was initiated with a focus on reforming the policies of exclusion directed at Catholics. The civil rights movement's marches became a sectarian battleground and British security forces were brought in to manage the growing unrest. Though some reforms were made by the Northern Ireland Parliament, under pressure from the British government to address the movement's demands, by the early 1970s, paramilitary groups representing warring ideologies were embroiled in an intense conflict with one another and with the British security forces. The central paramilitary groups during the conflict included a Republican group, the Provisional IRA, which were committed to seeking a united Ireland independent from Britain through militant means, and the Loyalist groups, the Ulster Volunteer Force, the Ulster Defense Association, and the Red Hand Commando, which were committed to maintaining unity with Britain. Various splinter groups emerged from these groups in later years of the conflict. The shooting of 13 civilians by British paratroopers during a civil rights march in Derry in January 1972 launched the domestic crisis into a more permanent form of instability. In March of the same year, the Northern Ireland Parliament (Stormont) was prorogued and direct rule of the region by the British government began. Several attempts were made to turn power over to a localized power-sharing administration but at different intervals both Nationalist and Unionist parties refused to accept the proposed arrangements.[2]

After an intense period of violence, the British government initiated the Anglo-Irish Agreement in 1985, which reiterated that the status of Northern Ireland remained dependent on the will of a majority, recognized the community of nationalists throughout Ireland, and provided the Irish government with a role in developing policy in the region. Though the Agreement was passed, talks among the Northern Ireland political parties and the Irish and British governments over the nature of a political settlement continued into the early 1990s with little consensus.[3] In August 1994, the IRA announced a complete ceasefire and the loyalist paramilitaries soon followed. At this moment, the beginning stages of peace negotiations were underway. After almost 30 years of conflict, and approximately 3600 lives lost, parties to the conflict signed the Belfast Agreement in 1998. The Agreement established the terms of a compromise, a power-sharing government in the region, and continued ties with Britain. By the end of October 2000, 433 political prisoners from both sides of the conflict (193 Loyalists, 229 Republicans, and 11 others) were released after an independent commission review process.[4]

In the years since the peace agreement, Northern Ireland continued to confront political instability and bouts of paramilitary violence. Intense debates also arose concerning the need for more formal processes of justice and reconciliation. Compensatory schemes for victims were established by the 1998 peace agreement through a national Victims Unit.[5] Several local peace initiatives also emerged to address various issues related to the conflict, including victims' rights, political prisoner and ex-paramilitary reintegration, youth programs aimed at dismantling sectarianism, the creation of memorials and storytelling projects. In 2007, a consultative project was commissioned by the Northern Ireland government to examine ways for the country to move forward and determine appropriate justice processes. The final report on this project, issued in 2009, recommended, among several other matters, public inquiries into state violations should not be established in the future.[6]

After the partition of Ireland in 1920, distinct legal systems were established in the northern and southern regions of the island. In Northern Ireland, the judicial sector falls under the common law legal system. The superior courts include the High Court, the Crown Court, and the Court of Appeal. The High Court primarily handles civil cases, while the Crown Court hears serious criminal matters, including murder, manslaughter, rape, and robbery.[7] The Court of Appeal is positioned above the High Court and Crown Court and cases may be further appealed from here to the House of Lords in London. The inferior courts manage more minor offenses and include county courts and magistrates' courts. Prior to prosecution in the High Court or Crown Court, committal proceedings are held in a magistrates' court to determine if there is prima facie evidence to proceed and, if so, the case proceeds to trial. A citizen can apply for a writ of habeas corpus on the grounds that his/her detention is believed to be unlawful, if access to a solicitor is denied, or if a person is maltreated during detention.[8] Habeas corpus applications are made to the High Court and thus are considered civil cases, as opposed to criminal proceedings.

The Attorney General in Northern Ireland is the chief law officer of the government whose main responsibility is advising the government departments and representing the government's interests in legal proceedings. The British prime minister has traditionally appointed this position. Prior to direct rule of the country by Britain in 1972, Northern Ireland retained its own Attorney General; between 1972 and 2010, however, the British

Attorney General acted for Northern Ireland.[9] In 2010, after policing and criminal justice powers were transferred from Britain to Northern Ireland, a local Attorney General was appointed by the Northern Ireland First Minister and Deputy First Minister.

The Attorney General is also responsible for appointing and removing the Director of Public Prosecutions (DPP). Prior to 1972, many prosecutions in Northern Ireland were conducted by police officers. The history of police conducting prosecutions in the United Kingdom stems from the UK Prosecution of Offenses Act 1879. This act established terms for the police to perform most of the investigations and prosecutions in criminal cases. However, through the Prosecution of Offences (Northern Ireland) Order 1972, the Office of the DPP was created to assume responsibility for serious criminal prosecutions. The police retained their investigative function and under this new framework, they submitted their investigation of a crime to the DPP (this body is now known as the Public Prosecution Service). Police officers in Britain were also largely responsible for prosecuting cases until the Crown Prosecution Service was created in 1985.[10]

The DPP in Northern Ireland decides whether a prosecution is justified, the charges, and initiates the committal proceedings in a magistrate's court (the pre-trial stage). If the DPP decides to commit a person for trial, all the necessary materials are sent to barristers of the Crown Counsel at the Belfast Crown Court, and one of these barristers prosecutes the case. The Crown Counsel represents the British government in all criminal cases. Though the creation of the DPP in 1972 was a marked improvement from prosecutorial power in the hands of the police, it has been argued that the state continued to largely investigate itself because the DPP relied heavily on the police for investigation and evidence, even in cases where the police were charged with a crime.[11] Since the DPP was appointed by and reported to the British Attorney General throughout the conflict years, there may have been space for government interference where the state was implicated. The lack of turnover within the DPP has also caused some human rights advocates in Northern Ireland to question its integrity in that there has been little room for reform.[12] For example, since 1972, only two people have headed the DPP. In contrast, DPP leaders in England are appointed every five years.

During the conflict and until very recently, the judges of the Court of Appeal, the Crown Court and the High Court in Northern Ireland were appointed and removed by the Queen on the advice of the Lord Chancellor, who is a Minister of the British Government, the Speaker of the House of

Lords, and appointed by the British prime minister.[13] The Lord Chancellor was generally responsible for overseeing the Northern Ireland Court Service, the administration for courts and tribunals in the country. In 2010, when policing and criminal justice powers were devolved from the British government to the Northern Ireland government, the Court Service became an agency under the Access to Justice Directorate of the Department of Justice for Northern Ireland.

The United Kingdom ratified the 1949 Geneva Conventions in 1957. The government did not, however, ratify the 1977 Additional Protocols until the conflict in Northern Ireland was effectively over, in January 1998. Similar to Sri Lanka, though the level of violence in Northern Ireland appeared to meet the threshold of conflict in Common Article 3, particularly in the early years of the war, the British government's consistent position was that the violence in Northern Ireland did not amount to internal armed conflict. Though the ICRC occasionally visited the prisons in Northern Ireland, the organization also did not formally acknowledge the applicability of Common Article 3 to the conflict. The delayed ratification by the British government of the Additional Protocols to the Geneva Conventions may have largely been intentional, as Protocol I granted prisoner-of-war status to combatants and Protocol II outlined the provision of amnesty to prisoners post-conflict.[14] The British government was thus in a convenient position in the early stages of the war to at some measure deny responsibility for actions that would have been construed as violations of international humanitarian law. Despite this, citizens utilized domestic criminal law and international human rights law to pursue human rights prosecutions.

The Emergency Institution in Northern Ireland[15]

The History of Emergency Laws in Northern Ireland

The history of Britain's use of emergency laws within Ireland goes further back than the history of emergency laws in Sri Lanka. Between 1800 and 1921, the British Crown implemented over 100 Coercion Acts in Ireland to quell violence and restore order.[16] The 1914–1915 Defense of the Realm Act and the 1921 Restoration of Ireland Acts, which established regulations for maintaining order in all the British colonies and Ireland, respectively, set an important precedent for emergency laws designed later to address the conflict in Northern Ireland. The 1922 Civil

Authorities (Special Powers) Act, created in response to growing political violence in Northern Ireland after the partition of the island, drew its provisions directly from the 1921 Restoration of Ireland Act.[17] Thus, the regulation of disorder and violence by the British government is part and parcel of the historical evolution of the Irish state and the creation of Northern Ireland.

The 1922 Civil Authorities (Special Powers) Act (SPA), remained in force in Northern Ireland until 1973, after it was made permanent by the Northern Ireland Unionist Government in 1933. In 1972, in response to a Belfast High Court ruling (*Regina (Hume and others) v. Londonderry Justices)*, which challenged the Northern Ireland government's claim that British armed forces in Northern Ireland were to act under the 1922–1943 SPAs, the British government immediately introduced a bill (Northern Ireland Act 1972) to retrospectively legalize all security force actions taken prior to 1972.[18] In this case, two Northern Ireland MPs, John Hume and Ivan Cooper, who engaged in a sit-down demonstration against the actions of the British troops in Derry, were charged with refusing to obey the order of an Army officer, who was acting under the power conferred on him by Regulation 38 of the SPA to disperse public assemblies.[19] The local magistrate convicted the MPs but they won their appeal in the Northern Ireland High Court. The High Court ruled that by conferring powers on the British Army, the emergency regulation was in fact not lawful given that the 1920 Government of Ireland Act did not allow the Northern Ireland government to order the armed forces of the Crown to take action. The 1972 Northern Ireland Act was eventually passed by both Houses in the British Parliament. The law was not an explicit amnesty law, nor did it contain specific immunity provisions similar to those issued in Sri Lanka. The objective of the law was to challenge the Northern Ireland High Court ruling by retroactively legitimizing the actions taken by the British armed forces in the *Regina (Hume and others) v. Londonderry Justices* case.[20] The law represents a significant moment in that as the British government assumed control over all functions of Northern Ireland through devolution in 1972, a tone was set concerning the legality of a British military presence in the region. The 1972 Northern Ireland Act was eventually repealed in 1999.

Immediately after the British government reintroduced direct rule over Northern Ireland, amidst growing political violence in 1972, it created the 1973 Emergency Provisions Act (EPA). This legislation re-enacted almost all of the provisions within the 1922 SPA, including measures related to

Table 3.1 A chronology of major emergency and counter-terrorism laws in the United Kingdom

Year	*Law*
1914–1915	Defense of the Realm Act (DORA)
1921	Restoration of Ireland Acts (ROIA)
1922	Civil Authorities (Special Powers) Act (SPA)
1939	Prevention of Violence Act
1973	Northern Ireland Emergency Provisions Act (EPA)
1974	Prevention of Terrorism Act (PTA)
1975	Northern Ireland Emergency Provisions Act (renewed)
1976	Prevention of Terrorism Act (renewed)
1978	Northern Ireland Emergency Provisions Act (renewed)
1987	Northern Ireland Emergency Provisions Act (renewed)
1989	Prevention of Terrorism Act (renewed)
1991	Northern Ireland Emergency Provisions Act (renewed)
1994	Criminal Justice and Public Order Act
1996	Prevention of Terrorism Act (renewed)
1998	Northern Ireland Emergency Provisions Act (renewed)
1998	Prevention of Terrorism Act (renewed)
2000	Terrorism Act (United Kingdom)
2006	Terrorism Act (United Kingdom) (renewed)

detention and internment.[21] The EPA was slightly amended in 1975 then re-enacted in 1978, 1987, 1991, and 1998 (see Table 3.1).

The 1974 Prevention of Terrorism Act was a United Kingdom-wide law rushed through Parliament with little debate or discussion after an IRA bombing in Birmingham, England. The law focused on the proscription of terrorist groups, exclusion orders, and powers of arrest and detention. This act also largely drew from existing legislation, including the 1939 Prevention of Violence Act, the 1922 SPA, and the 1973 EPA. The 1974 PTA was initially subject to biannual reviews in the British Parliament, but this was changed to annual reviews in 1976. It was re-enacted in 1976 and 1989, amended by the Criminal Justice and Public Order Act (1994), re-enacted in 1996, and amended and maintained in 1998.[22]

The use of laws from the colonial period by successive British and Northern Ireland administrations to regulate the conflict sustained a logic of impunity within the emergency institution. This logic granted legitimacy to the presence of British armed forces in the region and often the actions of said personnel in carrying out their duty to support the civil police forces. The logic of impunity built into historical emergency legislation was buttressed by two additional components of the emergency institution that emerged in the early years of the armed conflict: the regulation of inquests and the introduction of juryless courts.

Conversion: The Regulation of Inquests in Emergency Legislation and the Transfer of Inquest Provisions to Ordinary Legislation

As Chap. 2 demonstrates, successive administrations in Sri Lanka promulgated impunity through regulations on coroner's inquests and post-mortems, allowing for the disposal of victims' bodies without a proper inquest and for the police to have extensive control over the inquest process where security force personnel were implicated. Northern Ireland's emergency laws and Prevention of Terrorism Act, in contrast, do not contain explicit protection clauses for state actors. However, inquests were, for a time, regulated through emergency laws in Northern Ireland as a means to protect security forces from prosecution.[23]

The inquest procedure in Northern Ireland has undergone significant revisions since the early twentieth century. Historically, coroners had a central role in investigating sudden or unexpected deaths. The Coroners (Amendment) Act 1926 established that the police had the main responsibility of investigating and prosecuting unlawful deaths and coroners became a part of the investigative apparatus of the police. At a coroners' inquest, a jury had the power to issue an indictment of murder, manslaughter, or infanticide and the coroner could commit the accused for a criminal trial.[24] The Criminal Law Act of 1977 eliminated the right for coroners to issue determinations regarding indictments largely out of a concern that the rights of the accused would be compromised by the prior issuance of a verdict by the inquest jury.

Emergency legislation in Northern Ireland has included more explicit limitations on the inquest procedure. The 1922 SPA, which remained in force until 1973, included provisions that allowed the government to prohibit holding an inquest in a designated case or class of cases. It also enabled the Minister of Home Affairs to conduct an inquiry in lieu of an inquest and he/she could order a military court of inquiry instead of an inquest if military authorities requested it, all "for the purpose of preserving the peace and maintaining order."[25] This provision was modeled on Regulation 81 of the 1920 Restoration of Order in Ireland Act, which also remained in force until it was repealed by Westminster through the 1953 Statute Law Revision Act.[26] Concerns about the clauses in the 1922 SPA were raised in the Northern Ireland Parliament at the committee stage of the bill. One Member of Parliament stated: "If these inquests are prohibited it raises a suspicion that will enable the enemy to blacken us further as far as that may be possible."[27] Other members countered this allegation arguing that the government could not trust some coroners in the region and access to special powers was therefore necessary.[28]

The inquest provision in the 1922 SPA was later removed from the 1973 EPA, likely as a result of its controversial nature. Prior to this, however, questionable inquest provisions were incorporated into ordinary legislation, the Coroner's Act (Northern Ireland) 1959 and the Coroner's (Practice and Procedures) Rules 1963. Specifically, the 1959 Coroner's Act limited the coroner's investigation to the facts alone, namely who died and how he/she died, abolishing the prior power of an independent body to assess civilian deaths caused by the police and the armed forces (Public Records Office Northern Ireland). The act also replaced local authorities with the Minister of Home Affairs to oversee the functioning of the coroner's courts. Though some of these changes followed recommendations made by the government-sponsored Wright Committee Report, the elimination of the power of coroners to issue verdicts appears to be a direct response by the Northern Irish government to the escalating conflict situation.[29]

Rule 9 of the Coroner's Rules (Northern Ireland) 1963 stipulated that a person causing a death was a non-compellable witness. Thus, police or security officers who caused a civilian death by the use of force were never required to attend an inquest nor were they exposed to cross-examination or verification of their testimony in coroner's courts. Rule 17 of the Coroner's Rules allowed the inclusion of statements made by non-compellable witnesses, even though these statements were not given under oath and the witness was not required to be present.[30] Notably, there was no equivalent legislation in England or Wales during this time.[31]

The use of Public Interest Immunity Certificates (PIICs) in inquests has also diminished transparency in some state violence cases. Through the issuance of a PIIC by the Secretary of State for Northern Ireland or the Secretary of State for Defense, certain information can be deemed classified and therefore not available to a public court hearing. PIICs were used in a variety of state violence cases in order to exclude particular types of evidence, identified by government authorities as in the interest of national security, from the inquest proceedings. For example, concerns arose in cases where paramilitary members were killed by the British armed forces because some of the information withheld from the inquest as a result of the PIIC may have entailed important information on potentially illegal behavior by the government.[32] The PIICs made it difficult to conduct a full review of a case that concerned the state's culpability in not only potentially committing a crime against a civilian but also in planning out the crime in advance.

In the years leading up to the conflict, the Northern Ireland government strategically redeployed inquest clauses within emergency laws by placing them in ordinary legislation. This act of conversion served to address concerns about increasing controls over the inquest process and it enabled political actors to avoid judicial scrutiny. The normalization of these controls and the use of PIICs enabled state actors to skirt investigation and prosecution. Indeed, several civilian death cases between 1969 and 1994 were never subject to coroner inquests.[33] Coroners relied on the police to initiate an investigation and thus, the absence of an inquest and many times, the lengthy delays that followed the onset of an inquest, may have resulted from the reality that police personnel were leading and shaping a criminal investigation of their own colleagues.

The Criminal Prosecution Process in State Violence Cases: Juryless Courts

Given the previous discussion on the diminishing role of independent coroner inquests, it is evident that controls over the stages of investigation matters for human rights prosecutions. The nature of the criminal trial can also influence accountability outcomes and it can set the precedent for subsequent prosecutions of state actors. In Colombia, as Chap. 5 illustrates, the very definition of military jurisdiction in the Military Criminal Code, which was issued as an emergency decree, enabled military personnel to investigate and try their own in cases of serious violence against civilians for decades. This resulted in an almost complete lack of accountability during the first two decades of the Colombian civil war. In Northern Ireland, military courts were not utilized for cases of state violence. However, the type of criminal trial implemented in state violence cases, juryless courts, made it difficult for independent and external observers, specifically civilians, to weigh in.

After imposing direct rule in 1972, the British government requested a group of experts, under the leadership of Lord Diplock, to evaluate the legal processes in place that would address the increasing number of terrorist activities in Northern Ireland. The Diplock Report, resulting from this effort, included a recommendation that would become one of the most significant changes to the Northern Ireland court system during the crisis. On the basis of concerns of jury intimidation by paramilitary organizations and bias among jury members in a highly sectarian environment, the report suggested the creation of juryless courts for a series of particular offenses. The replacement court model, later referred to as Diplock courts, included a sole judge who would issue the final ruling and existing applicable rights of appeal were maintained.[34] This new legal process was adapted directly into Section 2 of the Northern Ireland EPA of 1973. The list of what are termed "scheduled offenses" in the EPA is lengthy and at the top of the list are common law offenses, including murder and manslaughter.[35] Several of the remaining offenses are related to terrorist activity and the majority of cases heard in the Diplock Courts were related to suspected terrorist crimes.

Most of the crimes analyzed in this chapter include what are termed "lethal force deaths." This term refers to cases in which the victims' deaths are caused by an agent of the state during the course of duty or while acting in pursuit of duty obligations to the state when force was wielded against a civilian.[36] Some of these deaths occurred amidst rioting or other situations of disorder, while others transpired during an arrest or confrontation between the state actor and the victim. Significantly, all lethal force deaths were prosecuted in juryless Diplock courts. The lack of a jury in these trials was significant to human rights prosecutions outcomes for several reasons, including the reality that one judge would be the only actor determining the "reasonableness" of the accused's decision to use lethal force. Additionally, because state actors are charged with ordinary criminal offenses in these cases (murder or manslaughter), judges are also alone in interpreting the applicability of ordinary criminal law in a conflict environment. Finally, most of the charges in these cases were murder, as opposed to manslaughter, and there was a serious reluctance on the part of judges to impose the requisite punishment in murder cases, life imprisonment, on members of the police and armed forces.[37] Thus, while state violence was not prosecuted in military courts, as it was for a significant period in Colombia, many of the cases involving civilian deaths at the hands of the state were brought before special juryless courts that were sanctioned through emergency legislation.

In lethal force prosecutions, the relevant law relied upon for assessing lethal force is Section 3 of the Criminal Law Act (Northern Ireland) 1967. Regarding use of force when making an arrest, Section 3 states, "A person may use such force as is reasonable in the circumstances in the prevention of crime, or in effecting or assisting in the lawful arrest of offenders or suspected offenders or of persons unlawfully at large."[38] There is no legislation regulating the use of lethal force in the context of a crisis situation. The police and military are trained in their own internal guidelines concerning how to assess imminent threats and using force to effect an arrest, but these are not binding in law. Thus, it is up to a judge, as opposed to a jury of civilians, to determine whether a member of the police or armed forces was acting reasonably under the circumstances.[39]

The court transcripts for prosecutions of lethal force cases demonstrate that judges are either struggling to assess how to square ordinary criminal law charges of murder or manslaughter with actions by state actors in a conflict situation, or the judges are explicitly biased in their support of state actors whom they view to be defending the nation against terrorist violence. For example, in the *R v. Jones* (1975) case, in which a British soldier was acquitted on the charge of murder for shooting and killing unarmed civilian Patrick Anthony McElhone as he ran away, Judge McDermott made the following comment:

> The Civil Power is charged with keeping the peace and in Northern Ireland the Army is acting in aid of the Civil Power. In some measure their rights and duties are to be gleaned from a consideration of the terms of the Emergency Provisions Act of 1973 and they are I believe protected if they act reasonably in various situations to do with carrying out their duties. On this occasion as far as the deceased is concerned, he was stopped and questioned, in my view properly, under section 16 of the 1973 Act and it was again in my view perfectly proper in the circumstances for the Sergeant to seek his recall for further questioning.
>
> In Northern Ireland there in fact exists a war or quasi war situation but the law remains the same, and one question that arises at the outset is, does this mean that the general wartime situation or the actual situation of a soldier on the ground is not a material or relevant factor? I have no doubt that both these factors are material and relevant. Mr Curran (the prosecutor for the Crown) is of course quite right when he says that the existence of the emergency does not give the troops carte blanche to shoot as and when they choose. But the existence of the emergency and the actual particular problem facing the soldier on the ground are relevant factors when assessing what is reasonable, because in any sphere of our law reasonableness is not some abstract, ill defined concept; reasonableness always depends on all the circumstances, not on a limited selection of them.[40]

Judge McDermott assesses the actions of the soldier in this case as lawful and not equivalent to murder by explicitly referencing the power to stop individuals for questioning enshrined in Section 16 of the 1973 EPA; McDermott then implies that the context of a war matters in his determination that shooting a civilian in the back is reasonable. Yet, there is no law for him to cite to support his conclusion that the use of lethal force was justified in this context. The judge, without input from other observers traditionally included in a jury trial, was the sole actor assessing what the crisis environment enables state actors to do in the performance of their duties.

A comparison case serves as a useful illustration of this point. In 1984, a juryless court convicted four off-duty members of the Ulster Defense Regiment (UDR)[41] for the murder of Adrian Carroll. What prompted a conviction in this case? One of the main distinctions was the accused were at no point claiming self-defense or the right to pursue an arrest of a suspected terrorist under emergency law. Because the accused were off-duty at the time of the crime, the use of force was not invoked in the trial. Thus, the initial trial judge, as well as the judge at the Court of Appeal in 1988, determined that the four men were guilty based on witness and defendant statements concerning intent, as opposed to the reasonableness of actions taken by security personnel during a crisis.[42] The *R v. Latimer* case went through several subsequent appeals. In 1992, three of the four UDR men were acquitted by the Court of Appeal while Neil Latimer's conviction was upheld. Latimer continued to appeal his conviction and in 2004 the conviction was maintained by the High Court of Belfast.[43] The Latimer case faced intense scrutiny and criticism over the course of several years. Police handling of the crime and evidence used in the case continues to be highly disputed today.[44] These two cases demonstrate that one of the central problems in prosecuting state violence involved legal ambiguity on "reasonableness" and the use of force in an emergency context.

By the mid-1990s, judges take a different tone regarding state violence in a few cases. The fairly widespread support for actions taken by the state in earlier cases is replaced with questions concerning the tendency among judges to conflate the lawful right to arrest suspected terrorists and the right to use lethal force. For example, in 1995, two Scot Guardsmen, Mark Wright and Jim Fisher, were convicted in the murder of Peter McBride. Peter McBride was shot and killed in 1992 not far from his home in the New Lodge Road area of Belfast. On the morning of his death, he was stopped and questioned by a commander of an army patrol in the area. After a short amount of time he fled from the patrol and was pursued on foot. McBride was told to halt and when he failed to do so, he was shot twice in the back. One of the accused claimed McBride was a threat because he believed the deceased was carrying a homemade bomb at the time.[45]

In his ruling on this case (*R v. Fisher and Wright*), Judge Kelly takes issue with conclusions made by Judge McDermott in the previously mentioned *R v. Jones* (1975) case. Judge Kelly comments:

> Dealing with Mr Smith's first submission on the factual basis that the deceased was running away but carrying a coffee-jar bomb and firearm, neither of which he had attempted to use against the accused or the patrol, either accused would have had the right to arrest the deceased, under section 18 of the Northern Ireland (Emergency Provisions) Act 1991 or section 26 of the Police and Criminal Evidence (Northern Ireland) Order 1989. In having a bomb or firearm in his possession, he was committing an offence, and an arrestable offence at that. What however creates considerable difficulty for me in this context of arrest, is the equating of the firing of aimed shots by a soldier at a fleeing suspect with intent to kill or cause him grievous bodily harm in order to 'stop' him with the effecting of a lawful arrest. Action of that kind does not seem to me to be the way of making an arrest. I doubt if it could be said that a police officer or civilian was in the process of making an arrest if, respectively, one fired aimed shots from his service revolver, or if the other fired aimed shots from his legally held shotgun at a fleeing criminal. To chase, catch, grab hold of and detain a suspect is what is commonly and I consider sensibly conceived to be the arrest of a fleeing criminal.[46]

Judge Kelly additionally comments on the matter of shooting a suspect in order to prevent the commission of a crime:

> My opinion was, and is, that the better view is that the shooting was lawful if, but only if, it was necessary to prevent imminent danger to life. I agree with Professor Glanville Williams (Textbook of Criminal Law (Second Edition) 504, fn 5) that, contrary to the view of Lord Diplock, there would then be evidence to found a defence of self-defence at common law, as well as under s 3. It is a very dangerous doctrine that would allow a fleeing person to be shot down because, if he gets away, sooner or later, he is likely to participate in acts of violence.[47]

Judge Kelly concluded that the two accused soldiers were guilty of murder with a mandatory term of life imprisonment. Only two years earlier, Private Clegg was also convicted of murder in the death of Karen Reilly and convicted for an attempt to wound Martin Peake. The two victims were shot while riding in a car that drove through an army checkpoint. Despite these convictions, these cases continue to cast a shadow on human rights prosecutions processes in Northern Ireland because in each case, the defendants were released early from their prison sentence; Wright and Fisher were released after three years and Private Clegg was released after two years.

The early releases in these cases illustrate an additional problem inherent in the prosecution of state violence cases. During the conflict, the crime of murder in ordinary criminal law was accompanied by a mandatory life sentence. There was great consternation among the judges in several murder cases about finding the accused guilty given the serious penalty of life imprisonment. Additionally, proving the intention of murder in lethal force cases was particularly difficult given the standard defense used by most of the accused was that they were facing an imminent threat to their own life in some way.[48] In some cases, judges commented that they would consider, or perhaps *should* consider, manslaughter as opposed to murder charges, but that their hands were tied because this involved legal reform, a matter outside their scope. For example, in an appeal by the Attorney General to the House of Lords regarding the outcome of the *R v. Jones* (1975) case, Viscount Dilhorne (one of the judges on the panel) issued this comment:

> The Attorney-General indicated that he would like it to be held that it was manslaughter, while I appreciate his reasons for doing so, I can find no escape from the conclusion that if a crime was committed, it was murder if the shot was fired with intent to kill or seriously wound. To hold that it could be manslaughter would be to make entirely new law. If a plea of self defence is put forward in answer to a charge of murder and fails because excessive force was used though some force was justifiable, as the law now stands the accused cannot be convicted of manslaughter. It may be that a strong case can be made for an alteration of the law to enable a verdict of manslaughter to be returned where the use of some force was justifiable but that is a matter for legislation and not for judicial decision.[49]

Additionally, in the *R v. Thain* case in 1984, where a soldier was convicted of murder, a judge in the Court of Appeal argued that the law on the use of force was vague and deserving of revision by Parliament. However, because he and the other appeal judges did not formally indicate that there was a legal matter of public importance on this issue, there was no further appeal to the House of Lords.[50] If a local parliament had been in place during the conflict, it is possible that legislation may have ensued regarding the problem of charges in these cases. However, because of direct rule by the British government, legislative reforms had to be taken up by Westminster. The ways in which certain Members of Parliament brought this matter to the attention of the British Parliament, discussed in the following section, is therefore significant.

Layering: Independent Oversight of Executive Emergency Powers and Regional Human Rights Court Rulings

Layering within an institution typically results when actors who wish to displace an institution have little capacity to do so as a result of weak veto power. When actors lack the capacity to dismantle the targeted institution, they work within the existing system to make change.[51] The institution's rules may be amended, revised, or added on to by those who wish to challenge the institution's undergirding logic. These incremental changes can have important impacts on the institution over time. In essence, institutions are not simply self-reinforcing entities. Rather, they are often sites of intense debate over the meaning, application, and enforcement of particular rules. Political actors and members of the judiciary are typically in a position to interpret, challenge, and enact an institution's rules. During the Northern Ireland conflict, the emergency institution was directly challenged through independent review procedures within British Parliament, contestation from members of Parliament and as a result of litigation at the European Court of Human Rights. Emergency rules concerning human rights prosecutions were amended over time as a result.

Independent Oversight of Executive Emergency Powers: Annual Reviews of Emergency Legislation

After the British government imposed direct rule over Northern Ireland in 1972, the country operated without a local parliament, though citizens were able to vote in British Parliament elections. A partial political administration was in place but the general lack of local political representation precluded the possibility of petitioning local leaders for change. In Sri Lanka, a brief, albeit short-lived, break in the pattern of impunity emerges when citizens elect a leader who ran on a platform of human rights protection and government accountability. This option was circumscribed in Northern Ireland and it mattered for debates on emergency laws and the impact of these laws on judicial proceedings. As a result of direct rule, members of the British Parliament created and amended the emergency and counter-terrorism laws enacted during the conflict. Though this arrangement suggests in theory that the executive may have weak veto possibilities in the context of parliament's power to scrutinize emergency laws, the British Conservative Party maintained a strong grip on governance throughout the conflict years, making it fairly difficult for oppositional positions to have significant sway. However, extensive parliamentary debates on emergency legislation were common and, as a result of push-back from the main opposition Labour Party, a series of independent reviews were conducted on each piece of emergency legislation. Some of these reviews resulted in amendments and revisions to the laws. In essence, though actors with fairly strong veto possibilities may seek to preserve the institution that serves their interests, they cannot completely prevent alterations of its rules or the layering of additional amendments.[52] The consistent review process produced an environment in which emergency legislation was under constant scrutiny. Human rights advocacy organizations were also given a platform to voice concerns and recommendations about the emergency institution, which directly influenced the reforms and demands made by the Labour Party. These organizations and their partners in the Labour Party challenged key aspects of the laws within the structure of parliamentary rules and debates.

Prior to the conflict, the 1922 SPA was debated in the Northern Ireland Parliament and at the time there was little opposition to its purpose or the wholesale adoption of language from prior emergency legislation. At the time, the Parliament was mainly comprised of Unionists (those in support of a union between Northern Ireland and Britain), and Nationalists (those in support of a unified and independent Ireland) were holding a boycott of the sitting government.[53] Though the London-based National Council on Civil Liberties (NCCL), later a key actor in litigation efforts, issued a report in 1936 seriously criticizing the SPA, and sectors of the nationalist community protested the measures, it was not until the civil rights movement of the 1960s that significant opposition emerged among some members of the Northern Ireland Parliament.[54] After direct rule of the country by the United Kingdom was introduced in 1972, members of the British Parliament took over the creation of emergency laws and they were then subject to annual reviews. Concerns over the legitimacy and effectiveness of emergency laws were routinely voiced during parliamentary debates.

During the conflict, every EPA was preceded by an independent review of the law's provisions and the issuance of recommendations, with the exception of the 1987 Act. The initiation of these reviews often followed calls from political leaders, including the Northern Ireland Secretary of State, or from opposition parties within the British Parliament, most notably the Labour Party. The Standing Advisory Commission on Human Rights (now the Northern Ireland Human Rights Commission) also produced reviews of each EPA and their recommendations are regularly mentioned in the parliamentary debates.

The independent reviews often included recommendations on curtailing or abolishing certain emergency or counter-terrorism laws. However, their conclusions typically supported the notion that an emergency did exist within Northern Ireland and thus, that the situation required extraordinary measures. For example, though both the 1975 Gardiner Committee report on the 1973 EPA and the 1983 Baker Committee report on the 1978 EPA recognized the laws' incursion on civil and political rights, and the growing permanency of the emergency regime, respectively, both reports concluded that the EPAs were legitimate and necessary.[55] The Shackleton and Jellicoe reviews of the Prevention of Terrorism Act in 1974 and 1976, largely initiated by the Labour Party's claim that emergency laws violated civil liberties in Northern Ireland, were limited in power given their narrow terms of reference.[56] Lord Shackleton did, however, make clear his concerns about the continued use of these measures in the region:

> The powers of arrest and detention of Section 12, including the extended detention, are regrettably necessary if the police are to be enabled adequately to prevent acts of terrorism of the kind we have experienced … Although it is not for me to judge what measures may, in the longer term, be necessary to deal with terrorism, I hope that the temporary concept of this legislation will not diminish. It would be highly regrettable if the view were to gain ground that these powers should in some way slide into part of our permanent legislation.[57]

Despite a broader trend by review committees to approve emergency laws during the Northern Ireland conflict, some of the reports' recommendations resulted in changes to government policy and practice. The following provides evidence of how the Labour Party and some of the political officials leading independent reviews, acted as agents of change, layering amendments, and revisions to the emergency institution on matters of human rights prosecutions.

The Bennett Inquiry is one of the earliest examples of the power of an independent oversight mechanism to check the abuse of emergency powers by security force personnel on the ground. The Secretary of State for Northern Ireland set up the inquiry in 1978 to investigate police procedures in the region and eventually the inquiry produced reforms concerning abusive interrogation practices. Though this inquiry was not created to look exclusively at the 1973 EPA, the comprehensive recommendations it issued targeted police mistreatment of those detained under emergency laws. Interview rooms used for interrogation were subsequently equipped with closed-circuit television cameras and the rights of detainees concerning medical assistance, representation by a lawyer and access to information about their arrest, were expanded.[58]

Additionally, members of the opposition Labour Party often played a central role in challenging the validity of the emergency institution. During the July and December 1980 debates in Parliament concerning the renewal of the 1978 EPA, Labour MPs argued that the government should enact a judicial review of the emergency law. The Conservative government promptly rejected this proposal. Labour MPs then demanded an independent review of the EPA "to ensure that the powers that it confers upon the security forces are consistent with the preservation of civil liberties and human rights, balanced by the maintenance of law and order."[59] The Baker Committee commenced a review in 1983 and it published a report in 1984. This report was significant in its attention to the aforementioned problem of interpreting the arrest powers of the police force in juryless courts.

The British government, led by the Conservatives, accepted the Baker Committee's recommendation that the armed forces' arrest powers under emergency legislation be based on "reasonable suspicion" as opposed to "suspicion." This amendment to Section 14 of the EPA narrowed the terms by which citizens presumed terrorists, or presumed linked to acts of terrorism, could be brought in. Soldiers were only able to arrest a person if they had reasonable grounds to suspect that he or she was culpable of an offense or was about to commit an offense.[60] This recommendation intended to address the reality that judges in juryless courts were granted wide discretion in interpreting police or soldiers' intentions to arrest a suspected terrorist and the decision to use lethal force. During a 1984 parliamentary debate on Baker's findings, members of the British Parliament extensively discussed the context of "reasonable suspicion" during arrests. For example, after the Secretary of State for Northern Ireland, Conservative Party member Douglas Hurd, asserted that all fatalities were fully investigated in Northern Ireland, a member of the Labour Party, Kevin McNamara, MP for Kingston upon Hull North, made the following comment on the killing of two IRA members in Derry:

> The Minister will appreciate that this point is especially sensitive. I realise that an inquiry is being made into the recent incident in Derry. But how do the security forces operate in stopping and shooting to kill a person when no warrant for his arrest has been issued—I refer to the reply that the Secretary of State gave me yesterday—and when he has not drawn arms? Does the right hon. Gentleman understand that that leads many people to think that the policy is shoot to kill and not stop and arrest?[61]

Mr. Hurd replied to Mr. McNamara:

> As I said, the policy is not shoot to kill. The existence or non-existence of a warrant is, of course, only part of the story....Of course it is. I have explained exactly how the rule of law applies.
>
> Much depends on the reasonable grounds for suspicion. But I shall not be drawn into commenting on the recent incident that the hon. Gentleman clearly has in mind. As I have said, all fatalities are investigated under the rule of law. The investigation of the two fatalities that the hon. Gentleman has in mind is proceeding, and it would be quite wrong for me to dwell on the matter.[62]

Thus, the impetus for altering the language in the EPA concerning grounds for arrest was bound up with knowledge on the part of the Baker Committee, and the MPs in the British Parliament, of the growing number of unarmed civilians killed by police or by members of the British armed forces stationed in Northern Ireland. The changes to emergency legislation that resulted from Baker's independent review process had a direct impact on human rights prosecutions in this case.

Between 1984 and 1988, members of the Labour Party also routinely challenged the PTA by citing its ineffectiveness in preventing terrorism and its infringement on civil liberties. For example, Mr. Gerard Kaufman, Labour MP for Manchester, Gordon, made the following comments in 1986 regarding the renewal of the PTA:

> Tonight the present Home Secretary agreed that this Act makes substantial inroads into ordinary civil liberties. That is why this Act is limited to a five-year life and must be renewed annually. This is why each year it is not the Opposition who have to make the case for annulment but the Government who have to make a conclusive case for renewal. The Home Secretary failed to make that case tonight, and the facts that he failed to provide for the House demonstrate clearly why that case cannot properly be made.
>
> In terms of preventing terrorism, this Act is a failure. Terrorism continues horrifically. The presence of the Prevention of Terrorism Act on the statute book, most unhappily, prevented neither the atrocity at Harrods nor the abomination at Brighton. Indeed, the very statistics published by the Government themselves demonstrate how little effectiveness this legislation delivers in return for the inroads it undoubtedly makes into civil liberties.[63]

The statistics referred to by Mr. Kaufman concern the percentage of people detained who were innocent of any crime and the high numbers of people detained without charge under the PTA. Some of these statistics were presented in the Jellicoe Report, which was tasked with reviewing the 1976 PTA.

Much of the discussion during this debate also concerned the controversial exclusion orders included in the PTA. The exclusion orders allowed for the transfer of suspected terrorists out of mainland Britain or out of Northern Ireland to other locations within the United Kingdom. The deprivation of the rights of innocent individuals, and their families in many cases, as a result of this provision produced heated debates within the British Parliament and the Standing Advisory Commission on Human Rights in Northern Ireland issued criticisms that this aspect of the PTA violated Article 8 of the European Convention on Human Rights, the right to a family life.[64] Despite condemnation of the PTA by Labour and human rights monitoring groups during the 1980s, Conservative governments continued to pass this law.

The Labour Party's contestation of emergency legislation continued with the 1989 and 1991 EPAs. Yet, similar to the trajectory of the PTA, little was altered in the actual law. Notably, Lord Colville, who was tasked with reviewing the EPA in 1989, made explicit his concerns about the problem of murder and manslaughter charges in lethal force cases. He recommended two key provisions which later became proposed amendments to the 1991 EPA: a clause mandating that the "Secretary of State shall make a code of practice in connection with the use of lethal force by police officers and members of Her Majesty's forces in dealing with suspected terrorists" with accompanying penalties for security personnel that violate this code[65] and a change in the structure of charges to allow alternative verdicts of manslaughter to be returned in cases where lethal force was seen as excessive.[66] Colville's recommendation on criminal charges was put to the Lordships' Select Committee on Murder and Life Imprisonment for consideration.[67] In the 1991 debate on the EPA, Colville's recommendation on this matter was formulated into Amendment 10, which had received support from the review committee and the Select Committee on Murder and Life Imprisonment. Discussions within the House of Lords debate illustrate the seriousness with which the matter was considered as well as the partisan divide concerning its necessity in emergency law. Lord Elton, a Conservative member of the House of Lords, made the following comments on Amendment 10:

> As a layman who has spent a good deal of time dealing with the law being framed in your Lordships' House, I find it extraordinary that a Bill which relates to Northern Ireland should be used to reinterpret a defence against murder and its treatment in the courts throughout the United Kingdom since the Bill deals with only a part of the United Kingdom. I find the intention equally disturbing—as I believe the effect would be—to change both the defence and the consequences to make them different in one part of the United Kingdom from another. I should have thought that the law on murder must be uniform throughout the United Kingdom. I believe that noble Lords would be ill-advised to accept either amendment.[68]

Lord Prys-Davies, a Labour member of the House of Lords, replied with the following:

> I now turn to Amendment No. 10. Given the present definition of the crime of murder, there is often no satisfactory way of dealing with cases in which the current rule about the legitimate use of lethal force as we understand that rule has been broken. The formal legal rule is that, where unreasonable force is deliberately used when some force could be justified, only a charge of murder is permissible. In practice, that makes it difficult for the prosecution to justify making a charge of murder in many cases because there is no realistic prospect of securing a conviction of murder against a soldier or a policeman who has used unreasonable force in self-defence, except in the most flagrant cases. The choice therefore appears to be a charge of murder or no charge at all.

> However, it is important in terms of public confidence that members of the security forces should not be seen by members of certain communities to be above the law. They should be seen to be amenable to the law, particularly in a case involving the killing of a person. The noble Lord, Lord Colville, recommended on more than one occasion that the law should be changed to permit a charge of manslaughter to be laid in cases in which some force can be justified in self-defence, but where lethal force has been unreasonably used.[69]

In the end, both amendments were withdrawn largely in response to what Lord Elton and others viewed as an untenable alteration to the existing emergency law and the potential for a lack of legal uniformity across the United Kingdom. It was implied that discussions would continue on the matter, in consultation with the Standing Advisory Commission on Human Rights, on how to proceed.[70] Proposals on this matter never made their way into emergency legislation, and the criminal law remains the same to this day.[71]

The debate in Parliament on criminal charges, initiated by an independent review process, is significant for understanding the conditions that can potentially produce institutional change. The review committee considered the troubling matter of lethal force incidents and the unclear parameters within criminal charges to be intimately connected to emergency legislation and its restrictions on human rights prosecutions. The fact that the EPA may have been revised to reflect the concerns raised by Lord Colville illuminates the importance of this oversight mechanism. The presence of strong veto possibilities on the part of the Conservative Party, and what appeared to be a broader concern that the British armed forces would be subject to differing codes of practice and penalty, limited the possibility of institutional change. Lord Colville's proposed amendments illustrate the important nexus between human rights prosecutions and the emergency institution.

During the debate on the 1991 EPA, Labour MPs also strongly criticized the EPA for undermining core aspects of democratic society and the abuse of emergency powers by those granted authority under it. In response to the Labour Party's assertions, Sections 61 and 62 of the EPA incorporated provisions that required the Secretary of State of Northern Ireland to make codes of practice on detention and treatment of individuals, and codes of practice on police powers of arrest, stop, and search. These provisions were short-lived. They were removed from the 1996

EPA on the basis that the codes were never actually created and that the powers of arrest, stop, and search were on the wane.[72] Secretary of State for Northern Ireland, Sir Patrick Mayhew, recommended that future review committees take up these provisions, but, in the end, they were not.

Finally, after Lord Colville conducted a review of the EPA in 1994, the British government incorporated one of his key recommendations into the 1996 EPA, which introduced silent video recording of interrogations. This marked an important step forward in response to the hundreds of torture allegations raised by detainees against police and security forces in prior years. During this same time period, Lord Lloyd was commissioned to assess whether there was a continued need for counter-terrorism legislation in the United Kingdom. Lloyd's review followed a series of legal challenges to the emergency regime brought by Northern Ireland citizens to the European Court of Human Rights (discussed in further detail below) and his mandate reflected the language of human rights more fully than past reviews. The terms of reference for the Lloyd Review were expanded to all emergency and counter-terrorism laws and it considered the United Kingdom's obligations to the European Convention on Human Rights and the International Covenant on Civil and Political Rights. In his report, Lloyd noted the UN Human Rights Committee's call for the elimination of emergency laws in Northern Ireland and the 1991 UN Committee Against Torture's concerns about detention practices. He also recognized that the emergency laws had tarnished the United Kingdom's international reputation in the realm of human rights protection. He therefore advised a reduction in powers of detention.[73]

In the end, in light of the waning conflict in Northern Ireland, Lloyd focused much of his review on the growing threat of *international* terrorism. As opposed to concluding that existing emergency laws be seriously amended or abolished, he recommended that in the face of global terrorism, all emergency and counter-terrorism laws should be consolidated into one act and rendered permanent. Shortly after the report was issued, the Labour Party gained a victory in the 1997 election. However, one year into its governance, the Northern Ireland community of Omagh experienced a horrific bombing set by the IRA. This prompted the Labour Party to sanction the continuation of emergency laws with little contestation. Following Lloyd's recommendations, the Labour government then created the 2000 UK Terrorism Act, which combined all emergency and counter-terrorism laws into one piece of legislation. The Terrorism Act was renewed in 2006 and it remains on the books today.

In contrast to the political context in Sri Lanka, which also granted strong veto possibilities to political actors wishing to maintain the status quo, a consistent review procedure in the British parliament allowed for contestation and incremental change within the emergency institution. At moments, these reviews may have simply operated as a means for the British government to legitimize its derogation procedures.[74] Yet, the nature of the parliamentary debates and the ways in which some of the concerns voiced by Labour made their way into legal reforms demonstrates that the presence of independent oversight mechanisms produced effects that likely would not have manifested if the review process were absent. The emergency institution was subject to layering that reflected societal and political pushback on abuse of arrest powers and lethal force deaths. The European Court of Human Rights also served as a site of contestation over the logic of impunity within the emergency institution.

The European Court of Human Rights Rulings on Emergency Legislation

The judiciary is often tasked with the interpretation and enforcement of institutional rules. It therefore can be an important vehicle for institutional change. Unlike the Colombian case (see Chap. 5), where after 1991 the Constitutional Court had judicial review powers to assess every state of emergency and subsequent emergency laws, no domestic court had automatic judicial review of the emergency institution in Northern Ireland. As a result, the European Court of Human Rights became a site where the validity of the emergency institution was called into question.

The Irish government brought one of the earliest cases to the European Court of Human Rights. In *Ireland v. United Kingdom* (1972), the government of Ireland filed a case at the European Commission concerning police use of ill-treatment and torture and the use of internment without trial. The Irish government asserted that the emergency powers in Northern Ireland exceeded what was required by the situation; that the powers were exercised in a discriminating manner; and that British police and security forces had engaged in torture and ill-treatment of detainees, a violation of Article 3 of the European Convention on Human Rights.[75] The commission ruled that the British interrogation practices in Northern Ireland constituted torture and inhuman treatment. However, the commission also found that the emergency powers in use met the requirements for the conflict situation and were not used in a discriminating way.

The Irish government appealed to the European Court of Human Rights, which gave a similar ruling to the commission, except it found that complaints of ill-treatment constituted inhuman or degrading treatment as opposed to torture. Though this ruling presented mixed outcomes for the applicant, the case set an important precedent; because the case was brought by another democratic state, it enhanced the legitimacy of the claims made against the British government concerning practices of torture and ill-treatment during detention. Both of these early cases were significant in drawing attention to the extent of the abuse of emergency powers and practice of inhumane treatment and torture by both the police and the British security forces stationed in Northern Ireland. In addition, the issues raised by the case directly influenced government policy. In particular, the cases influenced how security force personnel could perform their duties under emergency powers. For example, the British Parliament passed the Northern Ireland Act (1972), which authorized the Northern Ireland Parliament to "legislate in respect of the armed forces of the Crown in so far as that was necessary to the maintenance of peace and order in Northern Ireland."[76] After Ireland brought a charge against the British government in *Ireland v. United Kingdom* (1972) concerning ill-treatment of detainees, it brought a second charge in 1972 concerning the retrospective nature of the 1972 Northern Ireland Act. During the oral hearings, the Irish government withdrew their second petition after the British government agreed that no one would be prosecuted for actions that did not constitute a crime before the 1972 Act.[77] Additionally, *Ireland v. UK* (1972) pressured the British government to cease its use of the interrogation techniques under question while the commission deliberated the case, and the British government later told the Court that these particular practices would not be reintroduced.[78]

Once individuals were awarded the right to individually petition the European Commission on Human Rights in 1966, several applications were lodged concerning the validity of the SPA (1922). In the end, most applications were deemed inadmissible due to a failure by applicants to clearly articulate the claim, or due to attorneys' mismanagement of cases.[79] Several of the later challenges to emergency and counter-terrorism laws by Northern Ireland applicants in Strasbourg were also ill-fated due to the precedent set by *Lawless v. Ireland* in 1957. This case involved a challenge to Ireland's use of emergency laws, particularly the use of internment. The case examined whether derogation was justifiable and if the measures taken were "strictly required by the exigencies of the situation."[80] The

European Commission ruled in 1959 that there was a public emergency in Ireland at the time, though the few dissenters on the commission argued that the main activities of the IRA were largely in Northern Ireland. When the case went on to the European Court, it unanimously confirmed the commission's decision. The Court did not require significant evidence to support the claim that there was an emergency in Ireland, mainly relying on the Irish government's own assessment of the situation, understood as the margin of appreciation doctrine. This doctrine refers to the space granted by Strasbourg to national authorities when they are fulfilling their obligations under the European Convention on Human Rights. The Court has largely attempted to balance sovereignty of the member states with their obligations, and thus, the Court has often ruled that based on the British government's assessment of the conflict an emergency did exist in Northern Ireland and emergency rules should continue to be enforced.[81]

Four decades later, the Court would rule similarly in a case brought by the Belfast organization, the Committee on the Administration of Justice (CAJ). In *Marshall v. United Kingdom* (1998),[82] the CAJ submitted an application on behalf of a man who had been held in Castlereagh Holding Center for six days and two hours. Paul Mageean, his solicitor, argued that at that time, the security situation in Northern Ireland had changed considerably and the government should not be allowed to impose a permanent state of emergency. The Court found the application to be "ill-founded" because the detention was justified under the derogation notice issued by the British government. The Court ruled that the British national authorities were a better judge of the security situation than the Court and therefore deferred to the derogation. The court's ruling relied again upon the margin of appreciation doctrine.[83]

Though the Court supported the British government in several cases concerning the margin of appreciation doctrine, an accumulation of cases that challenged the emergency institution eventually produced alterations in the emergency institution's rules. In 1984, in the *Brogan v. United Kingdom*[84] case, an application made by four men detained in Northern Ireland for a period ranging from four to six days, challenged the provision within the PTA that allowed for a maximum seven-day detention of suspected terrorists. In 1987, the applicants gained a small success. The European Commission ruled four days, eleven hours was acceptable but five days, eleven hours was not. The European Court then ruled in 1989 that Article 5(3) of the European Convention on Human Rights (ECHR) had been breached in relation to all four applicants.[85] Though this was a clear success for the applicants and critics of emergency laws, the government's only response was to derogate again from the European Convention on Human Rights in order to justify extended detentions in future arrests.[86]

The *Brannigan and McBride v. United Kingdom*[87] case in 1989 followed up the British government's derogation notice with a challenge by two applicants who were held longer than four days while in detention in Northern Ireland. In 1991, the commission ruled that Article 5(3) had not been breached and that the 1988 derogation notice was valid. The European Court concurred in 1993. Notably, Amnesty International and CAJ made appeals to the European Court, arguing that if states are to be allowed a margin of appreciation when derogating from the Convention, the margin should be narrower the longer the emergency is in effect.[88] A few years later, Northern Ireland citizens won two more legal cases against the British government. The European Court ruled that the United Kingdom's EPA and PTA violated the European Convention concerning arrest powers, reasonable suspicion, access to a solicitor, and the court's right to draw inferences based on a detainee's silence.[89]

Though the European Court had fairly minimal enforcement power to pressure the British government to change emergency laws, the accumulation of cases at Strasbourg, and the handful of successful wins against the British government, did produce an impact. For example, after a growing number of cases were heard at the Court on emergency powers in the early 1970s, the 1922 SPA was repealed. The act designed to replace it, the Northern Ireland (Emergency Provisions) Act (1973), incorporated aspects of the ECHR, particularly in the area of administrative detention of suspected terrorists.[90] In addition, as discussed earlier, in direct response to the series of cases brought before the European Court, the British government tasked the Lloyd Review in 1996 to consider for the first time the necessity of emergency laws and the compatibility of the laws with the European Convention and the ICCPR, which resulted in reforms.

Human Rights Prosecution Data

Many of the domestic prosecutions early in the conflict were prompted by actions taken on behalf of victims' families by the Association for Legal Justice (ALJ) and the Northern Ireland Civil Rights Association (NICRA). The ALJ focused its efforts on two actions: the validity of emergency laws and security force powers, specifically misconduct of security forces in cases where criminal charges were brought against suspected terrorists;

and civil and criminal action against individual security force members for assaults, contested shootings, and other unlawful activities.[91] The organization helped victims and families to bring cases to court, they publicized state abuses and illegal actions in the press, and they wrote letters applying pressure on the British government. According to an attorney who worked with both organizations during this time, ALJ and NICRA operated relatively free from government threat or intimidation and were therefore quite successful in generating domestic and international attention on cases and applying pressure on political officials.[92]

In addition to criminal prosecutions, a number of families brought cases of torture to the civil courts. In many ill-treatment or torture cases, complainants tended to pursue the claim in civil courts for compensation because there was a lower evidentiary standard. In the early years of the conflict, interrogation techniques were not recorded, thus it was very hard to prove torture in a criminal trial.[93] If a complainant wished to file a writ of habeas corpus concerning mistreatment while he/she was unlawfully detained, the resulting trial would be a civil proceeding, held in the Belfast High Court.[94] According to the Attorney General of Northern Ireland, Sir Peter Rawlinson, within the first few years of the conflict, 150 civil actions were brought against the Crown for alleged assaults by security force members.[95] Many of the families that pursued this alternative form of accountability were supported by ALJ. In the end, however, very few of the civil cases were actually litigated; instead, most families were compensated through a settlement, which replaced a trial or any admission of guilt on the part of security forces. One of the attorneys who worked on some of these cases commented that people often felt this was the most they could do, even if they didn't want money from the government. Remarking on this trend, he argued that the settlements "simply allowed Britain to pay for the right to torture."[96]

In addition to the work of ALJ and NICRA, the Belfast-based CAJ, formed in 1981, forged important partnerships with international organizations such as the NCCL), Amnesty International, and Helsinki Watch, and these efforts were crucial in the 1980s for drawing attention to the trends in impunity in local courts. The NCCL helped CAJ gain lobbying access to the Labour Party as early as 1985 and it provided support when CAJ publicized government abuses.[97] The NCCL is mentioned repeatedly in parliamentary debates on accountability and emergency legislation, and the Labour Party often drew on the organization's work to support their arguments on the need for legal reforms.

In the early 1990s, CAJ made submissions to the UN Human Rights Committee and the UN Committee Against Torture concerning the conflict in Northern Ireland.[98] CAJ also organized a conference in 1991, which focused on the use of international organizations and treaties as a means to encourage government responsiveness to civil rights concerns.[99] The international partners in turn routinely applied pressure on the British government. Some of the domestic cases brought against the state in the early 1990s were initiated and/or supported by the NCCL. During a survey conducted by CAJ for a 2008 report on lessons learned from the Northern Ireland conflict, a participant commented, "One of the greatest safeguards in Northern Ireland was the ability to secure pressure on government from outside the jurisdiction."[100]

Security force members and police were responsible for the deaths of 363 civilians throughout the conflict in Northern Ireland.[101] Though other cases in this book include data on forced disappearance, there were no ***documented*** cases of state-perpetrated disappearances in the data sources used for this project. The British armed forces were responsible for the vast majority of state-perpetrated civilian deaths, approximately 81%, while the police were responsible for close to 15% of state-perpetrated civilian deaths. The remainder involved members of the UDR and the Royal Irish Regiment.[102] A total of 32 prosecutions charging 57 state actors for conflict-related civilian deaths were held between 1974 and 2014.[103] Within the 32 prosecutions, 35 of the 363 civilian deaths caused by the state were investigated, a prosecution record of 9.6%.

Thirty-five per cent of the security force members and police that were prosecuted were convicted. It is worth noting, as a comparison, that between 1984 and 1987, *civilians* who were prosecuted under scheduled offenses (outlined as terrorist offenses in emergency and counter-terrorism laws) were convicted on average in 93% of the cases; in non-scheduled offenses (other offenses not covered under emergency laws), civilians were convicted on average in 92% of the cases.[104]

The nature of the charges and the verdicts depicted in Table 3.2 demonstrate the problem of interpreting lethal force deaths within a juryless court system. The high number of acquittals for murder reflect what other research has carefully documented regarding the difficulty of utilizing ordinary criminal law for lethal force deaths in the context of

Table 3.2 Criminal charges and verdicts in Northern Ireland prosecutions, 1974–2014

Criminal charges	*Convictions*	*Acquittals*
Manslaughter	3	5
Murder	13[a]	27
Assault and bodily harm while in custody	2	4
Conspiracy to murder	1	1
Evading investigation of a murder	1	0
Total	**20**	**37**

[a]Note: Over half (8) of the total number of convictions for murder represent the four UDR men who were convicted for the murder of Adrian Carroll in 1983, and whose convictions were upheld during an appeal in 1988

an emergency.[105] The low number of manslaughter cases also reflects the problem of ambiguous language in the law on what is reasonable force during an emergency. Article 2 of the European Convention on Human Rights articulates that "deprivation of life shall not be regarded as inflicted in contravention of this article when it results from the use of force which is no more than absolutely necessary" in order to defend an individual or make a lawful arrest.[106] The specificity of the language in the Convention had limited impact in domestic proceedings, however, given the dualist legal system in place and the tendency for judges to consider the emergency setting as justification for the use of lethal force during an attempted arrest.

The majority of the victims in these cases were young Catholic men. In one particularly controversial criminal proceeding against Royal Ulster Constabulary (RUC) Constable John Robinson in 1984, though the two victims, Seamus Grew and Roddy Carroll, were found unarmed, Robinson admitted to firing 15 shots into their car as it approached a roadblock, reloaded then fired 4 to 5 shots at close range into the car because he believed he had been shot at and his life was in danger. It was revealed during the trial that the RUC had been engaged in a cover-up to hide the fact that anti-terrorist units were involved in the incident and falsely claimed that one of the victims had driven through the roadblock injuring an officer. Despite the presentation of this evidence, Robinson was eventually acquitted of murder.[107] The challenge to obtain a conviction, even when a fair amount of evidence to support a guilty verdict was presented, decreased the trust victims' families had in the Northern Ireland legal system over time.

When a British soldier was released in 1988 without a trial after being charged with manslaughter for the death of a civilian hit by a ricochet bullet, Seamus Mallon, deputy leader of the Nationalist Northern Ireland Social Democratic and Labour Party, stated, "The odds are stacked against an individual when there is a conflict of evidence involving the police or a soldier. Over the years this perception has seriously diminished confidence in the process of law."[108] Five years later in 1990, when two British soldiers, Lance Corporal Richard Elkington and Marine Andrew Callaghan, were acquitted of murdering Fergal Caraher when he drove through an army checkpoint after a verbal exchange with the soldiers, Caraher's widow Margaret stated, "We feel disappointed but not surprised. It was what we have come to expect from the judicial system in Northern Ireland."[109]

Members of the British armed forces and the RUC were prosecuted for civilian deaths early on in the conflict and at a fairly steady pace until the peace accord in 1998. In the last years of the conflict, prosecutions of security force members and police rise after a short lull. These prosecutions followed a period of intense lobbying by organizations, including the Belfast-based CAJ, British Irish Rights Watch, and Amnesty International, at the UN Human Rights Committee, the European Court and to the Special Rapporteur on Summary and Arbitrary Executions. It is likely that the increased pressure by these groups on the British government prompted a higher number of domestic prosecutions concerning extra-judicial killings within Northern Ireland (Graph 3.1).[110]

The low number of convictions overall are largely a result of the factors connected to the restrictions on accountability built into the emergency institution, including the regulation of inquests, the use of ordinary criminal law to judge lethal force cases (and a failure by the British government to initiate legal reforms on criminal charges after several public and political appeals to do so), and prosecutions in juryless courts. When examining convictions over time, we see a complementary pattern to the prosecution trends in that between 1992 and 1995, the period of intense lobbying at the UN and growing pressure on the British government via the European Court, there is a trend of slightly more consistent convictions (Graph 3.2). The patterns across the two graphs and the table on charges and verdicts illustrate a consistent and assertive attempt on the part of citizens and their legal representatives to push back against what is also visible in the data: the tendency for cases to never make it to the courts.

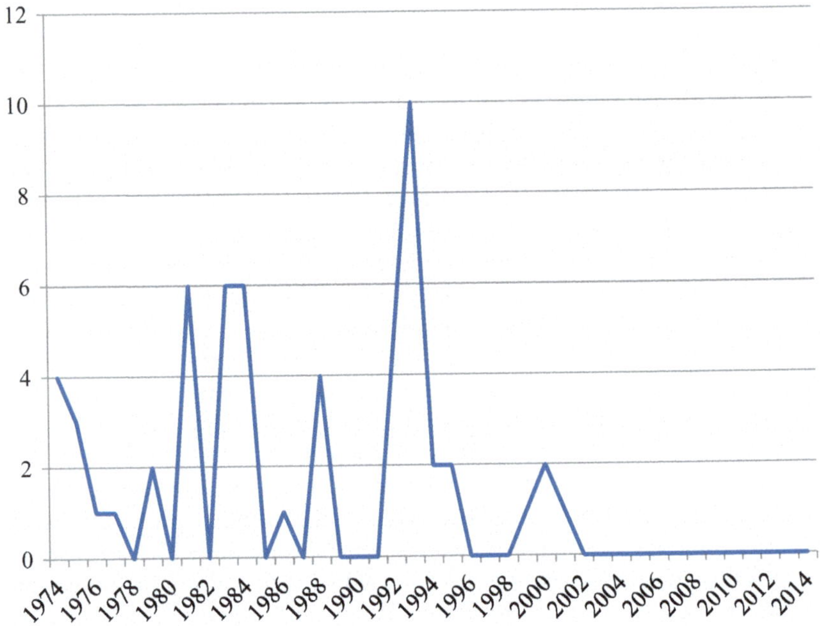

Graph 3.1 The number of state actors prosecuted per year in Northern Ireland

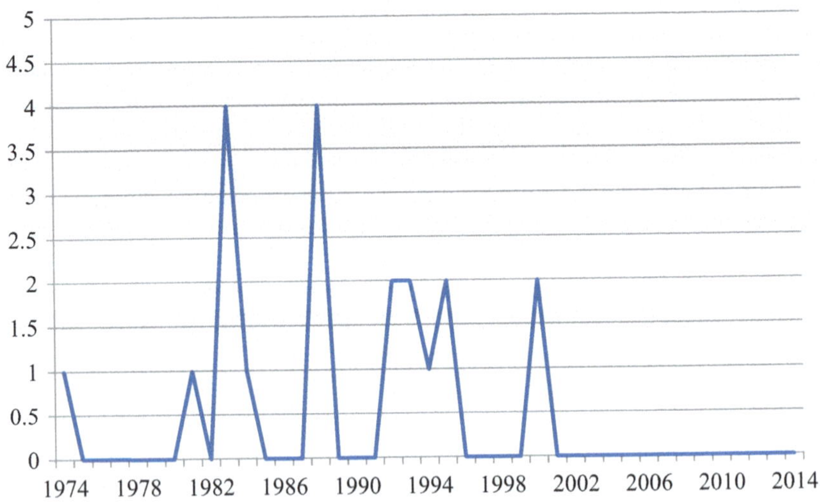

Graph 3.2 Convictions of state actors in Northern Ireland

Human Rights Cases at the European Court of Human Rights

Though the United Kingdom had ratified the ECHR in 1951, it was not binding upon the United Kingdom in domestic law until the UK-wide Human Rights Act came into force in 2000, a few years after the signing of the Belfast Accord. The United Kingdom did not have a Bill of Rights for citizens to draw on during the conflict. There are plans underway only recently to introduce a Bill of Rights in the United Kingdom to replace the 2000 Human Rights Act, but this move by the British government has been highly contested given it may mean a diminished relationship with the European Court of Human Rights. The 2000 Human Rights Act incorporated ECHR articles 2-12, 14 and 16-18, which include, among other rights, the right to life, freedom from torture, and the right to liberty and security. Thus, during the conflict, Northern Ireland citizens could invoke the ECHR in domestic courts but not as binding domestic law. Given the increasing number of acquittals in local courts and the restrictions on inquests, citizens and their legal representatives saw an opportunity to hold the British government accountable at a regional human rights court with presumably a stricter set of standards than local courts. It was within this climate that citizens mobilized to bring hundreds of cases to the commission in order to bolster their claims that human rights violations had been committed by members of the police and armed forces.

In order to pursue this route, applicants had to prove that every effort had been made to seek accountability in domestic courts. If a domestic remedy had been provided, as in the civil court settlements discussed earlier, the commission would often rule the case inadmissible. Though citizens and their legal representatives could make reference to treaty law in litigation, this law was not part of the terms of reference for judges assessing the case. The European Court of Human Rights thus became a venue for legal advocates to utilize human rights law to make arguments concerning state acts of violence and the right to a remedy. After 1966, individuals within the United Kingdom gained the right to submit individual applications to the European Commission. In the early years of the Court, all the applications were lodged with the European Commission with the potential to go on to the European Court. When the caseload facing the Court grew substantially in the 1990s, Protocol 11 of the ECHR was passed in 1998 to eliminate the commission while retaining the European Court of Human Rights as the sole judicial body.

NICRA and ALJ brought one of the earliest cases concerning ill-treatment by the police to the European Court. In *Donnelly v. United Kingdom* (1975), seven applicants alleged they were victims of ill-treatment while in police custody and they claimed that the practice of torture and inhuman or degrading treatment was systematic and widespread in Northern Ireland.[111] The European Commission declared the case admissible on April 5, 1973, and a small initial success was won. The commission ruled at this time that if an individual makes a complaint concerning systematic abuse as an administrative practice, the individual does not have to first exhaust domestic remedies because the question of the effectiveness of domestic remedies will be under consideration as well.[112] There was, in a sense, an assumption that given the nature of the claim, it would likely be difficult for an individual to win a domestic remedy. In the end, however, the commission ruled on December 15, 1975, that the alleged administrative practice of torture was not in violation of the European Convention on Human Rights because evidence had in fact not been presented to show that domestic remedies were ineffective or inadequate. This ruling was based on the fact that three of the seven victims were in the middle of civil proceedings in Northern Ireland concerning ill-treatment, and the remaining four had already been awarded some compensation through civil proceedings.[113] Thus, despite the fact that most families would have preferred a criminal trial in these cases, the Court saw the civil settlements as adequate and effective domestic remedies. The question of effectiveness in the investigation of state violence in domestic legal proceedings, and its relevance to the European Convention on Human Rights, would become the focus of several cases brought to the Court in the late 1990s after the peace accords were signed. These cases led to subsequent legal reforms concerning government accountability.

Post-conflict Prosecutions and Legal Reforms

A few years after the Belfast Accord was signed in 1998, several important cases brought against the state regarding civilian deaths at the hands of the security forces were successful at the European Court.[114] This may have resulted from the fact that the conflict was in the process of being resolved during this time, and thus the Court was willing to be stricter in their judgments against the British government. Some of these cases shaped policy concerning the domestic investigation and prosecution of state actors for conflict-related human rights violations.[115]

The common thread among the post-conflict cases was that the families and their legal representatives argued that the state had not conducted a full investigation of the deaths in order to ascertain whether state actors had behaved illegally when carrying out the killings. The European Court ruled that the British government had failed to satisfy the procedural aspects of Article 2 of the ECHR, which outlines the right to life and specifically stipulates when the use of force is considered necessary and legal. The Court also drew on Article 1 of the ECHR to argue that in order to secure citizens' rights within the convention, investigations of civilian deaths through the use of force must be thorough and effective. The Court laid out a list of requirements that would support the execution of an investigation that was aligned with the Convention. The requirements included: a stipulation that those who investigate the deaths are independent from the people who are implicated in the crime and not only in a hierarchical sense; the investigation must be completely thorough, drawing on multiple forms of evidence, in determining whether force was justifiable; the investigation must be prompt with attention to maintaining public confidence in adherence to the rule of law; and the investigation must be subject to some level of public scrutiny and next of kin must be involved to the greatest extent possible.[116]

The response from the British government to the Court's ruling, and its identification of definitive steps to take in future investigations, was fairly proactive. Specific changes to law and policy resulted, though not without contestation. Beginning in 1999, judges, as opposed to government ministers, were given the power to decide on the content that could be subject to a public interest immunity certificate (PIIC). In 2000, a Police Ombudsman was created to independently investigate complaints against the police and in 2002 the Public Prosecution Service (formerly the DPP) began to formally provide reasons if and when they decided not to prosecute a case involving civilian deaths at the hands of the state.[117]

Finally, in a move to establish an actual system for processing unresolved crimes that include state and non-state actor violence, including crimes of murder and rape, the Chief Constable of the new police service, Police Service Northern Ireland (PSNI), created a review team within the PSNI, which later became the Historical Enquiries Team (HET) in 2005. The HET included a team of mostly retired police officers from England, who were tasked with re-examining over 3000 unresolved deaths between 1968 and 1998 with the purpose of bringing some form of resolution to victims' families and to ensure that all evidentiary and investigative opportunities were exploited, a mandate outlined by the European Court of Human Rights for Article 2 compliance. The HET was not a traditional truth-seeking body in that it focused on micro-level information recovery, as opposed to a pattern of events; outside individuals were not invited to give testimony on the cases; and, if there was sound evidence to pursue criminal charges, the HET forwarded the case to the Public Prosecution Service.[118] As of summer 2010, approximately 1000 cases had been completed, but only a few cases had been forwarded to the Public Prosecution Service and one person had been formally charged. Staff from HET shared with me in 2010 that they were very careful to make it clear to families from the outset that prosecution was highly unlikely due to the length of time that had passed in most cases and due to problems of evidence. They explained that they focused on providing, to the best of their ability, information for the deceased's loved ones who often knew very little or had received conflicting and difficult reports over the years on the crime committed. The staff believed that most people did not want prosecution and preferred to receive information that resulted from a complete investigation. The staff cited the following examples to support this claim: some families wanted to know whether a priest was present to give last rites; and in the case of soldiers who died, families wished to know if they could contact colleagues of their loved one.[119] HET staff shared the results of a family survey they completed on satisfaction with the HET processes and feelings of trust among family members. Overall, in 2010, these numbers were quite high.[120]

By 2013, criticism of the HET had grown. In 2012, the Minister of Justice for Northern Ireland commissioned Her Majesty's Inspectorate of Constabulary (HMIC) to conduct an inspection of the role and function of the HET. It produced a formal report in 2013, including some of the following recommendations: improve accountability to the public and to the families involved (e.g., a formal complaints mechanism); conduct more thorough surveys of family members involved in HET processes (those surveyed were found to be somewhat handpicked, excluding those families who disengaged after some time and excluding families who were waiting on their final report); improve handling of state violence cases, and eliminate differential treatment of state violence cases and non-state violence cases; and improve and increase HET coordination with the Public Prosecution Service on state violence cases.[121]

In January 2015, the PSNI's Legacy Investigations Branch took over the remaining work within the HET. As of May 2015, 53 cases, relating to 86 deaths dating back to the early 1970s, were listed for inquest with an expectation that the number would rise in the coming years.[122] The Stormont House Agreement, which was published in November 2015 and lays out a series of steps for resolving various matters in Northern Ireland, attempts to address the possibility of a truth recovery body and a new investigations mechanism concerning the violence during the conflict years. Earlier proposals in the negotiations leading up to the Agreement argued that due to concerns from some sectors of the Northern Ireland community that the PSNI is not an independent body, the creation of a completely independent historical investigations unit might be necessary.[123] As of early 2017, there was no significant movement on this matter.

The spotty record of human rights prosecutions in the post-conflict setting demonstrates the challenge of pursuing human rights prosecutions decades after the crimes have taken place. While the European Court of Human Rights rulings on effective investigations of state violence in the late 1990s produced important reforms to the inquest and prosecution process, many of these reforms were implemented too late to have an impact on crimes committed decades earlier due to problems of evidence.

The Impact of Conversion and Layering on Human Rights Prosecutions

Layering altered some of the restrictions on human rights prosecutions within the emergency institution in Northern Ireland. Oversight mechanisms within Parliament and the European Court of Human Rights rulings produced revisions, amendments, and additions to clauses concerning interrogation practices, detention, and charges in lethal force civilian deaths. Layering did not, however, produce transformative change for three significant reasons. First, while the amendments addressed problematic aspects of juryless courts and expansive arrest and detention powers, both features of the emergency institution remained largely in place throughout the conflict. Independent oversight mechanisms were significant for eliciting scrutiny of the emergency institution, but the strong veto power of the Conservative Party made it difficult for those in the opposition to dismantle the institution. Layering results when change agents have little capacity to produce substantial institutional change either as a result of weak veto power or because bodies tasked with interpretation and enforcement of the laws are weak or absent. Second, as a result of conversion, tight controls over the inquest process remained in ordinary laws outside the scope of parliamentary reviews. Thus, while independent oversight was central for assessing the content of emergency laws, it did not scrutinize ordinary laws on coroners' rights and duties.

Third, though the European Court of Human Rights proved to be an important site for contesting the validity of emergency laws, in the end, the Court had minimal enforcement power in Northern Ireland. A local judicial review mechanism would have had greater capacity to interpret and enforce challenges to the emergency institution. Yet, had there been such a mechanism available to citizens in Northern Ireland, it would likely have been hampered by low levels of judicial independence. Many of the judges tended to support the actions of a majority Protestant police force and the British armed forces stationed in the region. The Northern Ireland case illustrates that the emergency institution is not simply self-reinforcing upon creation. Rather, it was a site of great contestation and debate by actors who aimed to challenge the logic of impunity embedded within it as well as those who wished to maintain the status quo.

Notes

1. Ruane, Joseph and Jennifer Todd. *The Dynamics of Conflict in Northern Ireland: Power, Conflict and Emancipation.* Cambridge: Cambridge University Press (1998).
2. Ruane and Todd (1998).
3. Ruane and Todd (1998).
4. McEvoy, Kieran. *Paramilitary Imprisonment in Northern Ireland: Resistance, Management and Release.* Oxford: Oxford University Press (2001).
5. Hamber, Brandon and Grainne Kelly. 2005. "A Place for Reconciliation? Conflict and Locality in Northern Ireland." Report 18, Democratic Dialogue, Belfast, Northern Ireland, 4–80.
6. Eames, Robin and Denis Bradley. 2009. Report of the Consultative Group on the Past.
7. Dickson, Brice. 1989. *The Legal System of Northern Ireland*, 2nd Edition. Belfast: SLS Legal Publications.
8. Dickson (1989).
9. Dickson (1989).
10. Dickson (1989).
11. Dickson (1989).
12. Interview 5, Belfast, Northern Ireland, 2009; Interview 7, Belfast, Northern Ireland, 2010.
13. Dickson (1989).

14. Ní Aoláin, Fionnuala and Colm Campbell. The Paradox of Transition in Conflicted Democracies, *Human Rights Quarterly* 27(1) (2005): 172–213.
15. Some of the arguments made in this section of the chapter were first published as an article. See Moira Katherine Lynch. A Theory of Human rights prosecutions and Emergency Law: Bringing in Historical Institutionalism, *Journal of Human Rights*, 14(4) (2015): 504–524.
16. Donohue, Laura K. *Counter-terrorist Law and Emergency Powers in the United Kingdom, 1922–2000.* Dublin, Ireland: Irish Academic Press (2001).
17. Donohue (2001).
18. Donohue (2001).
19. Boyle, Kevin, Tom Hadden, and Paddy Hillyard. *Law and State: The Case of Northern Ireland.* Amherst: University of Massachusetts Press (1975).
20. Boyle et al. (1975), Donohue (2001).
21. Donohue (2001).
22. Donohue (2001).
23. Donohue, 30.
24. Ní Aoláin, Fionnuala. *The Politics of Force: Conflict Management and State Violence in Northern Ireland.* Belfast: Blackstaff Press (2000), 137.
25. See Section 10(a) (b) (c), Civil Authorities (Special Powers) Act 1922.
26. Donohue, 18.
27. Donohue, 30.
28. Donohue, 30.
29. Ní Aoláin (2000, 142–143).
30. Ní Aoláin (2000).
31. A few years after the 1998 peace accord in Northern Ireland, the rules on inquests were altered so that witnesses suspected of involvement in a death could be compelled to attend an inquest (see Coroners (Practice and Procedure) (Amendment) Rules (NI) 2002 (SR 37)) and in 2006, a new Coroners' Service was created in Northern Ireland with the objective of expediting inquests (Dickson 2010, 271–272). The European Court of Human Rights cases that prompted these changes are discussed later in the chapter.
32. Ní Aoláin (2000, 163–164).
33. Ní Aoláin (2000, 152).
34. Dickson, Brice. *The European Convention on Human Rights and the Conflict in Northern Ireland.* Oxford: Oxford University Press (2010), 205.
35. Northern Ireland (Emergency Provisions) Act. (1973) Chapter 53 (London: Her Majesty's Stationery Office). [Online]. Available: www.legislation.gov.uk [17 June 2015].
36. Ní Aoláin (2000, 2).

37. Ní Aoláin (2000), Amnesty International. 1991. "United Kingdom: Killings by Security Forces in Northern Ireland." AI Index: EUR 45/12/91.
38. Criminal Law Act (Northern Ireland) (1967).
39. Ní Aoláin (2000).
40. *Regina v. Jones* (1975) Belfast Crown Court, 6–7.
41. The Ulster Defense Regiment (UDR) was created in 1970 as a locally recruited regiment of the British Army.
42. *R v. Latimer and others*, Court of Appeal 1988.
43. British Broadcasting Company (BBC). "Latimer's Conviction Upheld." February 9, 2004. http://news.bbc.co.uk/2/hi/uk_news/northern_ireland/3472439.stm (Retrieved November 2015).
44. Little, Ivan. "UDR Soldier Cleared of Catholic Murder," *Belfast Telegraph* February 19, 2015.
45. *Regina v. Fisher and Wright* (1995) Belfast Crown Court, 2.
46. *Regina v. Fisher and Wright*, 36.
47. *Regina v. Fisher and Wright*, 38.
48. Ní Aoláin (2000, 126–127).
49. *Regina v. Jones* (1976) Appeal at the House of Lords, 17.
50. Dickson (2010, 252).
51. Mahoney and Thelen, 17.
52. Mahoney and Thelen, 19–20.
53. Donohue (2001).
54. Donohue (2001, 115–116).
55. Donohue (2001).
56. Committee on the Administration of Justice. 2008. "War on Terror: Lessons from Northern Ireland."
57. Annual Human Rights Reports Submitted to Congress by the U.S. Department of State: United Kingdom. 1978.
58. Dickson (2010).
59. Donohue (2001, 177).
60. Dickson (2010, 101–102).
61. House of Commons Debate. HC Deb 20 December 1984 vol 70, col 578.
62. House of Commons Debate. HC Deb 20 December 1984 vol 70, col 578.
63. House of Commons Debate. HC Deb 19 February 1986 vol 92, col 420.
64. Dickson (2010, 90).
65. House of Lords Debate. HL Deb 06 June 1991 vol 529, col 823.
66. HL Deb 06 June 1991 vol 529, cc806-31.
67. House of Lords Debate. HL Deb 15 March 1989 vol 505, col 305–306.
68. HL Deb 06 June 1991 vol 529, col 823.

69. HL Deb 06 June 1991 vol 529, col 824.
70. HL Deb 06 June 1991 vol 529, cc806–31.
71. Dickson (2010, 251).
72. House of Commons Debate. HC Deb 09 January 1996 vol 269, col 38–39.
73. Donohue (2001).
74. Rolston, Bill and Phil Scraton. In the Full Glare of English Politics: Ireland, Inquiries and the British State, *British Journal of Criminology* 45 (2005): 547–564.
75. Hannum, Hurst. The Impact of European Human Rights Jurisprudence on the Conflict in Northern Ireland, in Eileen F. Babbitt and Ellen L. Lutz, eds., *Human Rights and Conflict Resolution in Context: Colombia, Sierra Leone and Northern Ireland*. Syracuse: Syracuse University Press (2009); Dickson (2010).
76. Boyle et al. (1975, 132).
77. Boyle et al. (1975).
78. Hannum (2009).
79. Hannum (2009), Dickson (2010).
80. Dickson (2010), European Convention on Human Rights (1950).
81. Dickson (2010).
82. *Marshall v. United Kingdom* (1998). European Court of Human Rights. HUDOC Database. www.echr.coe.int
83. Dickson (2010).
84. *Brogan v. United Kingdom* (1989) European Court of Human Rights. HUDOC Database. www.echr.coe.int
85. Article 5(3) of the ECHR mandates: "Everyone arrested or detained in accordance with the provisions of paragraph 1 (c) of this Article shall be brought promptly before a judge or other officer authorised by law to exercise judicial power and shall be entitled to trial within a reasonable time or to release pending trial. Release may be conditioned by guarantees to appear for trial" (ECHR 1950). Paragraph 1(c) states: "The lawful arrest or detention of a person effected for the purpose of bringing him before the competent legal authority on reasonable suspicion of having committed an offence or when it is reasonably considered necessary to prevent his committing an offence or fleeing after having done so."
86. Dickson (2010).
87. *Brannigan and McBride v. United Kingdom* (1989) European Court of Human Rights. HUDOC Database. www.echr.coe.int
88. Dickson (2010).
89. See *Fox, Campbell and Hartley* (1995) *v. United Kingdom* and *Murray (John) v. United Kingdom* (1996).
90. Boyle et al. (1975).

91. Boyle et al. (1975).
92. Interview 26 (Phone), 2011.
93. Annual Human Rights Reports Submitted to Congress by the U.S. Department of State: United Kingdom. 1993.
94. Dickson (1989).
95. Dickson (2010).
96. Int. 26, 2011.
97. Whelan, Leo J. The Challenge of Lobbying for Civil Rights in Northern Ireland: The Committee on the Administration of Justice, *Human Rights Quarterly* 14(2) (1992): 149–170.
98. O'Brien, Martin. 1996. "Northern Ireland at the United Nations, 1969–1996," Masters thesis, School of Law, Queen's University.
99. Whelan (1992).
100. Committee on the Administration of Justice, 88.
101. Committee on the Administration of Justice (2008).
102. Rolston, Bill. 2000. Unfinished Business: State Killings and the Quest for Truth. Belfast: Beyond the Pale Publications.
103. The prosecution data is based on my research of U.S. State Department reports, Belfast Crown Court transcripts, reports from the Committee on the Administration of Justice, Amnesty International, and Human Rights Watch, as well as media coverage of trial proceedings in the *Irish Times*, the *Guardian*, the *London Times*, the *Belfast Telegraph*, and other media sources.
104. Dickson (1989).
105. Ní Aoláin (2000).
106. ECHR (1950).
107. Jennings, Tony. 1984. "Agenda (Out of Court): Does Northern Ireland Now Have Final Courts of Justice?" *The Guardian (London)*, November 5.
108. Heast, David and Joe Joyce. 1988. "Ulster Killing Case Dropped," *The Guardian (London)*, September 28.
109. Bowcott, Owen. 1993. "Marines' Acquittal of Ulster Murder Brings Calls for Review of Law," *The Guardian (London)*, December 24.
110. O'Brien (1996).
111. Hannum (2009), Dickson (2010).
112. Dickson (2010).
113. Dickson (2010).
114. See *McKerr v. United Kingdom* (2002), *Kelly and others v. United Kingdom (2001) Jordan v. United Kingdom* (2003), *Shanaghan v. United Kingdom* (2001), *McShane v. United Kingdom* (2002), and *Finucane v. United Kingdom* (2003). Unlike the other cases, the Shanaghan Case involved a civilian death at the hands of a loyalist paramilitary member, but the investigation indicated there may have been collusion between the police and the paramilitary organization (Dickson 2010, 269).

115. An early civil case also involved a complaint to the commission regarding a violation of Article 2 in the ECHR. In *Farrell v. United Kingdom*, an Irish citizen, whose husband was killed by soldiers in Northern Ireland, made a complaint to the commission in 1983, after suing the Ministry of Defense in local civil courts and losing on appeal at the House of Lords (Dickson 2010, 253). After the commission accepted the complaint, the parties reached a "friendly settlement" and the British government agreed to pay Mrs. Farrell £37,500 and compensation towards legal costs (Yearbook of the European Convention on Human Rights, Vol. 27).
116. Dickson (2010, 269–270).
117. Dickson (2010, 271).
118. Lundy, Patricia. Exploring Home-Grown Transitional Justice and Its Dilemmas: A Case Study of the Historical Enquiries Team, Northern Ireland, *International Journal of Transitional Justice* 3 (2009): 321–340; Interview 9, Lisburn, Northern Ireland, 2010.
119. Int. 9, 2010.
120. A sampling of the survey results include: 92% of respondents viewed HET as sensitive; 72.8% felt the HET report was useful; 68.4% felt the HET process had been beneficial or very beneficial; 86% felt satisfied or very satisfied with performance of the team; and 95% viewed HET as professional (Int. 9, 2010).
121. Her Majesty's Inspectorate of Constabulary (HMIC). 2013. Inspection of Police Service of Northern Ireland Historical Enquiries Team.
122. McAleese, Deborah. "Dealing with the Legacy of the Troubles Could Take Us a Lifetime, Warns Top PSNI Officer," *Belfast Telegraph*. May 18, 2015.
123. Smith, Colletta. "HMIC Concern Over Accountability of PSNI's Legacy Investigation Branch," *BBC* June 24, 2015.

Bibliography

Amnesty International. 1991. United Kingdom: Killings by Security Forces in Northern Ireland. AI Index: EUR 45/12/91.

Annual Human Rights Reports Submitted to Congress by the U.S. Department of State: United Kingdom. 1978.

Annual Human Rights Reports Submitted to Congress by the U.S. Department of State: United Kingdom. 1993.

Bowcott, Owen. 1993. Marines' Acquittal of Ulster Murder Brings Calls for Review of Law. *The Guardian* (London), December 24.

Boyle, Kevin, Tom Hadden, and Paddy Hillyard. 1975. *Law and State: The Case of Northern Ireland*. Amherst: University of Massachusetts Press.

British Broadcasting Company (BBC). Latimer's Conviction Upheld. February 9, 2004. Retrieved November, 2015, http://news.bbc.co.uk/2/hi/uk_news/northern_ireland/3472439.stm

Brogan v. United Kingdom. 1989. European Court of Human Rights. HUDOC Database. www.echr.coe.int

Committee on the Administration of Justice. 2008. *War on Terror: Lessons from Northern Ireland*.

Criminal Law Act (Northern Ireland). 1967. Available: http://www.legislation.gov.uk/apni/1967/18/contents

Dickson, Brice. 1989. *The Legal System of Northern Ireland*. 2nd ed. Belfast: SLS Legal Publications.

———. 2010. *The European Convention on Human Rights and the Conflict in Northern Ireland*. Oxford: Oxford University Press.

Donohue, Laura K. 2001. *Counter-Terrorist Law and Emergency Powers in the United Kingdom, 1922–2000*. Dublin: Irish Academic Press.

Eames, Robin, and Denis Bradley. 2009. Report of the Consultative Group on the Past. Available: http://cain.ulst.ac.uk/victims/docs/consultative_group/cgp_230109_report.pdf

European Convention on Human Rights. 1950.

Hamber, Brandon, and Grainne Kelly. 2005. *A Place for Reconciliation? Conflict and Locality in Northern Ireland*, 4–80. Report 18, Democratic Dialogue, Belfast.

Hannum, Hurst. 2009. The Impact of European Human Rights Jurisprudence on the Conflict in Northern Ireland. In *Human Rights and Conflict Resolution in Context: Colombia, Sierra Leone and Northern Ireland*, ed. Eileen F. Babbitt and Ellen L. Lutz. Syracuse: Syracuse University Press.

Heast, David, and Joe Joyce. 1988. Ulster Killing Case Dropped. *The Guardian* (London), September 28.

Her Majesty's Inspectorate of Constabulary (HMIC). 2013. Inspection of Police Service of Northern Ireland Historical Enquiries Team.

House of Commons Debate. HC Deb 20 December 1984 vol 70, col 578.

———. HC Deb 19 February 1986 vol 92, col 420.

———. HC Deb 09 January 1996 vol 269, col 38–39.

House of Lords Debate. HL Deb 15 March 1989 vol 505, col 305–306.

———. HL Deb 06 June 1991 vol 529, cc806–31.

Interview 5, Belfast, Northern Ireland, 2009.

Interview 7, Belfast, Northern Ireland, 2010.

Interview 9, Lisburn, Northern Ireland, 2010.

Jennings, Tony. 1984. Agenda (Out of Court): Does Northern Ireland Now Have Final Courts of Justice? *The Guardian* (London), November 5.

Little, Ivan. UDR Soldier Cleared of Catholic Murder. *Belfast Telegraph*, February 19, 2015.

Lundy, Patricia. 2009. Exploring Home-Grown Transitional Justice and Its Dilemmas: A Case Study of the Historical Enquiries Team, Northern Ireland. *International Journal of Transitional Justice* 3: 321–340.

Mahoney, James, and Kathleen Thelen. 2010. A Theory of Gradual Institutional Change. In *Explaining Institutional Change: Ambiguity, Agency, and Power*, ed. James Mahoney and Kathleen Thelen. New York: Cambridge University Press.

Marshall v. United Kingdom. 1998. European Court of Human Rights. HUDOC Database. www.echr.coe.int

McAleese, Deborah. 2015. Dealing with the Legacy of the Troubles Could Take Us a Lifetime, Warns Top PSNI Officer. *Belfast Telegraph*, May 18, 2015.

McEvoy, Kieran. 2001. *Paramilitary Imprisonment in Northern Ireland: Resistance, Management and Release*. Oxford: Oxford University Press.

Ní Aoláin, Fionnuala. 2000. *The Politics of Force: Conflict Management and State Violence in Northern Ireland*. Belfast: Blackstaff Press.

Ní Aoláin, Fionnuala, and Colm Campbell. 2005. The Paradox of Transition in Conflicted Democracies. *Human Rights Quarterly* 27 (1): 172–213.

Northern Ireland (Emergency Provisions) Act. 1973. Chapter 53. London: Her Majesty's Stationery Office. Available: www.legislation.gov.uk. 17 June 2015.

O'Brien, Martin. 1996. Northern Ireland at the United Nations, 1969–1996. Masters Thesis, School of Law, Queen's University.

R v. Latimer and Others, Court of Appeal 1988.

Regina v. Fisher and Wright. 1995. Belfast Crown Court.

Regina v. Jones. 1975. Belfast Crown Court.

———. 1976. Appeal at the House of Lords.

Rolston, Bill. 2000. *Unfinished Business: State Killings and the Quest for Truth*. Belfast: Beyond the Pale Publications.

Rolston, Bill, and Phil Scraton. 2005. In the Full Glare of English Politics: Ireland, Inquiries and the British State. *British Journal of Criminology* 45: 547–564.

Ruane, Joseph, and Jennifer Todd. 1998. *The Dynamics of Conflict in Northern Ireland: Power, Conflict and Emancipation*. Cambridge: Cambridge University Press.

Smith, Colletta. 2015. HMIC Concern Over Accountability of PSNI's Legacy Investigation Branch. *BBC*, June 24, 2015.

Whelan, Leo J. 1992. The Challenge of Lobbying for Civil Rights in Northern Ireland: The Committee on the Administration of Justice. *Human Rights Quarterly* 14 (2): 149–170.

CHAPTER 4

"Resorting to Authoritarian Habits": Anti-terrorism Laws, State Violence, and Human Rights Prosecutions in Democratic Spain

In recent years, Spanish citizens have lobbied for a reckoning with the state's authoritarian past. Some sectors of society advocate for a truth commission, while others have organized the exhumation of mass graves in hundreds of sites across the country. The reopening of old wounds has shaken Spanish society and forced many communities to confront the notion that the democratic transition in 1976 after decades of repression under Franco may not be the "model" transition it was thought to be. While much of the recent truth-seeking focus is on the atrocities of the civil war (1936–1939) and the Franco regime that followed, this crucial moment in Spain's construction of historical memory begs important questions about the nature of Spanish democracy, particularly as it confronted periods of internal armed conflict. How did the Spanish government, as a new European democracy, manage the war with ETA? What did the post-transition administrations establish to ensure judicial accountability for state violations? This chapter examines the human rights violations committed by the state *after* Spain's democratic transition. Violence escalated between the Spanish government and the Basque separatist group Euskadi Ta

Aretxaga, Begoña. A Fictional Reality: Paramilitary Death Squads and the Construction of State Terror in Spain, in *Death Squad: The Anthropology of State Terror*, Jeffrey Sluka, ed. Philadelphia, PA. University of Pennsylvania Press (2000), 60

M. Lynch, *Human Rights Prosecutions in Democracies at War*, Human Rights Interventions,
https://doi.org/10.1007/978-3-319-96908-4_4

Askatasuna (ETA), or Basque Homeland and Liberty, during the transition and it continued for several years. Though the level of violence did not approximate the wars in the other cases in this book, Spain did experience internal armed conflict during the years 1980–1992.[1] ETA began using violence against the Franco regime years before the transition, but when the transition negotiations did not meet their demands for Basque independence, ETA continued their attacks on political officials and civilians. State-sponsored death squads carried out targeted extra-judicial killings against suspected ETA members. Many of these killings occurred in French towns bordering Spain, where several ETA members sought refuge. As the state significantly increased its arrests of suspected ETA members, ill-treatment and torture allegations from detainees surged. In an analysis of the state's use of violence during this time period, Basque anthropologist Begoña Aretxaga writes, "The state was both the law and its transgression….yet in the next moment it was the state against itself, as it were, or the good, democratic state against the bad state that was resorting to authoritarian habits."[2] The juxtaposition of democratic norms and institutions alongside the state's use of death squads and torture produced a crisis of identity for Spain during these years. More importantly, it shaped the trajectory of investigations and prosecutions of state human rights violations.

The emergency institution created in democratic Spain was comprised of anti-terrorist legislation, first issued as temporary decree laws. These laws did not contain inquest or immunity clauses; rather, protections for state actors who engaged in torture were built into the laws through the legalization of lengthy, unmonitored detention periods, known as incommunicado detention. Thus, the emergency institution's restrictions on human rights prosecutions mainly involved crimes of torture, not extra-judicial killings. The evolution of the emergency institution in Spain involved layering and conversion. Early on in the conflict, members of the main Basque political party questioned the ways in which anti-terrorism laws facilitated torture and encouraged impunity and, as a result, certain laws were amended or struck down. The Spanish government responded with conversion, a strategy of redeployment in which they first placed anti-terrorism laws in ordinary law, then permanently in the Penal Code. The government's use of conversion is significant in that, prior to their transfer to ordinary law, anti-terrorism measures were subject to parliamentary and judicial scrutiny reserved for crisis laws. Parliamentary oversight and judicial review of anti-terrorism measures was thus eliminated by the late 1980s.

This chapter analyzes the moments of layering and conversion within Spain's emergency institution to explain patterns of prosecution and to demonstrate the importance of analyzing gradual institutional change. Emergency and anti-terrorism laws are often dynamic and contested and, as a result, their effects on human rights prosecutions can be varied. While legal reforms established during Spain's democratic transition helped to facilitate prosecutions for state-sponsored killings during the 1980s and early 1990s, investigations and prosecutions of torture allegations were crippled by anti-terrorism laws that normalized and legitimized ill-treatment at the hands of the state.

The following chapter is organized as follows: the first section provides historical background to the Basque conflict in Spain; the second section discusses the history of the emergency institution in Spain and it explains how layering and conversion produced institutional change; the third section presents the prosecution data; the fourth section examines the conditions that spurred human rights prosecutions; and finally, the chapter concludes with a discussion on the legacy of the emergency institution on human rights prosecutions.

Historical Background to the Basque Conflict

The Basque region of Spain comprises four provinces in the north of the country, which include Vizcaya, Alava, Guipuzcoa, and Navarra, and some Basques consider the three French provinces that border Spain, including Soule, Labourd, and Basse Navarre, to also form part of the Basque Country. The relationship between the Basque region and Spain has been in tension for over a hundred years. Before Francisco Franco led a coup against the Second Republic in 1936, Basques attempted to negotiate autonomous status for the northern provinces, based on the region's economic success and a strengthening nationalism. During the Spanish civil war (1936–1939) that followed, Basques sided with Socialists and Communists in defense of their autonomy and the Republic. Their demand for self-rule, and much of their identity, including the Basque language (Euskera), was suppressed during the years of Franco's dictatorship (1939–1975).[3] An estimated 300,000 people lost their lives during the Spanish civil war, and under Franco's repressive regime, an estimated 400,000 people were imprisoned or forced to work in labor camps. Thousands were executed and over 100,000 people disappeared.[4]

Several youth groups formed in the Basque region to resist Franco's rule and to salvage Basque culture and identity, including a university student group called Ekin, which means "to act" in the Basque language.[5] Ekin joined with youth members of the Basque nationalist political party, Partido Nacionalista Vasco (PNV), to form ETA in 1958. ETA's initial aims were to challenge the Franco regime and seek Basque independence, and at first, its actions were confined to robberies, bombings, and property damage.[6] After 1968, however, as resistance to Franco's power strengthened, ETA increased the severity of its violence, engaging in various kidnappings and political assassinations.

Following Franco's death in 1975, opposition parties organized to develop plans for a democratic transition. The moderate political parties placed little emphasis on justice though there was a great deal of interest in creating democratic institutions to replace some of the existing government structures.[7] In contrast, Basque nationalists called for a total dismantling of the repressive institutions. In the end, as violence grew between left- and right-wing factions, and Spaniards began to fear further destabilization, the transition embodied a relatively cautious shift in power. Though the transition was not a ruptured transition, where previous power holders are marginalized, the development of a new constitution and corresponding democratic institutions did mark a major break with the authoritarian past. Spain did not employ justice processes, such as prosecutions or truth-seeking bodies, as it moved from decades of repression to democracy. The Amnesty Law of 1977 was a central demand from the democratic opposition, not Franco's allies. The new democratic government passed the law to permit the release of political prisoners, who were mostly ETA members, and to prohibit prosecution of those who committed human rights violations during Franco's regime.[8]

The 1978 Constitution, passed through a referendum, granted autonomous status to three Basque provinces (Vizcaya, Alava, and Guipuzcoa) now known as the Basque Autonomous Community and Navarra, as well as other regions of Spain, including Catalonia. This arrangement provided the Basque region with its own parliament and president, the power to collect and regulate taxes, and the freedom to establish its own police force, health-care system, and educational systems. The constitutional referendum received meager support from Basque citizens. Only 34.9% of Basques voted in favor of the constitution and the majority abstained from voting altogether. Among the remaining population in Spain, 87.9% supported the referendum and 7.91% opposed it.[9] The lack of reforms in the security sector and the co-optation of the Basque region within the Spanish state are argued to have fueled ETA's continued campaign of violence after the democratic transition. The sentiment within the Basque population that the Spanish transition was a failure is evident almost two decades later. In a 1994 poll, when asked if the transition made them proud, less than 50% of Basques responded yes, while over 80% of Spanish citizens responded yes.[10]

After the transition, Spain became a parliamentary democracy, whereby the monarchy holds the constitutional head of state and the head of government, the prime minister, is elected by the Congress. The Parliament, or Cortes Generales, is a bi-cameral body made up of the Congress (the lower house with a total of 350 seats) and the Senate (the upper house with a total of 266 seats). A party list proportional representation system is used for most elections with the exception of the Senate, which uses a plurality system. The two main political parties vying for power since the democratic transition include the center-right Partido Popular (PP) and the center-left Partido Socialista Obrero Español (PSOE). The Basque Nationalist Party (PNV) is a minority party in the Spanish Parliament but it is the largest political party in the Basque Autonomous Community and it has led the Basque regional government for over two decades (see Table 4.1).

During the years 1975–1992, Spain experienced intense violence between ETA and various right-wing groups that were covertly run by the state, including the GAL (Grupos Antiterroristas Liberación). The GAL was a state-sponsored death squad that targeted suspected ETA members during the 1980s through bombings, kidnappings, torture, and extra-judicial killings. Civilian mercenaries carried out most of the killings, though members of the police and security forces in the Basque region, and various members of the Spanish government, orchestrated the funding and the operations of this group. After the GAL violence dissipated, ETA continued a one-sided campaign of violence, involving political assassinations and targeted attacks on civilians, in the Basque region and throughout Spain from 1992 to 2010. Almost 900 lives were lost as a result of ETA's actions since the democratic transition.[11]

Spain ratified the Geneva Conventions in 1952 and the Additional Protocols in 1989. Though the International Committee for the Red Cross (ICRC) was active in Spain after the Spanish civil war (1936–1939), it was not a monitoring presence during the internal violence that followed the democratic transition. The internal war that transpired between

Table 4.1 A chronology of political parties/coalitions in power since the democratic transition in Spain

Year	*Political party/coalition in power*	*Prime minister*
1977	Unión de Centro Democrático (UCD) (minority government)	Adolfo Suárez González
1979	Unión de Centro Democrático (UCD) (with People's Alliance, Andalusian Party and Aragonese Party)	Adolfo Suárez González (1979–1981, then resigned) Leopoldo Calvo-Sotelo y Bustelo (1981–1982)
1982	Partido Socialista Obrero Español (PSOE) (majority government)	Felipe González Márquez
1986	Partido Socialista Obrero Español (PSOE) (majority government)	Felipe González Márquez
1989	Partido Socialista Obrero Español (PSOE) (with Canarian Coalition)	Felipe González Márquez
1993	Partido Socialista Obrero Español (PSOE) (with Convergence and Union Party and Basque Nationalist Party)	Felipe González Márquez
1996	Partido Popular (PP) (with Convergence and Union Party, Basque Nationalist Party and Canarian Coalition)	José María Aznar López
2000	Partido Popular (PP) (majority government)	José María Aznar López
2004	Partido Socialista Obrero Español (PSOE) (with United Left Party and Republican Left of Catalonia Party)	José Luis Rodríguez Zapatero
2008	Partido Socialista Obrero Español (PSOE) (minority government)	José Luis Rodríguez Zapatero
2011–present	Partido Popular (PP) (majority government)	Mariano Rajoy Brey

1980 and 1992 meets the broad definition of internal conflict identified in Common Article 3. However, there is no evidence that the Spanish government, ETA, or a third party invoked international humanitarian law during these years.

The Spanish government's approach to ETA's tactics has ranged from violent confrontation through the use of illegal death squads in the 1980s to expansive policies of arrest, detention, and extradition to periodic negotiation. ETA declared a series of ceasefires in the last two decades but they all ended in failure. In recent years, the demands from Basque nationalists have shifted from a focus on Basque independence toward a model of shared sovereignty.[12] Bilateral relations between political groups in Northern Ireland and the Basque region have also influenced ETA to devise a less violent strategy in favor of a purely political one.

In October 2011, an international conference was held in the Basque Country concerning the Basque question and plans for peace negotiations. Attendees included former UN Secretary General Kofi Annan and political actors from the Northern Ireland peace process. Immediately following the conference, ETA announced a permanent ceasefire and called for the French and Spanish governments to engage in dialogue in order to determine a solution to the conflict.[13] General elections were then held in November 2011, ushering in new political leadership with the PP. In the past, the Spanish government has consistently refused to negotiate with ETA while it remains active and armed. However, the weakening of ETA in recent years, and its recent commitment to a more definitive end to violence, is encouraging for many Spaniards.

The Spanish legal system is distinct from the legal system in the other cases in a few important ways. In particular, the criminal trial process is notably different. Criminal prosecution in Spain involves two phases: the judicial investigation (*instrucción*) and a trial in open court (*juicio oral.*) The first phase involves the investigation of the case under an investigating magistrate or judge. An investigation may be prompted by an accusation (*denuncia*) about an alleged offense by the police or an injured party or witness. It can also be prompted by a complaint (*querella*) made by an involved citizen, or in instances of alleged offenses against the public order or the public interest, an uninvolved citizen(s) can initiate a *querella*.[14] The evidence against the suspect is examined during this phase by the investigating magistrate and a state or public prosecutor (*fiscal del estado*), the latter of which reports to the Attorney General (Fiscal General del Estado). The incumbent government appoints the Attorney General.

Significantly, the state prosecutor in Spain does not have the exclusive right of prosecution in criminal proceedings. A case can also be brought by lawyers acting on behalf of the victim or his/her family (*acusación particular*), or lawyers acting on behalf of the general public (*acusación popular*). The former is understood as private prosecution, while the latter is known as the popular accusation or popular prosecution.[15] Defense lawyers represent the accused. During the investigation stage, the investigating judge has powers to seek further information from police or other authorities, and while he/she usually conducts the investigation in chambers, they can also visit crime scenes and interview suspects and witnesses.

The investigating judge decides whether a person should be indicted and he/she produces a report to a panel of judges on his/her recommendation (*auto de conclusión*). The panel of judges will then determine whether to proceed to trial or dismiss the case for lack of evidence. During the second phase of the criminal trial process, the investigating judge has no role in the trial (*juicio oral*) itself though he/she has a great deal of influence in directing the trajectory of the trial based on his/her investigative report. A different judge or judges with no previous contact with the case will preside over the trial. This judge determines the final judgment, verdict, and sentence.[16]

Two main courts have jurisdiction over the entire territory of Spain, including the Autonomous Communities. The Tribunal Supremo is the highest court in the country and it has five chambers: civil, criminal, administrative, social, and military. The Audiencia Nacional sits below the Tribunal Supremo and has jurisdiction in criminal, administrative, and labor matters.[17] Most of the cases involving members of the state-sponsored terror group, the GAL, were tried in the Audiencia Nacional. The court was specifically created in 1977 by the Real Decreto-Ley 1/1977 to centralize investigation and prosecution of terrorism cases.[18] This court has six examining magistrates and six trial chambers, and each is presided over by a three-judge panel. Crimes in this court's jurisdiction are not subject to trial by jury. All terrorism-related cases are tried in the Audiencia Nacional. One of the GAL cases, involving the kidnapping of civilian Segundo Marey, was tried in the Supreme Court because a Member of Parliament (MP) and former minister, Jose Barrionuevo, were indicted. A sitting MP can only be indicted if Parliament agrees to waive his/her privileges.[19] Before Barrionuevo was indicted, the Marey case was investigated at the Audiencia Nacional.

If a criminal trial is held in the Supreme Court, appeals can be made to the Constitutional Court. The Constitutional Court is generally tasked with interpreting the Constitution and one of its responsibilities is protection of the fundamental rights and freedoms enshrined in the Constitution; criminal cases concerning rights violations committed by the state may therefore at times proceed to the Constitutional Court. From the Constitutional Court, citizens can pursue their case at the European Court of Human Rights. Regional courts in Spain include the Tribunales Superiores de Justicia, which have jurisdiction in civil, criminal, administrative, and social matters within each of the Autonomous Communities, and the Audiencias Provinciales, which have jurisdiction in civil and criminal matters in the Spanish provinces.[20]

In contrast to Sri Lanka and Northern Ireland, relatively high levels of judicial independence were secured through the 1978 Constitution in Spain. Specifically, the constitution created the Consejo General del Poder Judicial (General Council of the Judiciary). This body is comprised of 21 members, including judges and lawyers, who are appointed by both chambers of Parliament, as opposed to the executive. These members elect the president of the Consejo, who is also the president of the Supreme Court, and they have the power to nominate the presidents of both the Tribunal Superiores de Justicia and the Tribunal Supremo (the Supreme Court). The Consejo is also responsible for promotions, sanctions, and suspensions of judges. The members of the Consejo hold their positions for five years, and with the exception of the president, cannot be re-elected.[21] Thus, there is far less opportunity in Spain for the executive to punish or dismiss judges whose decisions run counter to the interests of the incumbent government.

The Emergency Institution in Spain

Political leaders negotiating the transition had a great interest in avoiding crisis measures reminiscent of the Franco dictatorship, particularly those that centralized power within the executive and limited judicial independence.[22] Franco's death, the strong mobilization of civil society on the protection of rights, and subsequent democratic reforms resulted in the abolition of draconian laws. The rules and regulations of the emergency institution in the new democracy were created through two forms of law. First, the 1978 Constitution established clear provisions for protecting citizens from abuses committed by the executive or its security apparatus when the country faced a crisis. The Constitution also contained explicit clauses on emergency declarations and constraints on the executive. The Spanish government, however, never declared an emergency, and emergency measures were not enacted to regulate rising violence. Second, the Spanish government created anti-terrorism laws to regulate and address the increasing attacks by ETA. Specific clauses within the anti-terrorism laws that legitimized and encouraged incommunicado detention and expansive arrest powers enabled the use of ill-treatment and torture on suspected ETA detainees. Similar to the Sri Lankan and Northern Ireland cases, the facilitation of human rights violations by the police within these laws produced a logic of impunity within the emergency institution. Anti-terrorism laws became a site of contestation in the ensuing years and the government responded by entrenching them first in ordinary legislation, then permanently in the Penal Code.

Emergency Clauses in the 1978 Constitution

The suspension of civil rights concerning suspected terrorists was a regular feature of Franco's regime before the democratic transition. Franco imposed the first state of exception in 1956 in response to student protests in Madrid and this effectively continued until the democratic transition.[23] The Law of Public Order (1959) and the Decree on Banditry and Terrorism (1969) were central features of the emergency institution under authoritarian rule. Anti-terrorist laws were in effect under Franco during the early 1970s, and they were largely directed at the Basque region as ETA violence steadily increased.[24] In 1976, King Juan Carlos repealed a law created by Franco, the Law on Prevention of Terrorism.[25] Then, in 1977, the Royal Decree Law (RDL—4/1977) abolished the National Movement (Movimiento Nacional), the single regime party under Franco, and various related political institutions.[26] At this time, hundreds of individuals who had been accused of political crimes against the state remained imprisoned. Ahead of the 1977 parliamentary elections for the new government, three amnesty decrees were passed, and Parliament approved an amnesty law in 1977. Together, these provisions enabled the release of the majority of prisoners in the country, many of whom were Basque.[27] Spain ratified the International Covenant on Civil and Political Rights on April 27, 1977. By 1978, there were no anti-terrorist laws on the books.

The 1978 Constitution, created during the democratic transition, established clear criteria on the creation and regulation of emergencies and subsequent legislation. The suspension of certain rights is allowable if a state of emergency is declared, including the right to personal freedom (Article 17), the right to inviolability of the home and communications privacy (Article 18, clauses 2 and 3), freedom of residency and movement (Article 19), freedom of expression (Article 20, clause 1, subclauses a and d only, and clause 5), the right to meet (Article 21), the right to strike (Article 28, clause 2), and the right of workers and employers to adopt collective labor dispute measures (Article 37, clause 2).[28] Article 55 (2) of the Constitution states that an organic (ordinary) law may determine, with the participation of the courts and Parliament, the nature and to what extent Articles 17 and 18 may be suspended regarding investigations of terrorist groups. This clause also includes provisions for judicial accountability if powers under such a law are abused: "Unjustified or abusive use of the powers recognized in the foregoing organic law shall give rise to criminal liability where it is a violation of the rights and liberties recognized by law."[29]

Additionally, Article 116 stipulates that an ordinary law must be used to declare states of emergency and create emergency regulations. A declaration of emergency can only be issued by the government *after* the Congress has first authorized it, followed by approval from the Council of Ministers, which includes the prime minister, deputy prime minister, and other members of the Cabinet. The declaration has to state its effects, the specifics on applicable territory, and establish a clear duration, not exceeding 30 days. Extensions of 30 days are allowable through the same series of steps. Clause 6 of Article 116 clearly dictates the necessity of government accountability during emergency periods: "Proclamation of states of alarm, emergency and siege shall not modify the principle of liability of the Government or its agents as recognized in the Constitution and the law."[30]

Anti-terrorism Laws

Interim anti-terrorism laws were also developed by the Suarez government as Parliament worked on developing a new penal code and code of criminal procedure. These interim decree laws (*decretos-leyes*) were passed by parliament from 1978 to 1980. Decree laws are rules created by the Executive in times of urgency that have the force of law as permitted by Article 86 (1) of the 1978 Constitution. Limitations on these laws include: the decree cannot affect the basic institutions of the state, the civil rights and liberties outlined in Title I of the Constitution, the powers of the Autonomous Communities (e.g., the Basque region and Catalonia) or the general electoral regime. The Executive also must submit the decree law to Parliament for approval within 30 days.[31]

The interim decree laws during the late 1970s created expansive powers of arrest and detention in order to combat the increasing number of ETA attacks in the early years of democracy. The 1978 Decree Law 21/1978 was one of the first decrees that created conditions facilitating the use of torture on suspected ETA detainees. The Minister of Interior, Rodolfo Martín Villa, pushed the decree through without the required parliamentary approval after ETA assassinated a Bilbao journalist.[32] Under this law, suspected terrorists could be held without charge for more than 72 hours if police first notified judicial authorities. Decree Law 56/1978 then modified Decree Law 21 slightly and added a provision that allowed a judge to order incommunicado detention for as long as the investigation was underway (Table 4.2).[33]

Table 4.2 A selection of key anti-terrorism laws in Spain

Year	*Law*
1978	Decreto-Ley 21/1978 (June 20)
1978	Decreto-Ley 56/1978 (December 4)
1979	Decreto-Ley 3/1979 (January 26)
1980	Decreto-Ley 3/1979 (renewed for one more year)
1980	Ley Orgánica 11/1980 (replaces Decreto-Ley 56/1978)
1981	Law in the Defense of the Constitution (created after coup attempt)
1981	Ley Orgánica 4/1981, de 1 de junio, de los Estados de Alarma, Excepción y Sitio (never invoked)
1983	Ley Orgánica 14/1983 (December)
1984	Ley Orgánica 6/1984 (Habeas Corpus Law) (May 24)
1984	Ley Orgánica 8/1984 (December 26)
1988	Repeal of Ley Orgánica 8/1984
1995	Ley Orgánica 10/1995, de 23 de noviembre, del Código Penal (select provisions)

This moment in Spain's anti-terrorist legislation is significant to the matter of human rights prosecutions for a few key reasons. Decree Law 56 extended detention for up to ten days with permission from judicial authorities, and incommunicado detention allowed the authorities to detain a suspect without notifying family or an attorney for the length of the detention. Incommunicado detention immediately received significant criticism from rights groups[34] and it was also argued to be the reason for the growing allegations of torture in the 1980s.[35] In January of the following year, King Juan Carlos initiated Decree Law 3/1979, which created penalties for supporting terrorist actions or groups verbally or in writing and the law increased punishment for terrorist crimes.

Layering and Conversion: Resistance from Basque Politicians and the Transfer of Anti-terrorist Measures into Ordinary Law

Torture is prohibited in Article 15 of the Constitution and thus, the Spanish government had an incentive at the time to consider how they would combat the perception they were engaging in serious human rights violations via the anti-terrorism laws. After a few years of issuing decree laws, the government developed *ordinary* laws that simply mirrored the anti-terrorism decree laws. Expansive powers of arrest and the sanctioned use of ten-day incommunicado detention were no longer codified in temporary crisis laws; rather, they were part and parcel of any other ordinary law regulating the lives of Spanish citizens.

The first of these laws, Organic Law 11/1980, retained the provisions in Decree Law 56. It was passed by Parliament with overwhelming support; of the 350 members, only 2 voted against and 7 Basque deputies abstained.[36] The ordinary law also allowed for increased interceptions by the police into private communication among citizens and more severe penalties for those publicly supporting terrorism, or those suspected of supporting terrorism. Arrests of suspected ETA terrorists, who primarily were Basque, doubled between the years 1979 and 1981.[37]

In 1981, after the military attempted a failed coup by storming the Congress for several hours, Parliament passed two additional measures, which operated to entrench crisis legislation in the everyday functioning of Spain's nascent democracy. The Law for Defense of the Constitution, passed in 1981, broadly expanded the definition of terrorism to include any attack on the Spanish nation or its identity, even non-violent activities, and the government was granted the power to close the doors of media organizations that appeared to be in support or defense of terrorist groups.[38] The same year, Parliament passed Ley Orgánica 4/1981 de los Estados de Alarma, Excepción y Sitio, which granted more control to the executive in declaring states of siege or emergency in ways that slightly contradicted provisions in the Constitution. The latter law was never invoked.

In 1984, the Spanish Parliament introduced Organic Law 6/1984, or the Habeas Corpus Law. This law established the right of a detainee, his/her spouse, companion, or guardian in case of a minor, the Public Prosecutor, the Defensor del Pueblo (Ombuds Institution), and the instructing judge, to file writs of habeas corpus regarding the lawfulness of a detention.[39] While in theory this law appeared to address the growing number of torture allegations from detainees, in practice, it was incredibly difficult to challenge the legality of detention. Existing anti-terrorist laws established incommunicado detention as a priori legal. Additionally, writs of habeas corpus in cases of detained suspected terrorists were only reviewed by judges at the Audiencia Nacional, as opposed to the local judge where the individual was detained. This meant that the same judge that first ordered the detention was also the judge reviewing the habeas corpus claim.[40] Most attorneys therefore viewed habeas corpus petitions to be ineffective and they were rarely filed after this law was enacted.

The political party in power, the PSOE, held a majority in the Spanish Parliament from 1982 until they were ousted by the PP in 1996. As a result, the continued enactment of anti-terrorism legislation during these years was largely sanctioned. There was, however, some pushback from members of the Basque Parliament. Up until 1986, the oldest Basque party, the PNV (Basque Nationalist Party), led the Basque Parliament through a narrowly held majority. The PNV had a history of resisting Franco's rule, but it largely separated itself from radical nationalism which was taken up by other parties, including Herri Batasuna. The Basque Parliament posed challenges to key anti-terrorism laws in the early 1980s, but efforts waned after the PNV split and lost substantial support in the 1986 elections. This forced the party to form a coalition with the Basque wing of the Spanish socialist party, PSE.[41] Two particular moments of resistance on the part of the Basque Parliament are noteworthy given both actions resulted in the elimination of proposed anti-terrorism strategies.

In May 1983, Minister of Interior José Barrionuevo and Director of State Security Rafael Vera, announced Plan ZEN (Zona Especial del Norte or Special Northern Zone), which was approved by the Spanish Parliament in September. The plan sought increased funding to crack down on terrorism in the Basque region through the media, political groups, and police operations. However, the Basque Parliament refused to cooperate with the plan and it passed a resolution stating its opposition. Plan ZEN was dismantled shortly afterwards.[42]

A year later, Organic Law 8/1984 (December 26) was introduced, which maintained the terms of earlier laws and added several harsher provisions. The law authorized government bans on political parties and other groups led by convicted terrorists. It also increased the penalties for terrorist offenses and equated public support of terrorism with violent acts by issuing similar penalties.[43] The severity of the measures within this law caused some Basque political leaders to denounce it as Francoist. Eventually, in 1985, the Basque parliament asked the Constitutional Court to declare unconstitutional 10 of the law's 22 articles. The Court agreed to review the law and in its 1987 verdict, it declared some articles unconstitutional. However, by this time, parts of the law had lapsed based on a deadline written into the law, and after large support from most political parties in the Spanish and Basque Parliaments, with the exception of two Basque parties, the government repealed the remainder of the articles.[44]

The Transfer of Anti-terrorism Laws into the Penal Code

Anti-terrorist legislation became increasingly normalized by the late 1980s. In November 1987, the González administration introduced legislation to repeal Organic Law 8/1984 and transfer most of its provisions into the regular penal code. Incommunicado detention was also effectively reduced from ten days to five.[45] Organic Law 8/1984 was completely repealed in 1988. Between 1988 and 1995, stand-alone anti-terrorist laws ceased to exist because this was largely unnecessary. Terrorism matters were folded into the existing criminal code and plans were set to overhaul the criminal code entirely.[46] On November 23, 1995, Organic Law 10/1995 was passed by Parliament as the new penal code and it remains the penal code to this day. Terrorist crimes are defined in the regular Criminal Code (Código Penal), and the Code of Criminal Procedure (Ley de Enjuiciamiento Criminal) establishes the powers of law enforcement agencies and judicial authorities to investigate crimes of terrorism, while at the same time proscribing the rights of terrorist suspects.[47]

The 1995 Penal Code maintains expansive powers of arrest and detention regarding suspected terrorists and it broadens the definition of terrorism. Article 571 of the Criminal Code defines terrorists as those who are belonging, acting in the service of or collaborating with armed groups, organizations or groups and whose objective is to subvert the constitutional order or seriously alter public peace.[48] The definition is further expanded and generalized through Article 553, which allows police to immediately detain people when there is an order to do so, when they are caught in the act of committing a crime, when a fleeing criminal takes refuge in a building, or, in exceptional cases, when people are ***presumably involved*** in actions related to crimes listed in Article 384 bis (this includes crimes committed by a person related to a terrorist group or crimes committed by individual terrorists).[49] Article 577 stipulates that even those who do not belong to a terrorist group but who contribute to actions that subvert the public order, or commit crimes listed as related to terrorism, will be subject to the same penalties as those persons identified as terrorists. Finally, Article 574 broadens but fails to clarify that any person who belongs to or collaborates with an armed or terrorist group who commits "any other offense" with any of the purposes outlined in Article 571 will be subject to the same penalties identified for terrorist acts.[50] The penalty identified for most of these crimes is 15–20 years. Summarizing the preceding list of articles in the Penal Code, a staff member at a Basque human rights organization commented, the terrorism definition is like a "flexible suit, a suit that can fit anybody."[51] The large number of Basques that have been detained and released at a later point, many of whom have claimed torture in private or made formal complaints, reflect in some measure the impact of the Penal Code's ambiguous language on people's lives.

The provisions for incommunicado detention in the Penal Code, as well as shifts in jurisdiction for terrorist-related crimes, amplified concerns about continuing patterns of torture and impunity after the mid-1990s. Article 520 bis (2) allows for incommunicado detention of a terrorism suspect for up to five days upon a judge's authorization within 24 hours of the arrest.[52] Article 527 (a) stipulates that detainees subject to incommunicado are provided with the assistance of an official appointed lawyer (not one of their own choosing) and an examination by a state-assisted forensic physician. Articles 527 (c) and 520 (6) (c) stipulate that incommunicado detainees do not have the right to confer in private with their lawyer and they can only meet with a lawyer of their choice after formal charges are presented and the incommunicado detention is lifted.[53] Since 1988, through Organic Law 4/1988, cases related to terrorism have been exclusively heard by the Audiencia Nacional in Madrid. Before this moment, local judges would determine the terms of detention and hear any complaints of ill-treatment after periods of incommunicado detention.[54]

The centralization of processing these cases does not necessarily immediately indicate a breach of detainees' rights. However, an organization in the Basque community that has documented cases of torture for several years has found that when individuals experienced ill-treatment while they were detained in local police stations and they were admitted to the hospital, medical personnel were often less willing to send these persons back to police knowing the abuse would likely continue. In Madrid, hundreds of miles from the Basque Country, the organization found that such safeguards for hospitalized detainees were largely absent.[55] Thus, there is concern among not only organizations following this issue but also detainees' families, that the processing of suspected terrorism detainees in Madrid likely facilitates the employment of ill-treatment as well as impunity since incommunicado detention is codified in the Penal Code.

Finally, the fact that the penalties for state officials engaging in the practice of torture are minimal is arguably an additional incentive on the part of state actors to continue these practices.[56] The penalties for torture are outlined in the reformed 1995 Penal Code. Article 174 of the Penal Code states: "Any public official that commits torture to obtain information or a confession, or for any act he has committed or is suspected of committing, or for any reason based on discrimination, involving physical or mental suffering, will be punished with imprisonment from 2 to 6 years if the attack is severe, 1 to 3 years if it is not and there will be a penalty of disqualification from public office from 8 to 12 years."[57] This was in fact an improvement from the long-standing 1882 Penal Code, which had weaker penalties for the crime of torture and ill-treatment. In many cases, prosecutions held after the 1995 Penal Code went into effect had to rely on the earlier penal code because the crimes were committed while that code was in force.[58]

Though the UN Commission on Human Rights declared in a 2003 resolution that "prolonged incommunicado detention may facilitate the perpetration of torture and can in itself constitute a form of cruel, inhuman or degrading treatment or even torture,"[59] the incommunicado detention regime in Spain continued in the 2000s, with some alterations. In 2003, the Penal Code was reformed to allow for a second forensic doctor to examine detainees held incommunicado, and a reform to Article 509 allowed a judge to extend the detention an additional five days for individuals suspected of membership in a terrorist group or suspected of having committed a crime with two or more individuals.[60] In response to criticism from the UN and other bodies, the Spanish government reported that between 2002 and 2003, the vast majority of incommunicado detainees were held for 72 hours, only a quarter of detainees were held five days, and in one case, a detainee was held for more than five days.[61] A few years later in 2006, two proposals were submitted to the Spanish Congress in April and September, backed by almost all of the minority parties, demanding the elimination of the incommunicado regime. Votes from the PSOE (then the leader of government) and the PP, the opposition party at the time, blocked the proposal.[62]

The introduction of legal safeguards a few years later provided a response to government inaction on the issue. The "Garzón Protocol" was developed by Judge Garzón and allows for constant video surveillance, family visits and examinations by doctors of the detainees' choice, for detainees held in incommunicado detention. It only becomes applicable through a judicial decision in an individual case, so it often does not apply from the moment of arrest.[63] Compliance with the protocol appeared to be inconsistent in the first few years of the protocol's employment. As of 2011, only one-third of the investigating judges on terrorism cases had applied the protocol.[64] In another significant development, the Basque Autonomous Police Forces had almost completely phased out the use of incommunicado detention in terrorism cases by the end of the 2000s, as a form of best practice.[65]

The persistence of anti-terrorism measures in Spain, particularly the incommunicado regime, in both temporary and ordinary legislation produced routinely high rates of torture allegations. Extensive documentation over close to 30 years by Spanish and Basque NGOs, Amnesty International, Human Rights Watch, UN special rapporteurs, the European Committee for the Prevention of Torture and Inhuman or Degrading Treatment or Punishment (CPT), and the UN Committee Against Torture (CAT), produce evidence of a range of ill-treatment strategies employed by the police and security forces, some of which are extremely violent. Employment of "*la bolsa*," asphyxiation by the use of a plastic bag over the head, is common; electrodes have often been applied to parts of the body, including the genitals; sexual abuse of women increased over time; "*la bañera*," immersion of the head in water, has been used; and, finally, threats of execution, rape, or other bodily harm have also been routinely cited.[66] Members of the Spanish government as well as the judiciary have regularly explained to UN special rapporteurs and other investigators that torture allegations are a decades-long strategy employed by ETA to sabotage the investigation of terrorist crimes. As a result, in some cases, judges have outright dismissed or ignored detainees' complaints of mistreatment.[67]

Through layering and conversion, the emergency institution in Spain gradually evolved from a set of temporary crisis laws to ordinary legislation and finally as a permanent part of the Penal Code. Tracing the evolution of these laws demonstrates how while at first these measures were subject to parliamentary and judicial scrutiny reserved for temporary crisis laws, their transfer to ordinary legislation, and the Penal Code shielded them from mechanisms of oversight established by the Constitution. The normalization of incommunicado detention made it difficult for victims and their families to pursue investigations and prosecutions. As a result of the design and implementation of anti-terrorism laws, prosecutions for extra-judicial killings proceeded in the 1980s and early 1990s, while investigations of ill-treatment and torture allegations suffered under the shadow of the emergency institution.

Human Rights Prosecution Data

"El fuego no le llegó"[68]

A total of 40 prosecutions were held between 1976 and 2014 concerning state violence against citizens. The prosecutions for ill-treatment and torture largely involved police personnel, while the GAL crimes involved a range of state actors, including high-ranking members of an incumbent PSOE government, a chief of police, governors, and members of the military. Of 151 state actors prosecuted, 125 individuals were convicted and 26 were acquitted. The majority of the prosecutions, 32, were for crimes of ill-treatment and torture; 7 prosecutions addressed murder and related crimes, and 1 trial involved kidnapping charges. Twenty-two state actors were convicted for the GAL crimes in trials spanning from 1991 to 2003.

Prosecutions for Crimes of Ill-Treatment and Torture

Proving the systematic use of torture was incredibly difficult in Spain because of the routine use of incommunicado detention and the allegations from government, law enforcement, and some judicial actors that ETA suspects harmed themselves in order to concoct evidence of torture. The narratives surrounding torture were, as a result, highly contested among Spanish citizens, Basque citizens, political officials, and detainees. When I spoke with members of Basque human rights organizations about these conflicting narratives, one individual described the imprint of ill-treatment on Basque society:

> So many people have suffered torture in the Basque country. So many that it is often people sitting next to you. So people in Basque country know what can happen at police stations. They know this well.[69]

The interviewee added, when the Spanish media covers cases of incommunicado detention, detainees are often described as "singing." Singing indicates the detainee provided a confession during detention and often the entire confession is printed in the paper.[70] For some family members, this is very painful. A confession implies that coercion or force may have been used, particularly if they believe their family member is innocent of the crime. The media has also reported that detainees are weaker than they used to be. Such reports suggest to families of detainees that their loved ones have likely been exposed to harm while in detention and, further, that members of the public and the Spanish media are not concerned nor are they outraged that a democratic government is engaging in such practices.[71]

The number of prosecutions over a 30-year period does not come remotely close to reports of ill-treatment and torture complaints in the Basque Country.[72] The available data on torture complaints is sporadic and inconsistent across both local and international reports. Some organizations collect only judicial complaints, while others collect testimonies from victims that did not report ill-treatment to a judge or other investigator. The latter data is important because throughout pages of testimony gathered by TAT (Torturaren Aurkako Taldea), a Basque NGO, it becomes clear that victims are afraid to report anything if the perpetrator(s) remain in the room during a questioning by medical experts or judicial personnel.[73] Amnesty International did not report regularly on complaints in the 1980s, though in 1984, it found that the government received 137 complaints of torture.[74] According to annual reports produced by TAT, the average number of torture allegations in the Basque Country between 1992 and 2007 was about 90 per year.[75] The TAT data comports somewhat with more recent findings. A 2013 report completed by the Basque government on human rights violations committed in the Basque region between 1960 and 2013 found that on the matter of torture, between 1979 and 2013, there is a real absence of sufficient data. In the analysis, the authors found that the positions on torture "are very different, ranging from total denial of its existence to those who record 10,000 cases."[76] Through their own research, they identify 5500 public complaints of torture during these years. The total includes complaints made to a judge and those made public but not through a formal complaint.

If we compare this estimate to the data gathered for this book on human rights prosecutions, knowing that 5500 public complaints of torture may have involved one or more perpetrators, the level of impunity comes in to focus. Thirty-two prosecutions were held between 1976 and 2014 for crimes of ill-treatment and torture, involving 119 members of the Guardia Civil, the National Police and local police officers. The prosecution rate is therefore abysmally low, at 0.6%. Unsurprisingly, the majority of prosecutions involved claims of ill-treatment and torture that transpired during incommunicado detention. In a study covering the years 2000–2008, the Basque government's Human Rights Directorate found that the frequency of ill-treatment and torture allegations among 957 incommunicado detention cases was just over half. 634 people claimed ill-treatment or torture and 446 of these people filed a judicial complaint. The study also found that Guardia Civil officers, who were defendants in most of the prosecutions, were associated with the worst forms of violence against detainees.[77]

Though the overall number of prosecutions is low, conviction rates are quite high. Ninety-five members of the police forces were convicted (80%)

for ill-treatment or torture and 24 police officers (20%) were acquitted. The sentences have historically been quite minimal. This is partly a result of the 1886 and revised 1995 penal codes, which outline weak penalties for these crimes. It was not uncommon for a sentence to include mere months in detention and a handful of years of disqualification from the profession. The outlier sentences of harsher penalties often manifested after the involvement of a private or people's prosecutor who recommended the maximum allowable punishment. Additional common features of these trials include both the granting of promotions to convicted perpetrators, either during an appeal or after serving a short sentence, and government-issued pardons. For example, in 1997, three members of the Guardia Civil were convicted for torturing ETA member Kepa Urra. They were sentenced to four years in prison and a ban from employment for six years. In 1999, they won an appeal at the Supreme Court and had their sentences reduced. One of the defendants was promoted a short time later, despite the fact that he was not exonerated through the appeal. All three were awarded pardons and a promotion was awarded to an additional officer after his suspension had lapsed.[78]

There are a low number of trials in the 1980s, and the prosecutions that do occur result largely from citizens bringing the cases themselves, as opposed to the public prosecutor. The numbers of police that are prosecuted jump and remain relatively high during the 1990s and this can be explained by increased activity on the part of private prosecutors and growing attention from international human rights bodies on the severity of the problem in a European democratic state.[79] In 1991, the CPT visited Spain for a two-week period to gather evidence on the growing number of torture complaints. In 1996, CPT presented a damning report to the Spanish government in 1996 detailing abundant evidence of ill-treatment and torture at the hands of the Guardia Civil and other police forces, as well as the need to drastically reform prison conditions. Spain ratified the Convention Against Torture in 1987 and in the early 1990s, the UN Human Rights Commission issued reports on unresolved cases of abuse and detention conditions. In 1994, the UN CAT agreed for the first time to review a case in which an ETA member sentenced to over 2000 years alleged he was tortured in 1990.[80] In 1997, the UN CAT issued an extensive report with recommendations regarding the serious problem of torture in Spain, not only in the Basque region but also in other parts of Spain. Finally, after additional visits to Spain by the CPT in 1994, the Spanish government agreed, after a long delay, to publicly release the

CPT's report and the government response.[81] The years 1997 and 1998 include two of the highest numbers of police prosecuted for ill-treatment and torture, 15 and 23, respectively (Graph 4.1).

The prosecutions for torture drop off precipitously after 2001. This reflects a relative shift in the political conditions in Spain. Allegations of torture *in all of Spain* increase during this period, with an average of 700 cases per year. Many of these cases involve migrants, suspected Al Qaeda members, Muslim citizens, and individuals arrested after participating in social movement demonstrations. The cases linked to the Basque conflict go down considerably during this period (2004–2012), accounting for only 8% of data gathered by the Spanish organization, Coordination Group for the Prevention and Denunciation of Torture.[82] The history of conflicting narratives on the existence and persistence of torture in Spain is likely to come to an end altogether given recent efforts to push this legacy in to the light. After the Basque government released its 2013 report on human rights violations in that region spanning 50 plus years, a collective of Basque and Spanish organizations, medical experts, psychologists, psychiatrists, and academics, completed a comprehensive study on the use of torture during incommunicado detention. The authors interview

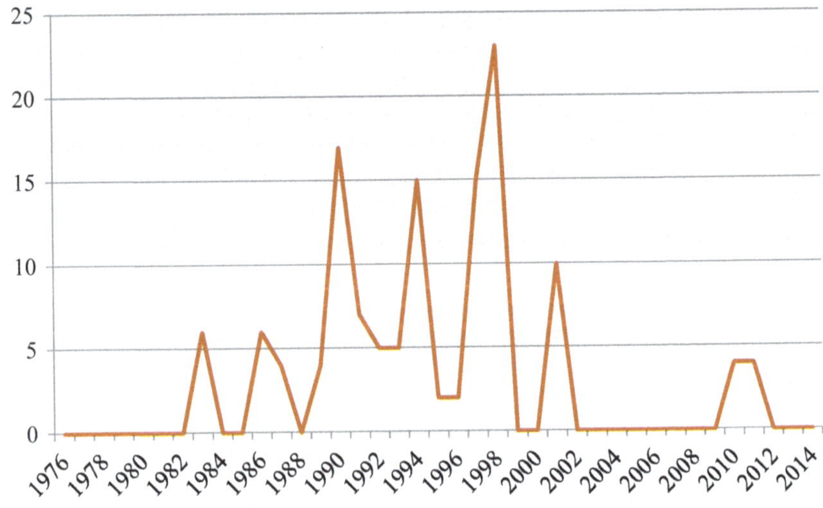

Graph 4.1 The number of police prosecuted for ill-treatment and torture in Spain

victims, gather data, and assess physical and psychological impact on a sample of individuals. The conclusions and recommendations are the most comprehensive to date in the country's history regarding this issue. In the authors' own words: "The assessments show a significant level of credibility, coherence and are conclusive evidence of interrogations in which coercion techniques improper of a democratic State are used."[83]

Prosecutions for the GAL Crimes

In addition to the torture allegations made against police during the early post-transition years, the first "dirty war" was also under way. Several right-wing groups, including AAA (Alianza Apostólica Anticomunista), BVE (Batallón Vasco-Español), ED (Extrema Derecha), and GAE (Grupos Armados Españoles), engaged in violent attacks against suspected ETA members and other civilians in the early years of the democratic transition (1975–1981). Though they operated outside the government, these groups were often sponsored or condoned by the post-Franco administrations.[84] Thirty-eight people died at the hands of these groups, and the majority of deaths were committed by the BVE, a group that formed in 1975 to target ETA.[85] Between 1983 and 1989, a covert state-sponsored death squad that identified themselves as the GAL waged a second "dirty war." Some analyses of this time have argued that it is difficult to prove whether the lack of purges in the police and military forces during the transition led to the second dirty war, given that other European governments also utilized such practices without prior dictatorships.[86] Others have argued that the lack of reform in the security arena likely caused policies, personnel, and practices from the authoritarian regime to carry over to the democratic administration.[87]

In addition to the 38 deaths caused by right-wing death squads in the early years of transition, the GAL was responsible for the deaths of 28 individuals between 1983 and 1989. Guardia Civil and police unrelated to the GAL were responsible for the deaths of four ETA members in 1982 and 1996. Thus, in total, state actors and members of state-sponsored terror groups were responsible for 70 civilian deaths related to the Basque conflict. Twenty-two of these deaths were investigated and prosecuted, a record of 31%. The majority of victims in these cases were ETA members or suspected ETA members, and many of the latter turned out to have no affiliation with ETA.

The first prosecution for extra-judicial killings by the state occurred in 1981. Iturbe and Zabala, members of the BVE, were convicted in 1981 for seven murders and two attempted murders.[88] Though the judicial investigations of the GAL's actions began as early as 1983, the first prosecution related to the GAL did not commence until 1991. The GAL trials were significant in that 22 state actors, including a former Minister of Interior, the Director of State Security, the civil governors of two Basque provinces, the Chief of Police in Bilbao, and an army general, were convicted for crimes related to a state-sponsored death squad. Several mercenaries (civilians) of French, Portuguese, and African descent who worked for the GAL were convicted as well. The investigations and the trials were neither swift nor without controversy, spanning the years 1983–2003. Five main trials were held throughout this time to address the GAL violence and to investigate the state's complicity in the GAL's actions. The private and people's prosecutions played a role in the first investigation against Bilbao Police Superintendent José Amedo Fouce and his deputy Michel Dominguez. Both were convicted in 1991 for six attempted murders, illegal association, falsification of documents, and public use of assumed names, and sentenced to 108 years.[89] They were released through a partial pardon after serving less than two years but were then convicted again in 1998 for the kidnapping of civilian Segundo Marey.

The private and people's prosecutions were also present in the 1998 Segundo Marey kidnapping trial, during which the former Interior Minister, José Barrionuevo, former Director of State Security, Rafael Vera and Julian Sancristobal, former Civil Governor of Vizcaya and former Director of State Security, were convicted and sentenced to ten years.[90] The seven other individuals convicted, including the Police Chief of Bilbao, received shorter sentences. A central part of the corroborative evidence against the suspects, however, was the Interior's failure to effectively investigate the Marey case. Barrionuevo and Vera were barred from holding public office for 12 years and fines totaling 30 million pesetas were levied against them and the other defendants to compensate the victim. However, after serving 105 days in prison, Barrionuevo and Vera received a reduced sentence of three years. Then, the PP agreed to a partial pardon for Barrionuevo and Vera in 1998, because during this time they were issuing ETA prisoner releases under a ceasefire and they faced pressure to produce a bipartisan position on a possible resolution to the Basque question.[91]

The third trial in 1999 addressed the 1984 murder of Basque doctor Santiago Brouard. Lieutenant-Colonel Rafael Masa and Julian Sancristobal were convicted for organizing and funding the murder but were released only a few months later pending new investigations.[92] The difference between the sentences for state actors and civilians is stark in this case. Ismael Miquel Gutierrez, a civilian police informer, was convicted earlier that year and sentenced to 45 years for recruiting a mercenary to murder civilian Robert Caplanne in 1985.

The fourth trial in 2000 involved the kidnapping and murder of two young ETA members, Lasa and Zabala, almost two decades earlier. This was one of the most closely followed cases by the public. After years of little information concerning the victims' disappearance, their bodies were discovered. General Galindo, Julen Elgorriaga (PSOE Civil Governor of Guipuzcoa during the GAL period), Felipe Bayo (a Guardia Civil agent), Enrique Villalobos Dorado (a Guardia Civil sergeant), and Guardia Civil Colonel Angel Vaquero were convicted in April 2000 for kidnapping and murdering of the two victims.[93] Galindo was sentenced to 71 years, Elgorriaga sentenced to over 60 years, and the remaining suspects received slightly shorter sentences. General Galindo was released after five years in 2006 for health reasons.[94]

The most recent trial was held in 2003 and involved a revisiting of the Brouard case. José Amedo, José Luis Morcillo (a civilian businessman), and Rafael Masa were acquitted for the murder of Santiago Brouard.[95] The investigation of this case passed through several magistrates' hands, and its sustained life over the years is largely due to efforts made by the victim's families' lawyer, private prosecutor Txema Montero.[96]

Setting the Stage: Legal Reforms and Human Rights Prosecutions

Legal reforms during the democratic transition empowered citizens to exercise their rights in holding the state to account. Additionally, as a result of careful negotiation by political actors during the democratic transition to establish a judicial sector that broke with the former authoritarian regime,[97] judges became powerful autonomous players in the pursuit of prosecutions against the state. The judiciary in Spain was established as formally independent with a high degree of judicial assertiveness, a move that stemmed from previous years of judicial activism resistant to the

Franco regime.[98] A tone was set in this regard by a particular clandestine group of judges and prosecutors, Justicia Democrática (Democratic Justice) that organized in the final years of the Franco regime to promote judicial independence, freedom for civil society groups, and civil rights protections. This group took various actions to combat authoritarian rule both within and outside of the judicial sector. One such action included prosecuting members of the police for violations of criminal procedure, which likely prompted the Franco regime to amend the Law of Criminal Procedure to create a separate protected jurisdiction for the police.[99] In a fairly prescient move, Justicia Democrática also circulated recommendations for judicial and legal reforms, including a strong criticism of the Franco regime's attempt to institute a policy of extended detention without charge, and they made efforts to align Spain's criminal procedure with other European countries.[100] Both judges and prosecutors within this group were forced to transfer to remote judicial posts as a result of their activism, including a young prosecutor, José María Mena, who, among other charges, was accused of investigating torture.[101] Some of the arguments made by Justicia Democrática over the years were brought into negotiations on the 1978 Constitution.

One of the most significant legal reforms to arise from the democratic transition is the right to private prosecution. Though the public right of citizens to prosecute existed for several centuries in Spain, and the 1882 Law of Criminal Procedure also established similar provisions, some key changes emerged that facilitated later human rights cases. First, Article 125 of the 1978 Constitution establishes that citizens have the right to engage in popular prosecution (and participate in a jury) as a form of engaging in the administration of justice. Second, Article 19(1) of the 1985 Law on Judicial Power (Ley Orgánica 6/1985, del Poder Judicial) established the right of Spanish citizens to issue a popular accusation, which involves an accusation by a person who is not directly related to the crime. Finally, in addition to rights outlined in the 1882 Law of Criminal Procedure that establish that a private prosecutor can be any victim, the 1978 Constitution adds that a victims' lawyer fees must be paid by the accused if he/she is convicted, unless the accusation was found to be dishonest.[102] The rights for victims to be present in the criminal trial process vary greatly by country, but generally the right to private prosecution enables victims to participate in various stages of the criminal trial process under the advice of an attorney, who formally acts as the private prosecutor. The private prosecutor can request investigations and challenge the public prosecutor's decision to dismiss a case. The presence of a private or people's prosecutor can shape the trajectory of a trial and, at times, the outcome of a case, by representing the interests of parties other than the state.[103]

The judicial reforms during the democratic transition in Spain produced ripe conditions for human rights prosecutions in two key ways: Spanish judges willing to pursue investigations of state-sponsored death squad activity collaborated with French judges across the border in the early years of democracy to hold state actors to account; and citizens, including victims, their families, and advocacy organizations, took advantage of the right to private and popular prosecution in cases of torture and extra judicial killing, particularly where the state prosecutor or the government refused to bring charges or were obstinate during trial proceedings. The latter point is particularly significant in that there has been little scholarly work on the use of private prosecution for human rights cases after the democratic transition.[104]

The political context was certainly important for human rights prosecutions. In the mid-late 1990s, an opposition political party pushed for members of the incumbent government to be prosecuted for the extra-judicial killings as a form of political strategy. The opposition party's influence in leaking information to the media was particularly powerful. However, no matter how serious the violence under investigation nor how great the pressure applied by a rival party, prosecutions would not have moved forward unless members of an autonomous judiciary had the will and the means to continue their work, and unless citizens had the ability to push back on key matters of evidence and sentencing when the public prosecutor was slow or unwilling to act. The following presents the chronology of the GAL investigations and the prosecution of ill treatment and torture cases.

The First Stage of the GAL Investigations: 1985–1992

Many Spaniards view the prosecution of 22 state actors for GAL violence as the manifestation of competition between two major political parties, the center-right PP and the center-left PSOE. After the PSOE won a third election in 1993, the PP grew uneasy. By this point, the violence between ETA and the GAL had reached its peak and the GAL investigations were in the news on a regular basis. PP party insiders have since admitted that they believed they had to oust Prime Minister Gonzalez through other means because they were failing to do so through the normal election process. Thus, the PP devised a political strategy, using financial and media resources, to see that Gonzalez was brought to trial on GAL charges, and, ideally, to ensure his imprisonment.[105] Ultimately, the PP succeeded in tarnishing the PSOE administration enough to obtain power in 1996, though they failed in their pursuit to see Gonzalez behind bars. Instead, several top political officials took the fall for Gonzalez, including the Interior Minister and the Director of State Security.

Though the PP played a key role in pushing investigations of the PSOE in 1993, between 1985 and 1992, lengthy investigations of the GAL and one key trial had already taken place.

What, then, initially prompted an investigation of the government's ties to a dirty war against ETA? Specifically, in a climate of brutal and illegal use of violence against civilians by a presumably democratic government, what conditions made human rights prosecutions possible?

Mercenaries of Portuguese, French, and African descent, hired by the Spanish police, were responsible for carrying out most of the GAL killings. Because the GAL operations were largely conducted just over the Spanish border in the southern French provinces, the French judicial system played an important role in the beginning. In the mid-1980s, French judges in Bayonne (Labourd province) prosecuted several mercenaries, and these individuals increasingly began to reveal important information about their superiors in the police force, including who organized the targets and who funded the GAL operations.[106] In particular, the focus narrowed in on Police Superintendent of Bilbao, José Amedo Fouce, one of the first state actors to be prosecuted for GAL crimes. In November 1987, two French judges, Armand Riberolles and Christophe Seys, held a special hearing in Madrid with Spanish magistrate, Carlos Bueren, during which they interrogated Amedo.[107] At this time, two investigative journalists, Ricardo Arques and Melchor Miralles, both working for the newspaper *Diario 16*, handed over a significant number of documents they had gathered from an anonymous tip that provided detailed information on the GAL's strategies and resources. This prompted Judge Bueren to initiate a more in-depth investigation of Amedo. Soon afterward, Judge Castro Meije took on the case against Amedo and his deputy, Michel Dominguez, but Judge Meije quickly resigned. Judge Baltasar Garzón replaced Castro and from this point forward, he became one of the central players in the GAL investigations.[108]

In the early years of democratic governance, the Spanish government had a difficult time gaining cooperation from the French government in combating ETA on the border. The Gonzalez administration initially struggled to obtain help from the French to extradite ETA members from the French Basque region to Spain. The French government eventually issued a statement demonstrating their willingness to be a bit more cooperative on this front, and it has been argued that France's hesitation stemmed from their desire to first see improvements in Spain's human rights record before increasing the extradition of ETA members.[109] Others have argued that the eventual shift to a more collaborative extradition policy resulted from the ideological affinity between the French and Spanish socialist governments in the mid-1980s.[110] Spain's entry to the European Economic Community (EEC) in 1986 also may have granted it legitimacy in the eyes of the French government. Combatting ETA was perhaps not only about eliminating a political threat for the Gonzalez administration; ETA's violence may also have been seen by outsiders as preventing Spain from becoming "European."[111]

Despite some of these early tensions between the two governments, French judges, particularly in the border town of Bayonne, appeared to have few qualms coordinating an investigation with Spanish judges on the GAL crimes and its chain of command.[112] Judicial will on the French side of the border to pursue the GAL investigations appeared to be matched with the same degree of enthusiasm on the Spanish side. One of the central barriers, however, confronting victims of state violence in democracies at war is the reality that the state is ultimately investigating itself. Unsurprisingly, some pressure was applied on the judges investigating the case. Garzón was later recruited as an ally by the prime minister during the investigations, though in the end, this did not stall his efforts; there were also conflicting viewpoints in the judicial sector when investigations first began as to whether national security trumped government accountability for abuses.[113] The opportunity for victims and other members of society to present charges against a person in the public sector, through a private or popular prosecution, was therefore important to some of the initial investigations and prosecutions of the GAL crimes.

During the investigation of Police Superintendent José Amedo Fouce, led by Judge Garzón in the mid-late 1980s, 101 citizens brought a claim against Amedo because they felt that the state prosecutor was not moving forward with the case.[114] This claim formed the popular prosecution side of the case, led by attorney Fernando Salas. In the summer of 1989, the popular prosecution went a step further than Judge Garzón, by calling for the trial of two of Amedo's superiors, Miguel Planchelo (head of police anti-terrorist intelligence in the Basque region) and Martinez Torres (chief of police intelligence under PSOE). Though neither was prosecuted in this trial in the end, Planchelo was later convicted in the Marey kidnapping trial. During the 1991 trial of Amedo and Dominguez (Amedo's deputy), Miguel Castells, the private prosecutor on behalf of GAL victims, worked to ensure that the detailed statements made by GAL mercenaries in the French prisons were incorporated into the proceedings despite the fact that for security reasons the French government refused to transport the prisoners to the court to deliver their testimony in person.[115] Both Amedo and Dominguez were repeatedly identified as mercenary contractors in these statements. The popular and private prosecutors also took a stronger stance against the defendants during the trial proceedings than the state prosecutor, José Aranda. Popular prosecutor Salas "directly accused the government of creating the GAL," and private prosecutor Castells argued that the existence of the GAL was much worse than ETA because it tarnished the legitimacy of the state.[116] In the end, Amedo and Dominguez were convicted for organizing two violent attacks in which several people were injured, and they were acquitted of the Garcia Goena murder, one of the GAL's civilian victims.

A private prosecutor was also important in the Lasa and Zabala investigation, which began in 1995. The private prosecutor, Iñigo Iruin, represented the families of Lasa and Zabala, two ETA members kidnapped and murdered in 1983. The PSOE government had refused to declassify key documents from the CESID (Centro Superior de Información de la Defensa), the Spanish military intelligence service, which many believed would show the GAL chain of command and evidence of death squad orders in southern France. Iruin appealed to a specialized chamber of the Supreme Court, the Third Chamber of the Supreme Court for Judicial Review of the Central Administration (La Sala Tercera de lo Contencioso-administrativo del Tribunal Supremo), for a judicial review of the government's refusal to declassify these documents.[117] On April 10, 1997, the Supreme Court judges ruled that some of the CESID papers would be declassified while others would not (due to their ability to affect the security of the state). Though this ruling left some gaps in evidence for the prosecutors, notably the audiotapes, which would have provided actual names, generally Iruin's efforts provided access to key evidence for both the Marey and Lasa and Zabala trials.[118]

The Second Stage of the GAL Investigations: 1993–2003

After violence reached its peak between the GAL and ETA in the early 1990s, and as it became clear that the PSOE administration was intimately involved in orchestrating covert death squads, public support for PSOE weakened. The PP proceeded to unseat the PSOE in the 1996 presidential elections, albeit through a fairly narrow victory. The PP obtained 38.8% of the votes while PSOE obtained 37.6%. It was after the PSOE gained power for the third time in the 1993 elections that the PP began to devise a strategy for taking down Prime Minister Gonzalez in order to win at the polls in 1996. The PP's tactics involved manipulating the right-wing media for political gain.[119] This second stage of the GAL investigations and the trials involved more of a *complot* (conspiracy) than the first stage; as one journalist covering the trials explained to me, what the PP wasn't doing publicly in Parliament to oppose the PSOE, they did through right-wing media outlets to link the PSOE government to the GAL crimes.[120] *El Mundo*, a right-leaning newspaper, was central in driving much of the information concerning the GAL cases during this time. The initial years of GAL investigations linking sections of the PSOE government, the police and security force members to the GAL demonstrate that the PSOE administration had a hand in the violence, though as one journalist explained to me, the PP "would have loved to have done it themselves."[121]

The PP's manipulations produced a fairly damaging environment for the PSOE but the continued efforts of Judge Garzón and State Prosecutor Jesus Santos on the GAL cases were critical during these years. Garzón intensified his investigation of high-ranking government officials in the early 1990s largely after Amedo and Dominguez, who were convicted in 1991, divulged names and details of government involvement.[122] Garzón also eventually submitted a report to the Supreme Court in 1995 suggesting that charges be brought against Interior Minister Barrionuevo and Prime Minister Gonzalez. Though Garzón faced some obstruction from his judicial superiors at various moments, his efforts along with Santos led to the trials in 1998 and the early 2000s of significant actors in Gonzalez's administration. In the end, 22 state actors were convicted for the GAL crimes.

Prosecutions of State Actors for Torture and Ill-Treatment

The first prosecutions for torture and ill-treatment during detention occurred in 1983. Though hundreds of complaints are made after this point, only four or five prosecutions are held in the following years up through 1990. The slow start in prosecutions early on in Spain's shaky democracy can be explained by a few key factors. Though some judges were willing to pursue the GAL investigations during roughly the same timeframe, a large swath of the judicial sector was obstinate when it came to torture or ill-treatment cases, and much of it stemmed from the belief that ETA detainees fabricated ill-treatment as a form of political strategy.[123] In the years before Organic Law 4/1988 moved all terrorism-related cases to the Audiencia Nacional in Madrid, there were some exceptions to this rule among Basque judges that heard torture complaints directly from detainees.[124] For example, convictions were obtained in 1986 in two cases involving six policemen accused of torture and ill-treatment, and these were issued by judges in the Basque region, specifically the Audiencias Provinciales in Bilbao and in San Sebastián.[125] A 1991 report completed by 40 attorneys in the Navarre region of the Basque Country found that during the 1980s, the state had largely failed to investigate cases of torture. The report concludes that the prosecutions that *had* occurred in the 1980s resulted from legal actions taken by victims themselves and their families. In several cases, an *acusación particular* was used to initiate criminal charges against police officers and members of the Guardia Civil.[126]

Data collection and analysis of trials held during the 1980s and 1990s confirm the findings of the attorneys' report. For example, in 1989, the two most prominent cases concerning torture involved an *acusación particular* and an *acusación popular*, the latter of which refers to criminal charges brought by individuals, groups, or organizations not associated with the victim. The *acusación particular* was brought by detainee Julian Nazar and his attorney. Nazar alleged that he suffered ill-treatment during detention in 1985 under the care of police officer Juan Nuñez Santiago. Despite medical forensic documentation that Nazar had suffered several bruises and abrasions, the trial resulted in an acquittal.[127] The *acusación popular* that concluded the same year resulted in a conviction. The former head of Bilbao police, Francisco Alvarez Sanchez, was found guilty of the charge of corruption for covering up the unlawful removal of a detainee's torture complaint.[128] He was sentenced to six years of disqualification from his profession. Additionally, in 1991, an *acusación particular* was employed in three distinct torture prosecutions against a police commissioner, a sergeant and captain of the Guardia Civil, and lower level members of the Guardia Civil, all of which ended in acquittal.[129]

The significance of citizens' rights to the *acusación particular* and *acusación popular* in torture cases is also evidenced in later torture prosecutions. In a 2001 trial, eight of ten Civil Guards were found guilty of torturing seven Basque citizens in 1980. Each was sentenced to between 4 and 20 months of imprisonment, between 4 and 20 years of disqualification from the profession, and each victim was awarded one million pesetas as well as coverage of trial costs.[130] During the trial, the public prosecutor recommended an acquittal of all the defendants except one, and during the proceedings, the accused refused to respond to the charges brought by the *acusación particular* and the *acusación popular*, only speaking to the judge and his own attorney. The attorneys working on behalf of the individual and popular complaints countered the public prosecutor's recommendation of acquittal by demanding harsher sentences and lengthier terms of disqualification than was typical of torture cases. In the end, though the judge did not meet all of the attorneys' demands, the penalties were some of the harshest issued by a court up until that point. For example, Guardia Civil Lucio de Sosa Robledo, identified by the victims as one of the torturers, was recommended for acquittal by the public prosecutor working on the case. After the individual and popular attorneys presented evidence, the public prosecutor changed his mind and suggested one month's imprisonment and one month's disqualification from employment. The individual and popular attorneys responded with a recommendation of 36 months of imprisonment and 36 years of disqualification; in the end, the judge found the defendant guilty on 5 counts and thus ordered 20 months of imprisonment and 20 years of suspension from employment.[131]

State Violence Cases at the European Court of Human Rights

The first judgment concerning Spain at the European Court was in 1988 (*Barbera, Messegue, and Jabardo v. Spain*)[132] in which the government of Spain was found to have violated Article 6 (right to a fair trial) in its handling of the transfer of detainees from Barcelona to Madrid and the court proceedings that followed. Cases heard at the Court involving Spain gradually increased from this moment. Another judgment was made in 1989 and in the 1990s, 20 judgments were handed down. During the 2000s, the Court issued over 60 judgments. As of January 2016, the total number of judgments involving Spain was 481. In contrast, the total number of judgments at the Court involving the United Kingdom is 1954.[133]

The European Court of Human Rights did not play a role in scrutinizing the anti-terrorism laws or their impact on human rights prosecutions. Cases involving allegations of torture against the state were first heard decades after complaints began in the Basque Country. In a 2004 case, *Martinez Sala v. Spain*, the European Court of Human Rights ruled that a failure to conduct a thorough and effective investigation into the applicant's allegations of torture and ill-treatment resulted in a violation of Article 3 of the European Convention on Human Rights (ECHR).[134] In a similar ruling, on September 28, 2010, the Court ordered the government to pay 23,000 euros to ETA member Mikel San Argimiro Isasa for not having undertaken an "effective investigation" into his complaint of torture, which he suffered in Madrid after his arrest for planting a car bomb in 2002.[135] The Court indicated that the government had violated Article 3 of the ECHR from a procedural point of view due to the lack of investigation, but it had not violated it from a substantive point of view since there were no conclusions that torture had in fact taken place. The Spanish government complied and awarded compensation. On March 8, 2011, the Court issued effectively the same ruling in the case of *Beristain Ukar v. Spain*,[136] and the government was again directed to provide compensation to the victim.[137]

In 2012, the Court ruled again that the procedural aspects of Article 3 had been violated in the *Otamendi Egiguren v. Spain* case. The individual who brought the complaint, Martxelo Otamendi Egiguren, was the publication director of a Basque daily newspaper and was arrested in 2003 on charges of membership and collaboration with ETA. He was cleared of these charges in 2010. Otamendi alleged that he had experienced several forms of ill-treatment during incommunicado detention. The Court ruled in the applicant's favor arguing that Spanish authorities had disregarded his complaint and it emphasized that forensic medical examinations of persons held incommunicado should be significantly improved.[138] Most recently, in 2014, the Court ruled on two cases whose complaints included alleged ill-treatment while held in incommunicado detention. The *Etxebarria Caballero v. Spain* and *Ataun Rojo v. Spain* cases were filed at the Court in 2012 and 2013, respectively. In 2014, the Court concluded unanimously that Article 3 of the ECHR had been violated on account of the lack of an effective investigation into the applicants' complaints of ill-treatment. The Court noted in its conclusions that given the lack of sufficient evidence, which resulted from the absence of an in-depth investigation of the complaints, it could not determine that ill-treatment had occurred.[139] The rulings by the Court in these cases resemble those brought by Northern Ireland citizens against the British government concerning the lack of effective investigation into unlawful killings by the state.

A recent Court ruling in 2009 reflected a growing concern in the Basque community that the Spanish government was increasingly restricting the civil and political rights of those fighting for a separate Basque state. In 2003, the Basque political parties, Herri Batasuna and Batasuna were banned via the 2002 Political Parties Law (Ley Orgánica 6/02 June 27th). Local bans on certain Basque civil society groups preceded this law. The government justified its decision arguing that the parties had links to ETA. One of the attorneys who worked on the European Court case commented to me that the same could have been said of, Herri Batasuna in the 1980s but the party was not banned then. He believed the ban was the government's response to a perceived political threat, a powerful and growing leftist movement.[140] The Basque political parties' attorneys took the case to the European Court of Human Rights and claimed violations of Article 10 (freedom of expression) and Article 11 (freedom of association). In the end, the Court ruled in favor of the ban, citing Articles 10 and 11 had not been violated given that the mission of the parties, in their affiliation with ETA, constituted a threat to Spanish democracy.[141]

One of the only European Court of Human Rights cases that emerged from the period of GAL violence involved an application concerning Article 10, freedom of expression. The nature of this complaint reflects the significance of a citizen's right to challenge state human rights violations in a court of law in the face of deafening silence. In 1985, Miguel Castells, an MP and also the private prosecutor that worked on behalf of GAL victims, filed an application with the Court after he was convicted for denouncing in a newspaper article that the right-wing death squads were not being investigated. Castells had been convicted at the Spanish Supreme Court and he lost his appeal at the Constitutional Court. The European Court ruled in favor of Castells in 1992 determining that there had been a violation of Article 10 (freedom of expression) and the Court directed the Spanish government to pay Castells three million pesetas (approximately 23,000 US dollars) for costs and expenses.[142]

"We Are Still Looking for Bones"[143]

Many of the people I spoke with in the Basque Country urgently discussed the civil society efforts underway to exhume the remains of those disappeared or killed during the Franco regime. This citizen-led reckoning had cast a long shadow over Spanish democracy and not only in the Basque region. Significantly, for many Basques, these efforts to literally unearth the authoritarian past were intimately connected to the years of state violence that followed the democratic transition. The high levels of torture practiced on Basque citizens and the GAL violence against suspected ETA members had felt, to many, like a continuation of the Franco regime. The blatant obstructions to justice, particularly in cases of torture, was a signal to victims, their families, and the wider Basque community that democracy had not yet been won.

This chapter reveals an important tension at the heart of the Spanish case: while legal reforms during the 1976 transition created pathways for human rights prosecutions, the creation of a new emergency institution in the form of anti-terrorism laws restricted prosecutions for torture. Though anti-terrorism laws were initially subject to parliamentary and judicial review as temporary crisis laws, once they were transferred permanently to the Penal Code in the late 1980s, oversight was greatly minimized. Additionally, the inclusion of incommunicado detention in anti-terrorism provisions provided legitimacy and cover to state actors engaging in torture during the detention period. A close examination of the emergency institution in Spain reveals the importance of analyzing the origin and purpose of these laws and how they underwent gradual change. While two forms of serious human rights violations were conducted by the state in the early years of democracy, extra-judicial killings and torture, the government used anti-terrorism laws to facilitate and avoid judicial scrutiny in the latter. The evolution of anti-terrorism laws illustrates how those who benefit from the logic of impunity will fight to maintain the status quo in the face of external oversight mechanisms. Transferring arrest and detention powers, which were strictly created for a crisis period, into a permanent feature of the Penal Code enabled the government to remove itself from the spotlight and continue its war against detainees. Anti-terrorism laws in Spain underwent gradual change, not from an exogenous shock but from endogenous sources: contestation over the rules on incommunicado detention. Change resulted not only when opponents challenged anti-terrorism laws. Indeed, the most significant alterations emanated from government's strategies to normalize incommunicado detention and avoid judicial scrutiny.

Notes

1. The Uppsala Conflict Database (UCDP) evaluates the existence of internal war within countries, measured by at least 25 battle deaths per year. Though ETA committed violence against the Franco regime in its final years of existence, Spain did not reach this threshold until a few years later.
2. Aretxaga, 60.
3. Woodworth, Paddy. *Dirty War, Clean Hands: ETA, the GAL and Spanish Democracy*. Cork: Cork University Press (2001); Idoiaga, Gorka Espiau. 2006. "Special Report: The Basque Conflict, New Ideas and Prospects for Peace," United States Institute of Peace.
4. Aguilar, Paloma. Justice, Politics and Memory in the Spanish Transition, in de Brito, Gonzalez-Enriquez and Aguilar, eds., *The Politics of Memory*. Oxford: Oxford University Press (2001); Davis, Madeline. Is Spain Recovering Its Memory? Breaking the *Pacto del Olvido, Human Rights Quarterly* 27(3) (2005): 858–880.
5. Aiartza, Urko and Julen Zabalo. 2010. "The Basque Country: The Long Walk to a Democratic Scenario," Berghof Series, Resistance/Liberation Movements and Transition to Politics; Woodworth (2001).
6. Idoiaga (2006).
7. Aguilar (2001).
8. Aguilar (2001).
9. Aiartza and Zabala (2010).
10. Aguilar, 117.
11. COVITE (Colectivo de Victimas del Terrorismo en el Pais Vasco). 2010. Listado: Victimas Mortales del Terrorismo. www.covite.org
12. Idoiaga (2006).
13. Gurruchaga, Inigo. "Viewpoint: ETA Move Raises Hopes and Stakes," *BBC News*, October 20, 2011. www.bbc.co.uk (Retrieved February 2, 2012).
14. Woodworth (2001); Merino-Blanco, Elena. *Spanish Law and Legal System* (2nd edition) London: Sweet and Maxwell (2006).
15. Pérez Gil, Julio. "Private Interests Seeking Punishment: Prosecution Brought by Private Individuals and Groups in Spain," *Law and Policy* 25(2) (2003): 151–172; Merino-Blanco (2006).
16. Woodworth (2001).

17. Merino-Blanco (2006).
18. Aguilar (2001); Scheinin, Martin. Report of the Special Rapporteur on the Promotion and Protection of Human Rights and Fundamental Freedoms While Countering Terrorism, Mission to Spain, UN Human Rights Council, A/HRC/10/3/Add.2, December 16, 2008.
19. Woodworth (2001).
20. Merino-Blanco (2006).
21. Merino-Blanco (2006).
22. Hilbink, Lisa. "The Constituted Nature of Constituents' Interests: Historical and Ideational Factors in Judicial Empowerment," *Political Research Quarterly* 62(4) (2009): 781–797.
23. Vercher, Antonio. *Terrorism in Europe: An International Comparative Legal Analysis.* Oxford: Clarendon Press (1992).
24. Aguilar (2001); Encarnación, Omar G. Democracy and Dirty Wars in Spain, *Human Rights Quarterly* 29 (2007): 950–972.
25. Clark, Robert P. *Negotiating with ETA: Obstacles to Peace in the Basque Country, 1975–1988.* Reno: University of Nevada Press (1990), 38.
26. Aguilar, 110.
27. Clark (1990, 38).
28. Constitución Española (1978).
29. Constitución Española (1978).
30. Constitución Española (1978).
31. Merino-Blanco (2006).
32. Clark (1990, 40).
33. Amnesty International Annual Report (1979).
34. Amnesty International Annual Reports (1978–1981), Clark (1990).
35. International law does not out-right prohibit the use of incommunicado detention but the UN Human Rights Committee issued General Comment No. 20 in 1992 that recommends provisions be taken against this practice since it is seen as likely to increase the incidence of torture and ill-treatment (HRW 2005, 24).
36. Clark (1990, 42), Amnesty International Annual Report (1981).
37. Clark (1990).
38. Clark (1990).
39. Amnesty International. 1985. "Spain, The Question of Torture: Documents Exchanged by Amnesty International and the Government of Spain."
40. Human Rights Watch. 2005. Report on Spain's Counter-terrorist Laws, 38.
41. Clark (1990, 19).
42. Clark (1990, 57); Interview 13, Oñati, Spain, 2010; Interview 14, Oñati, Spain, 2010.
43. Clark (1990, 64).

44. Clark (1990, 65).
45. Clark (1990).
46. Merino-Blanco (2006).
47. Human Rights Watch (2005).
48. Código Penal Española (1995).
49. Torturaren Aurkako Taldea (TAT). Torture in Basque Country. 2001 Report, 253–255.
50. Código Penal Española (1995).
51. Int. 13, 2010.
52. Scheinin (2008).
53. Scheinin (2008).
54. Torturaren Aurkako Taldea (2001, 255–256).
55. Int. 13, 2010.
56. Torturaren Aurkako Taldea (TAT). La Tortura en Euskadi. 1991 Report.
57. Código Penal Española (1995).
58. Amnesty International. 1999. Spain: A Briefing on Human Rights Concerns in Relation to the Basque Peace Process.
59. Human Rights Watch (2005).
60. Human Rights Watch (2005, 25).
61. Human Rights Watch (2005, 28).
62. Behatokia (Basque Observatory of Human Rights). Comments to the UN Human Rights Committee Report (2007).
63. Scheinin (2008).
64. Interview 19A, Minneapolis, Minnesota, 2010.
65. Scheinin (2008).
66. Scheinin (2008).
67. Scheinin (2008, 17).
68. The English translation of this quote is "the fire did not reach him." A journalist I interviewed who covered the GAL trials is referring to the fact that though the GAL investigations hotly pursued Prime Minister Felipe Gonzalez, he managed to avoid prosecution (the fire). Those directly under Gonzalez, however, were not so lucky, and they likely took the fall for the prime minister (Interview 19, Santoña, Cantabria, Spain 2010).
69. Interview 13, Oñati, Spain 2010.
70. Int. 13, 2010.
71. Int. 13, 2010; Int. 14, 2010.
72. This data does not include torture complaints from the rest of Spain during this period.
73. Torturaren Aurkako Taldea (TAT). Dossier Torturas. 1989 Report; Torturaren Aurkako Taldea (TAT). La Tortura en Euskadi. 1991 Report; Torturaren Aurkako Taldea (TAT). 1992 Annual Report; Torturaren Aurkako Taldea (TAT). Torture in Basque Country. 2001 Report.

74. Amnesty International Annual Report, 1984; Annual Human Rights Reports Submitted to Congress by the U.S. Department of State: Spain. 1984.
75. ARGITUZ, Spanish Association of Neuropsychiatry, Ekimen Elkartea, GAC, Community Action Group, Jaiki-Hadi, Osasun Mentalaren Elkartea (OME), Asociación por el Derecho a la Salud (OSALDE), Department of Social Psychology (Basque Country University). 2013. Incommunicado Detention and Torture: Assessments Using the Istanbul Protocol.
76. Carmena, Manuela, Jon Mirena Landa, Ramón Múgica, and Juan M Uriarte. 2013. Base Report on Human Rights Violations in the Basque Country Case (1960–2013). Office of the Secretariat General for Peace and Social Harmony, the Basque Government.
77. Carmena et al. (2013).
78. Annual Human Rights Reports Submitted to Congress by the U.S. Department of State: Spain. 1999.
79. This finding is in line with Powell and Staton's (2009) argument that states that ratify the Convention Against Torture will only feel bound to this commitment if domestic legal enforcement is strong.
80. Annual Human Rights Reports Submitted to Congress by the U.S. Department of State: Spain (1994).
81. Annual Human Rights Reports Submitted to Congress by the U.S. Department of State: Spain (1997).
82. ARGITUZ et al., 29.
83. ARGITUZ et al., 233.
84. Woodworth (2001, 46).
85. COVITE (2010).
86. Aguilar (2001).
87. Encarnación (2007).
88. Woodworth (2001).
89. Annual Human Rights Reports Submitted to Congress by the U.S. Department of State: Spain (1991), Woodworth (2001).
90. Woodworth (2001), Annual Human Rights Reports Submitted to Congress by the U.S. Department of State: Spain (1998).
91. Woodworth (2001).
92. Woodworth (2001).
93. Woodworth (2001).
94. Behatokia (2007).
95. Woodworth, Paddy. "GAL verdict concludes investigation into Spanish dirty war crimes: A ruling this week may consign government-backed death squads to history," *Irish Times*, June 27, 2003.
96. Woodworth (2001).

97. Hilbink (2009, 787).
98. Hilbink, Lisa. 2012. "The Origins of Positive Judicial Independence," *World Politics* 64(4): 587–621.
99. Hilbink, Lisa. 2007. "Politicizing Law to Liberalize Politics: Anti-Francoist Judges in Spain's Democratic Transition," in Terence Halliday, Lucien Karpik and Malcolm Feeley, eds., *Fighting for Political Freedom: Comparative Studies of the Legal Complex and Political Change*. Oxford: Hart Publishing, 413–414.
100. Hilbink (2007, 414 and 421).
101. Hilbink (2007, 417).
102. Pérez Gil, 156.
103. Pérez Gil (2003); Michel, Verónica and Kathryn Sikkink. 2013. "Human Rights Prosecutions and the Participation Rights of Victims in Latin America," *Law and Society Review* 47(4): 873–907.
104. Pérez Gil (2003) provides a very useful explanation of the history of private prosecution in Spain and its use at the end of the twentieth century, but the analysis does not cover the use of private prosecution during the GAL trials or in torture prosecutions.
105. Maravall, José. 2003. "The Rule of Law as a Political Weapon," in Adam Przeworksi and José Maravall, eds., *Democracy and the Rule of Law*. Cambridge: Cambridge University Press; Interview 13, Oñati, Spain 2010; Interview 14, Oñati, Spain 2010; Interview 17, Bilbao, Spain 2010; Interview 19, Santoña, Cantabria, Spain 2010.
106. Woodworth (2001).
107. Interview 19, Santoña, Cantabria, Spain 2010.
108. Woodworth (2001).
109. Clark (1990, 59–60).
110. Vercher (1992, 398).
111. Aretxaga (2000).
112. Clark (1990); Int. 19A, 2011.
113. Woodworth (2001).
114. Int. 19A, 2011; Woodworth (2001).
115. Woodworth (2001).
116. Woodworth (2001, 240).
117. Woodworth (2001, 320).
118. Woodworth (2001, 329).
119. Maravall (2003); Int. 13, 2010; Int. 14, 2010; Int. 17, 2010; Int. 18, 2010, Int. 19, 2010.
120. Int. 19, 2010.
121. Int. 17, 2010.
122. Woodworth (2001, 256).
123. Scheinin (2008).

124. Torturaren Aurkako Taldea (1989, 1991).
125. Torturaren Aurkako Taldea (1991).
126. Torturaren Aurkako Taldea (1991, 15).
127. Torturaren Aurkako Taldea (1989, 80).
128. Torturaren Aurkako Taldea (1989, 81).
129. Torturaren Aurkako Taldea (1991).
130. Torturaren Aurkako Taldea (2001, 227).
131. Torturaren Aurkako Taldea (2001, 228).
132. *Barbera, Messegue, and Jabardo v. Spain* (1988). European Court of Human Rights. HUDOC Database. www.echr.coe.int
133. European Court of Human Rights. HUDOC Database. www.echr.coe.int
134. *Martinez Sala v. Spain* (2004). European Court of Human Rights. HUDOC Database. www.echr.coe.int; Scheinen 2008.
135. *San Argimiro Isasa v. Spain* (2010). European Court of Human Rights. HUDOC Database. www.echr.coe.int
136. *Beristain Ukar v. Spain* (2010). European Court of Human Rights. HUDOC Database. www.echr.coe.int
137. The precedent for ruling on effective investigation concerning torture or ill-treatment is the 1998 Court judgment, *Assenov v. Bulgaria.*
138. *Otamendi Egiguren v. Spain* (2012). European Court of Human Rights. HUDOC Database. www.echr.coe.int
139. *Etxebarria Caballero v. Spain* (2014) European Court of Human Rights. HUDOC Database. www.echr.coe.int; *Ataun Rojo v. Spain* (2014). European Court of Human Rights. HUDOC Database. www.echr.coe.int
140. Interview 18, Bilbao, Spain 2010.
141. *Herri Batasuna and Batasuna v. Spain* (2009). European Court of Human Rights. HUDOC Database. www.echr.coe.int
142. *Castells v. Spain* (1992). European Court of Human Rights. HUDOC Database. www.echr.coe.int
143. Int. 13, 2010.

Bibliography

Aguilar, Paloma. 2001. Justice, Politics and Memory in the Spanish Transition. In *The Politics of Memory*, ed. de Brito and Gonzalez-Enriquez and Aguilar. Oxford: Oxford University Press.

Aiartza, Urko, and Julen Zabalo. 2010. *The Basque Country: The Long Walk to a Democratic Scenario.* Berghof Transitions Series, Resistance/Liberation Movements and Transition to Politics. Berghof Conflict Research. Berlin.

Amnesty International. 1985. *Spain, The Question of Torture: Documents Exchanged by Amnesty International and the Government of Spain*. London: Amnesty International Publications.

———. 1999. Spain: A Briefing on Human Rights Concerns in Relation to the Basque Peace Process.

Amnesty International Annual Report. 1978.

Amnesty International Annual Report. 1979.

Amnesty International Annual Report. 1980.

Amnesty International Annual Report. 1981.

Amnesty International Annual Report. 1984.

Annual Human Rights Reports Submitted to Congress by the U.S. Department of State: Spain. 1984.

Annual Human Rights Reports Submitted to Congress by the U.S. Department of State: Spain. 1991.

Annual Human Rights Reports Submitted to Congress by the U.S. Department of State: Spain. 1994.

Annual Human Rights Reports Submitted to Congress by the U.S. Department of State: Spain. 1997.

Annual Human Rights Reports Submitted to Congress by the U.S. Department of State: Spain. 1998.

Annual Human Rights Reports Submitted to Congress by the U.S. Department of State: Spain. 1999.

Aretxaga, Begoña. 2000. A Fictional Reality: Paramilitary Death Squads and the Construction of State Terror in Spain. In *Death Squad: The Anthropology of State Terror*, ed. Jeffrey Sluka. Philadelphia: University of Pennsylvania Press.

ARGITUZ, Spanish Association of Neuropsychiatry, Ekimen Elkartea, GAC, Community Action Group, Jaiki-Hadi, Osasun Mentalaren Elkartea (OME), Asociación por el Derecho a la Salud (OSALDE), Department of Social Psychology (Basque Country University). 2013. Incommunicado Detention and Torture: Assessments Using the Istanbul Protocol.

Ataun Rojo v. Spain. 2014. European Court of Human Rights. HUDOC Database. www.echr.coe.int

Barbera, Messegue, and Jabardo v. Spain. 1988. European Court of Human Rights. HUDOC Database. www.echr.coe.int

Behatokia (Basque Observatory of Human Rights). 2007. Comments to the UN Human Rights Committee Report.

Beristain Ukar v. Spain. 2010. European Court of Human Rights. HUDOC Database. www.echr.coe.int.

Carmena, Manuela, Jon Mirena Landa, Ramón Múgica, and Juan M Uriarte. 2013. Base Report on Human Rights Violations in the Basque Country Case (1960–2013). Office of the Secretariat General for Peace and Social Harmony, the Basque Government.

Castells v. Spain. 1992. European Court of Human Rights. HUDOC Database. www.echr.coe.int

Clark, Robert P. 1990. *Negotiating with ETA: Obstacles to Peace in the Basque Country, 1975–1988*. Reno: University of Nevada Press.

Código Penal Española. 1995.

Constitución Española. (1978). Available: https://www.boe.es/legislacion/documentos/ConstitucionCASTELLANO.pdf

COVITE (Colectivo de Víctimas del Terrorismo en el Pais Vasco). 2010. Listado: Victimas Mortales del Terrorismo. www.covite.org

Davis, Madeline. 2005. Is Spain Recovering Its Memory? Breaking the *Pacto del Olvido*. *Human Rights Quarterly* 27 (3): 858–880.

Encarnación, Omar G. 2007. Democracy and Dirty Wars in Spain. *Human Rights Quarterly* 29: 950–972.

Etxebarria Caballero v. Spain. 2014. European Court of Human Rights. HUDOC Database. www.echr.coe.int

Gurruchaga, Inigo. Viewpoint: ETA Move Raises Hopes and Stakes. *BBC News*, October 20, 2011. Retrieved February 2, 2012, www.bbc.co.uk

Herri Batasuna and Batasuna v. Spain. 2009. European Court of Human Rights. HUDOC Database. www.echr.coe.int

Hilbink, Lisa. 2007. Politicizing Law to Liberalize Politics: Anti-Francoist Judges in Spain's Democratic Transition. In *Fighting for Political Freedom: Comparative Studies of the Legal Complex and Political Change*, ed. Terence Halliday, Lucien Karpik, and Malcolm Feeley, 413–414. Oxford: Hart Publishing.

———. 2009. The Constituted Nature of Constituents' Interests: Historical and Ideational Factors in Judicial Empowerment. *Political Research Quarterly* 62 (4): 781–797.

———. 2012. The Origins of Positive Judicial Independence. *World Politics* 64 (4): 587–621.

Human Rights Watch. 2005. Report on Spain's Counter-terrorist Laws.

Idoiaga, Gorka Espiau. 2006. *Special Report: The Basque Conflict, New Ideas and Prospects for Peace*. Washington, DC: United States Institute of Peace.

Interview 13, Oñati, Spain, 2010.

Interview 14, Oñati, Spain, 2010.

Interview 17, Bilbao, Spain 2010.

Interview 18, Bilbao, Spain 2010.

Interview 19, Santoña, Cantabria, Spain 2010.

Interview 19A, Minneapolis, Minnesota, 2010.

Maravall, José. 2003. The Rule of Law as a Political Weapon. In *Democracy and the Rule of Law*, ed. Adam Przeworksi and José Maravall. Cambridge: Cambridge University Press.

Martinez Sala v. Spain. 2004. European Court of Human Rights. HUDOC Database. www.echr.coe.int

Merino-Blanco, Elena. 2006. *Spanish Law and Legal System*. 2nd ed. London: Sweet and Maxwell.

Michel, Verónica, and Kathryn Sikkink. 2013. Human Rights Prosecutions and the Participation Rights of Victims in Latin America. *Law and Society Review* 47 (4): 873–907.

Otamendi Egiguren v. Spain. 2012. European Court of Human Rights. HUDOC Database. www.echr.coe.int

Pérez Gil, Julio. 2003. Private Interests Seeking Punishment: Prosecution Brought by Private Individuals and Groups in Spain. *Law and Policy* 25 (2): 151–172.

Powell, Emilia Justyna, and Jeffrey K. Staton. 2009. Domestic Judicial Institutions and Human Rights Treaty Violation. *International Studies Quarterly* 53 (1): 149–174.

San Argimiro Isasa v. Spain (2010). European Court of Human Rights. HUDOC Database. www.echr.coe.int

Scheinin, Martin. Report of the Special Rapporteur on the Promotion and Protection of Human Rights and Fundamental Freedoms While Countering Terrorism, Mission to Spain, UN Human Rights Council, A/HRC/10/3/Add.2, December 16, 2008.

Torturaren Aurkako Taldea (TAT). Dossier Torturas. 1989 Report.

———. La Tortura en Euskadi. 1991 Report.

———. 1992 Annual Report.

———. Torture in Basque Country. 2001 Report.

Vercher, Antonio. 1992. *Terrorism in Europe: An International Comparative Legal Analysis*. Oxford. Clarendon Press.

Woodworth, Paddy. 2001. *Dirty War, Clean Hands: ETA, the GAL and Spanish Democracy*. Cork: Cork University Press.

———. GAL Verdict Concludes Investigation into Spanish Dirty War Crimes: A Ruling This Week May Consign Government-Backed Death Squads to History. *Irish Times*, June 27, 2003.

CHAPTER 5

The Constitutional Court, Military Jurisdiction, and Human Rights Prosecutions in Colombia

A Colombian attorney, Eduardo Carreña Wilches, who has worked on human rights cases for a few decades, told me that in his experience there were no more than 50 attorneys, out of roughly 200,000 in the entire country, who were regularly working on human rights cases.[1] The threats and violence against human rights attorneys was so great that it effectively succeeded in bringing down the number of prosecutions. The fact that a number of prosecutions transpired at all in this case demands a nuanced explanation. The other cases in this book have illustrated that a logic of impunity is, to a greater or lesser extent, embedded in emergency laws. Colombia is unique in that the emergency institution consists not only of the standard state of emergency declarations and the accompanying laws that regulate a crisis. The emergency institution also includes executive decrees that promulgate particular legal reforms. One of the most significant legal reforms to emanate from emergency decrees in this case includes revisions to the military criminal codes. At key moments before and after the civil war commenced in 1965, presidents issued emergency decrees that amended existing military criminal codes, and these alterations had a deep impact on human rights prosecution outcomes in Colombia. Specifically, the amendments gave military courts jurisdiction over virtually all criminal offenses committed by military and police personnel against civilians. As a result of this key feature of the emergency institution in Colombia, prosecutions for human rights

M. Lynch, *Human Rights Prosecutions in Democracies at War*,
Human Rights Interventions,
https://doi.org/10.1007/978-3-319-96908-4_5

violations were almost non-existent in the first 20 years of the war, and in the handful of cases concerning torture and extra-judicial killing of civilians that were brought before military courts in the early 1980s, acquittals were the norm. This chapter traces a shift from prior years of government impunity to a period in the mid-late 1990s when human rights prosecutions emerged and steadily increased over time. As a result of two key factors, judicial review of emergency legislation and judicial independence among judges on the Constitutional Court, the military criminal code was gradually displaced during the 1990s. A series of court rulings slowly eroded the logic of impunity, and in response the government created a new military criminal code reflective of human rights standards. As a result of gradual displacement, human rights prosecutions were steadily transferred from military courts to ordinary courts and the number of trials as well as convictions increased.

Colombia is currently in the process of implementing a comprehensive peace accord. A central pillar of the accord concerns the terms of justice for the most serious violations. I interviewed several members of the human rights community one year before the peace accord became finalized. One member of a research and advocacy organization commented to me, for Colombia to submit to the pressures from the Inter-American Commission on Human Rights to abide by international human rights law through investigation, prosecution, and punishment for every human rights abuse, would mean that the country would be in violation of these laws forever. In his view, the prosecution of everyone is simply not possible.[2] On the same subject, a human rights attorney explained to me that she sees no other way for Colombian society to move forward. She could not forget the victims she represented and it was difficult for her to reflect on their stories as the state and the Fuerzas Armadas Revolucionarias de Colombia (FARC) negotiated justice compromises during the peace talks. She did not see how Colombians would be able to coexist without a major reckoning.[3] This chapter's findings on the conditions shaping human rights prosecutions during the Colombian civil war provides key insights on how justice is negotiated in conflict transitions and how legal and political structures that remain through the transition will continue to shape justice outcomes.

The chapter is organized as follows: the first section provides historical background to the conflict; the second section discusses the historical evolution of the emergency institution; the third section details the conditions for gradual displacement; the fourth section discusses human rights prosecutions and emblematic cases; and the fifth section provides concluding comments on the status of transitional justice laws and the peace process in Colombia.

Historical Background to the Conflict in Colombia

Colombia has a long history of both violent conflict and an active legal culture. In fact, the intertwining of these two aspects of Colombian society produced unique trends in accountability that reverberates today. Though other conflicts transpired before the commencement of La Violencia (1946–1965), these years mark a key moment in the country's experience of violence in that they instigated the eventual formation of guerrilla groups whose Marxist roots and goals of social revolution would shape the war that continues today. La Violencia began after Jorge Eliécer Gaitán, a populist Liberal leader, was assassinated in Bogotá. The murder led to riots and increased polarization between Liberals and Conservatives, and the violence expanded to rural communities.[4] La Violencia was largely waged among civilians, often between classes and contending political affiliations, and the nature and locus of the violence varied significantly over the years.[5] Though Liberals and Conservatives often appeared to have similar positions on a number of political issues, and historically they both have been characterized by elitism and patron-client networks, there are a few key differences. The Conservatives tend to claim stronger ties to the Catholic Church and political officials often proclaim religiosity, while Liberals are largely secular and thus more leftist on social policies including family planning and marriage. Additionally, while the Conservatives have been somewhat resistant to agrarian reforms, the Liberals have taken the lead in revolutionizing economic policy, most notably in the 1960s under President Carlos Lleras Restrepo.[6]

The National Front, created in 1957, sought an end to La Violencia by establishing a government structure in which power would be shared between the two major political parties, Liberal and Conservative. Though this agreement put an end to the period of La Violencia, the elite-dominated democracy that resulted produced an entrenched system of political exclusion. The years of alternating power between two major parties created a virtual ban on third-party formation or a strong opposition faction and thus, during the 1960s, guerilla groups, such as the FARC, strengthened in their call for widespread social and political reforms (Table 5.1). This

Table 5.1 Political parties in power during the Colombian conflict

Years	*Political party*	*President*
1958–1962	Liberal	Alberto Lleras Camargo
1962–1966	Conservative	Guillermo León Valencia Muñoz
1966–1970	Liberal	Carlos Lleras Restrepo
1970–1974	Conservative	Misael Pastrana Borrero
1974–1978	Liberal	Alfonso López Michelsen
1978–1982	Liberal	Julio César Turbay Ayala
1982–1986	Conservative	Belisario Betancur Cuartas
1986–1990	Liberal	Virgilio Barco Vargas
1990–1994	Liberal	César Gaviria Trujillo
1994–1998	Liberal	Ernesto Samper Pizano
1998–2002	Conservative	Andrés Pastrana Arango
2002–2010	Colombia first	Álvaro Uribe Vélez
2010–	National unity	Juan Manuel Santos Calderón

closed political system also fomented the birth of additional revolutionary groups, for example, Movimiento 19 de Abril (M-19), Ejército de Liberación Nacional (ELN), and Ejército Popular de Liberación (EPL).[7] The executive gained increasing swaths of power during these years through state of siege decrees and as a result of laws granting the president the authority to make political appointments (as opposed to holding local elections). Some electoral reforms emerged in the 1980s, and as a result, a third party, the Unión Patriótica (UP), attempted to make inroads in the political sphere. Close to 3000 UP members were assassinated in the following years and high levels of violence became the central strategy for guerilla groups seeking political reforms.[8]

The civil war changed in character during the 1980s for a few key reasons. First, drug trafficking surged and the FARC began relying solely on the drug economy for its revenues. Second, the conflict took on a new form when the military began organizing paramilitary factions to confront the FARC. Paramilitarism grew from a counter-insurgent operation force to a fully formed political actor by the late 1990s, the Autodefensas Unidas de Colombia (AUC).[9] The high number of civilian killings since the mid-1990s has been at the behest of paramilitary factions (75%), while less than 5% of the violence has been at the hands of the state's armed forces, and 20% has been committed by the guerillas.[10] One of the most destabilizing factors for human rights prosecutions in the last 20 years has been the growing number of human rights activists, attorneys, and judges murdered each year. Judges and lawyers working on state violence cases were increasingly targeted in the 1980s and 1990s. A 1992 study by the Commission of Colombian Jurists found that between 1970 and 1991, an average of 26 judges and lawyers were assassinated and harassed every year, the majority of which were those working on criminal cases related to paramilitary violence.[11] Since the mid-1990s, on average, a human rights defender has been murdered each month.[12]

Despite the increasing levels of violence over time, several administrations initiated peace negotiations with guerilla groups between 1982 and 2002. Additionally, the Uribe administration began, for the first time, talks with the AUC in an effort to put in place the large-scale demobilization of paramilitary factions.[13] These initial efforts led to a string of laws during the 2000s that some have characterized as attempts at transitional justice.

The assassinations and harassment of human rights defenders reflects the fact that what had become a strengthening legal human rights community by the 1980s was regarded as a serious threat to the actors perpetrating the violence. The robust legal culture in Colombia is often argued to reach back to Francisco de Paula Santander, a general during the Wars of Independence from Spain. After the Spaniards were defeated, Santander became a political leader that was largely responsible for designing the structure of the new Republic's political administration. As a result, he became known as *el Hombre de las Leyes* (the man of the laws).[14] Since that time, Colombia has often been associated with Santander due to early and strong legal institutions. These institutions had significant meaning in the decades that followed. The elite nature of politics that emerged in the early twentieth century, and then cemented through the National Front pacts, has prompted citizens to seek redress and solutions from the judicial branch. In essence, mobilization through political channels is seen as either too dangerous or a dead end, and thus, for some sectors of society, the courts have come to represent the only means for empowerment.[15]

The creation of the Fiscalía through the 1991 Constitution resulted in the transformation of the Colombian legal system from an inquisitorial system to a prosecutorial system. In the former, judges are tasked with the investigation of the case, and there is little coordination with law enforcement agencies, whereas, in the latter, the prosecution and the defense present the evidence and a judge plays a more neutral role in trial proceedings.[16] Importantly, the Fiscalía was tasked with special duties to investigate and prosecute government officials on criminal matters; law enforcement could no longer pursue an arrest, conduct a search, or violate a person's privacy without a prosecutorial order.[17]

Though human rights attorneys working within and outside the Fiscalía pursued accountability for state violations in the ordinary courts, much of the legal mobilization that led to institutional change within the emergency apparatus in Colombia involved petitions at the Constitutional Court and challenges to decisions on jurisdiction by the Consejo Superior de la Judicatura (CSJ). The Colombian court system includes four supreme judicial bodies. The Corte Suprema de Justicia (Supreme Court) functions as a court of cassation to quash lower court decisions and its judges are selected by their peers from nominees of the Superior Judicial Council for eight-year terms. The Consejo de Estado (Council of State) is the highest court of administrative law and it settles jurisdictional conflicts among departments and municipalities and between them and the government. The judges are selected through the same process as the Supreme Court. The Corte Constitutional (Constitutional Court) was first created by the 1991 Constitution and it is tasked with reviewing the constitutionality of laws as well as some executive decrees; it is responsible for reviewing processes related to the *tutela*, which allows citizens to make a complaint concerning a fundamental rights violation without an attorney; and it decides on the constitutionality and enforcement of international treaties.[18] Finally, the CSJ (Superior Judicial Council) includes two chambers: one that administers the civilian judiciary and one that resolves jurisdictional conflicts that arise between courts. The 13 judges that sit on the CSJ serve 8-year terms. They are selected by the other three high courts and by Congress from nominees put forth by the Executive.

A few key additional bodies are mandated to check state abuse of power. The Procurador General de la Nación is appointed by the Senate from a list generated from the president and the highest courts. The Procurador is tasked with, broadly, protection of the rule of law and he/she can hold public officials liable for civil, labor, military, criminal, administration, or disciplinary infractions. The Procurador can only issue administrative sanctions, but since 1991, it can pass on cases to the Fiscalía for criminal investigation and prosecution. The 1991 Constitution also created an independent body to monitor and defend rights protected under the Constitution, the Defensoria del Pueblo. Congress appoints the Defensor for a four-year term from a list created by the president.[19] Both of these institutions played a role alongside citizens and human rights lawyers who pursued judicial accountability for human rights violations through petitions to the Constitutional Court.

The Emergency Institution in Colombia

States of siege (or states of emergency) were part and parcel of life in Colombia dating back to the nineteenth century. The 1886 Constitution granted the president power to declare states of siege and to establish special laws (*decretos legislativos*) to regulate order and place restrictions on civil liberties during a crisis.[20] During the first half of the twentieth century, Colombia experienced several phases of violence, notably the period of La Violencia (1946–1965). During this period, and after the civil war commenced in 1965, emergency rule was the norm. These laws provided cover to state actors through the provision of strong arrest and detention powers and some emergency decrees included explicit language protecting government actors from judicial scrutiny.[21]

The History of Military Criminal Codes

Accountability for human rights violations and emergency institutions are often intertwined as a result of immunity provisions within emergency legislation or the provision of legal cover to security personnel through the expansion and legitimization of their powers during a crisis. In Colombia, even before the civil war erupted in 1965, emergency decrees were also used to expand the power of military courts, to extend the jurisdiction of military courts, and to define offenses within military criminal codes. The first Military Code in 1881 was passed by Congress and it was not part of an emergency decree. It set the terms for military court organization, laid out court procedures, and defined offenses. According to this code, military courts could not try security personnel for ordinary offenses, except in a few circumstances, and sanctions were to be administered if the military courts were seen as abusing their power on this issue.[22]

The first military criminal code established by emergency decree was issued in 1905, Law No. 28. This code "authorized the military courts to try ordinary offenses committed by military personnel and members of the rebel forces during the 'Thousand Days War' (La Guerra de los Mil Días)."[23] The significance of this law is not necessarily readily apparent, yet it set a precedent for later human rights cases and jurisdictional battles that continue today. First, this law enabled military courts to prosecute their own personnel for crimes that are not solely related to service ("ordinary offenses"). Service in this context is typically defined narrowly in that military courts typically prosecute offenses related to orders given within military command that are part of upholding the purpose of the military institution. For example, human rights violations committed by military personnel, such as the massacre of unarmed civilians in a village, arguably goes against the purpose of the military institution and it violates the interests of society. By expanding the scope of offenses that could be considered by military courts, the 1905 law established terms that would later matter greatly in cases where military officials were alleged to have committed or directed serious human rights violations.[24] Second, the 1905 law made it permissible for military courts to prosecute civilians. In essence, both provisions gave an enormous amount of power to military courts to rule on the majority of state violence cases and cases concerning state security.[25]

Between 1931 and 1950, three different codes of military justice were created via emergency decrees and the provisions concerning jurisdiction from the 1905 law remained in these codes. Additionally, military jurisdiction was extended to the Colombian National Police through several emergency decrees between 1952 and 1954. This is notable because in addition to the entrenchment of emergency legislation during the first half of the twentieth century, the majority of crimes committed by military and police personnel in the country were defined and arbitrated by the security apparatus tasked by the state to regulate the violence.

The 1958 Code of Military Criminal Justice retained most of the provisions in the 1950 Code and it was made permanent in 1961 through Law No. 141.[26] The offenses defined in the 1958 code were separated into three categories: strictly military offenses, common military offenses performed during service, and common crimes. Strict military offenses included such crimes as violations of military honor, abandonment of post, insubordination, and attacks on peers. Common crimes included those applicable to civilians, such as rebellion, riot, and conspiracy. The crimes listed as related to "service" are the most instructive for understanding why fierce debates concerning the content of these codes and military jurisdiction multiplied as the civil war became more violent and the language of human rights became an instrument of justice. The crimes listed as related to service include: homicide, personal injury, crimes against the civilian population, the latter of which includes *devastación*, looting and extortion, and crimes against international law.[27] Colombia ratified several key international treaties in the years immediately following the 1958 Code of Military Criminal Justice, including the International Covenant on Civil and Political Rights (1969), the American Convention on Human Rights (1973) and later, Colombia ratified Protocol II of the Geneva Conventions (relating to the protection of victims of non-international armed conflicts) in 1995. The human rights enshrined in these treaties provided fuel to later debates on the legitimacy of military jurisdiction and "service-related" offenses as defined in the 1958 Code.

The clauses on service-related crimes within the 1958 Code facilitated a logic of impunity within Colombia's emergency institution by condoning serious human rights violations against civilians. The 1958 Code of Military Criminal Justice remained permanent until the Barco government issued a new code in 1988 through a request for emergency powers. The 1988 Military Criminal Code further entrenched a logic of impunity within Colombia's emergency institution. Article 291 gave sole jurisdiction to military courts for typical human rights violations such as torture, extra-judicial killing, and arbitrary detention. The effects of this new code were devastating. Families that wished to seek justice for human rights violations were effectively blocked out from participating in military court proceedings and the Code had no provisions concerning the right for civilians to bring civil actions for damages at the military courts.[28]

The Early Years of Judicial Review: The Supreme Court

The common law emergency oversight model argues that government accountability can be strengthened when judicial actors are given power to subject emergency powers to scrutiny and strike down laws that enable abuse of emergency powers.[29] In Sri Lanka, there is evidence of judicial review in a few key cases and yet, due to the increased ability for the executive to appoint and influence judicial positions, the scrutiny rapidly disappeared. The common law emergency oversight model for government accountability is a significant tool for checking executive abuses during a crisis, but the judicial sector is never completely independent of political control. Judicial review of emergency legislation can lead to institutional change or continuity, depending on the political context and the level of independence granted to the courts. Judicial review in Colombia throughout the civil war reflects this reality. During the first 25 years of the civil war (1965–1990), the Supreme Court had powers of judicial review concerning emergency legislation. Between 1958 and 1980, the Supreme Court was extremely lenient in its assessment of emergency declarations and it did not question the military courts' jurisdiction over civilians who were accused of sedition.[30] The Supreme Court began to declare some emergency decrees unconstitutional in the 1980s and, importantly, in March 1987, it ruled that the article in the Military Criminal Code allowing civilians to be tried by military courts for political crimes was unconstitutional.[31] However, there was no change during this period to the military criminal code concerning violent offenses committed by security personnel against civilians. The complete absence of human rights prosecutions during this time reflects the restrictions on accountability in the code.

Though the 1958 Code of Military Criminal Justice defined the military courts' jurisdiction in a sweeping manner, a higher court, the Disciplinary Tribunal, possessed the authority to settle questions and debates concerning whether certain offenses should be tried in civilian or military courts and the scope of service-related acts. Between 1972 and 1987, the Disciplinary Tribunal was tasked with settling conflicts of jurisdiction and its interpretation during this time was largely in favor of state interests. For example, one of the key distinctions it made was that during peacetime, military officials should be tried for ordinary offenses within ordinary courts; but, during conflict, all offenses by military personnel were seen as falling within military court jurisdiction.[32] In other words, any act of military personnel during war was argued to be service-related, despite the fact that some of the crimes committed during this period involved murder, torture, and forced disappearance.[33] The 1988 Military Criminal Code granted authority on jurisdictional battles to the Supreme Court, and between 1987 and 1989 the Supreme Court did on occasion question the right of military courts to prosecute human rights cases. In other cases, however, the Supreme Court declared forced disappearances and cases involving massacres as "service-related." There was no consensus at this time on what constituted "service" and yet, there were rumblings of a new understanding and awareness of the distinction between "strict military offenses" and human rights violations. A progressive interpretation of jurisdiction within a framework of international human rights law obligations strengthened with the creation of the 1991 Constitution a few years later.

The Conditions Shaping Gradual Displacement of the Emergency Institution

> Military criminal justice has been very ineffective in bringing to trial and sentencing violators of human rights from among the ranks of the State defence and security bodies. [...] It is noticeable, as has happened on previous occasions, that a misconceived "*esprit de corps*" has led to concealment, made investigation difficult, planted obstacles throughout the proceedings and ended up preventing justice from being done. In addition, in many cases, the decisions reached by the military courts openly contradict rulings by the Procuraduría General de la Nación [on disciplinary matters], [...] What is needed is a thorough re-thinking of the way in which members of the Armed Forces should be tried.[34]

The political landscape changed dramatically for Colombia in 1991. A few years earlier, after President Barco proposed holding a plebiscite, and President Gaviria created a 72-member constituent Assembly, a new era of participatory democracy was ushered in and sanctioned through unprecedented inclusion and consensus of several political and social groups.[35] The result of this collaboration was the 1991 Constitution, a document that made significant changes to the discourse on rights, the regulation of emergency powers, and judicial review. The 1991 Constitution introduced a new Bill of Rights, strengthened direct democracy, through the creation of referendums and recalls, and created the *acción de tutela*. The growing attention to human rights norms and legal doctrine in the 1980s was given credence through Article 93 of the Constitution, known as the *bloque de constitucionalidad*. Article 93 stipulates that international treaties and conventions related to human rights prevail over contrary norms in the domestic legal system, and the rights and duties set forth in the Constitution must be interpreted in conformity with the international human rights treaties ratified by Colombia.[36] Additionally, the 1987 Supreme Court ruling that determined military courts, even in times of internal war, should be prohibited from investigating and prosecuting civilians, was codified in Article 214 of the Constitution.

The Constitution also promulgated the creation of several human rights bodies, including the Fiscalía General de la Nación (Office of the General Prosecutor) and the Defensor del Pueblo (Ombudsman). The Fiscalía became even more significant in relation to human rights cases when, in 1995, the Human Rights Unit was created to tackle the backlog of state and paramilitary crimes, including massacres, disappearances, and torture. The Human Rights Unit has been credited with helping to increase the number of human rights prosecutions after 1997.[37]

However, the work of the Human Rights Unit would not have been possible if it did not have jurisdiction over human rights cases. Though the 1991 Constitution was a watershed moment regarding participatory democracy and rights, one of the main obstructions to justice, military jurisdiction over human rights cases, remained intact via Article 221 of the Constitution. This article grants special jurisdiction to military courts for offenses committed by military and police during active service.[38] Thus, in the years immediately following 1991, human rights abuses committed by military personnel largely remained in the hands of military courts. The empirical data analyzed in this chapter demonstrates that the upward trend in prosecutions does not begin until after 1997 (see Graph 5.1). In order to make sense of this, it is necessary to examine the alterations that were made to the emergency institution as a whole and, specifically, to the Military Criminal Code, during this period.

In Colombia, the executive wielded consistently strong veto power concerning emergency legislation, but the judicial review powers granted to the Constitutional Court in 1991 produced an environment in which the military criminal code was continuously under attack. Petitions brought to the Constitutional Court by citizens and leaders in the human

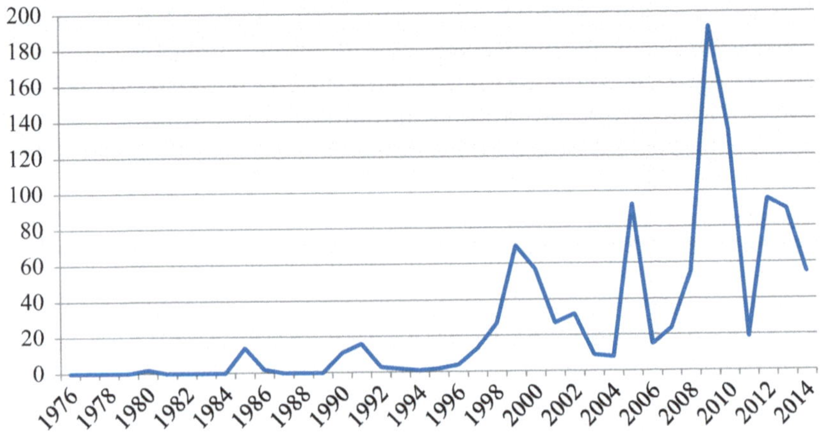

Graph 5.1 The number of state actors prosecuted per year in Colombia

rights community challenged the logic of impunity within the Military Criminal Code. Court rulings produced tighter controls and limitations on what the military could define as "service" and which human rights cases the military courts could litigate. In only a matter of eight years, the Constitutional Court's rulings led to the creation of a new Military Criminal Code and a rise in human rights prosecutions. Gradual displacement unfolded in Colombia as citizens petitioned the Constitutional Court to eliminate the logic of impunity within the military criminal code.

The Absence of Independent Oversight of Executive Emergency Powers

Though the Congress in Colombia possesses the power to amend, add, or repeal emergency legislation, historically it has largely approved these laws. This trend of rubberstamping the executive's promulgation of crisis decrees reflects one of the central debates about Colombian democracy: the absence of a true political opposition.[39] The National Front pacts between 1958 and 1986 granted significant power to the two main parties, Liberal and Conservative, and the result of this model of alternating power meant that the winning political party often held a majority in Congress. Additionally, the failure by the elite-dominated two-party system to incorporate marginalized groups meant that any opposition to the effects of emergency policies on civil society was rarely considered. Congress grew increasingly more ineffective and less powerful during the National Front Years due to a culture of clientelism. The dominant parties were generally unwilling to initiate substantive change, and the president possessed the power to control legislation on key issue areas, including the economy and national security.[40]

The closed political climate that resulted from the National Front pacts produced resistance in the form of electoral activism and guerilla movements. The former's culminating act was the creation by university students of *la séptima papeleta*, which called for a constitutional convention. When President Barco placed his weight behind this initiative and it was put to a public vote, 89% of the voters supported it.[41] The resulting 1991 Constitution stripped away the clientelistic aspects of the former political system and it considerably strengthened elements of participatory democracy. The Constitution also placed strict time limits on the duration of states of emergency, it prohibited the suspension of fundamental rights during a crisis period and it granted Congress the power to repeal, amend, or add to emergency decrees during the first year of its operation.[42] Yet, the "electoral hegemony"[43] of the two traditional political parties remains to this day. The ability for the executive to dictate policymaking, particularly in the realm of national security, remains a problem, and much of this results from the reality of conflict in which these political actors operate. Despite the persistent legacy of strong veto possibilities in the Colombian political system, the 1991 Constitution created flexibility in the interpretation and enforcement of the emergency institution through the creation of the Constitutional Court.

Judicial Independence on the Constitutional Court

Judicial review is not inherently progressive, as is evident in the previously discussed Supreme Court rulings on emergency laws during the 1980s. However, beginning in 1991, key rulings from the Constitutional Court eroded the historically permanent state of emergency and transformed the military courts' control over human rights cases. The Constitutional Court's rulings altered the impact of emergency laws on human rights prosecutions in two distinct ways: beginning in 1992, it challenged the status quo by questioning the content and legitimacy of emergency declarations made by the executive and rubberstamped by Congress and, in some cases, the Court nullified the declaration altogether. The Court also regularly and consistently chipped away at the military courts' grip on human rights cases through several key decisions on jurisdiction and definitions of "service" within the military criminal code. Judges that sit on the Constitutional Court are not wholly independent from the government. They are elected by the Senate for eight-year terms from lists generated by the president, the Supreme Court, and the Council of the State. Those who, in the year prior to the election, are members of the Cabinet or judges on the Supreme Court or Council of the State are not eligible for positions on the Court. In this regard, it is somewhat surprising that judges would challenge the emergency institution. Why then, did the Court take on the issue of military jurisdiction in several rulings?

The Court was progressive in its first decade largely because the mandate it was given was highly progressive. All questions of constitutional rights were in the hands of the Court and it could annul other judges' decisions on these matters. Additionally, the powers of the Court built on a long history of judicial review, meaning the political community already had a familiarity with courts wielding large amounts of power.[44] The Court also had enormous financial and technical support to carry out its mandate. It was, for better or for worse, set up to be a super court.

Change Agents: Citizens Petition the Constitutional Court

One of the central features of the Court's mandate is deciding on citizen petitions regarding unconstitutional laws and practices. Article 241 of the Constitution, which identifies the functions and powers of the Constitutional Court, empowers citizens to directly engage in matters of constitutional rights. The Court decides on petitions of unconstitutionality brought by citizens concerning laws, amendments, and decrees, or for errors of procedure in a law's formation or, in some cases, law implementation.[45] The Constitution also mandates that the Procurador General weigh in on every petition and it allows other interested parties, including citizens and state actors, to submit statements defending or opposing the constitutionality of the law or decree in question.[46] With the exception of one case, beginning in the mid-1990s, citizens submitted most of the petitions regarding the unconstitutionality of the Military Criminal Code.[47]

Yet, the provision of this right to petition the Court does not necessarily mean it will be exercised by citizens or even known to them. The Constitutional Court was able to effect change within the emergency institution not only because its mandate granted citizens the right to question the logic of impunity inherent within the Military Criminal Code. Institutional change also resulted from the fact that citizens were made aware of their constitutional rights and received support and resources from a strong legal human rights community.

The historically strong legal culture in Colombia is not insignificant to the institutional change within the emergency institution during the 1990s. Many years prior, in addition to the development of other forms of rights activism, including land rights and peasant rights, a legal human rights community began to grow. Several NGOs formed during the 1970s and 1980s as the violence steadily increased. One of the first major human rights groups to emerge in the late 1970s, the Permanent Committee for the Defense of Human Rights, held public forums on human rights for the public and organized meetings with government officials. A short time later, the Centro de Investigación y Educación Popular (CINEP) initiated some of the first efforts to document and catalog human rights abuses in addition to providing the growth of the human rights community in rural areas. Due to conflicting objectives and generational differences, many of the early groups splintered. A group of new rights and advocacy organizations that emerged throughout the 1980s had varying mandates but they were unified in their practice of producing human rights knowledge based on law. Human rights reporting became a central tool of organizing reliable and accurate claims for victims of abuse, and these processes were not without controversy.[48] Some of the main organizations to embody these practices, including the José Alvéar Restrepo Lawyers' Collective (Colectivo de Abogados), the Colombian Commission of Jurists (CCJ), and the Intercongregational Commission for Justice and Peace, still exist today.

During the 1980s, CCJ and Colectivo had little power to alter the reality that military courts had jurisdiction over all offenses performed by the military and National Police. Though Colombia had ratified the International Covenant on Civil and Political Rights in 1969 and the American Convention on Human Rights in 1973, there was no actual venue at the domestic level to make these claims given the barriers presented by military jurisdiction. The 1991 Constitution changed the landscape in this regard in a few key ways. The creation of the Fiscalía and the Defensor del Pueblo established institutions that were tasked with the investigation of rights violations committed by the state. Through Article 241, the Constitution additionally provided citizens the means to challenge decrees such as the Military Criminal Code. Finally, through Article 93, the *bloque de constitucionalidad*, the Constitution established the recognition of international human rights law as superior to domestic legal norms. Taken together, these factors strengthened the ability of the legal human rights community to transform the logic of impunity within Colombia's emergency institution.

The *bloque de constitucionalidad* provided a tangible resource upon which the legal human rights community could mobilize and it helped to expand the coalition of individuals and groups who would have a stake in the constitutionality of emergency decrees, and more specifically, the compatibility of international human rights law and international humanitarian law with aspects of the Military Criminal Code. Access to the norms within international human rights law raised the expectation of success among citizens and human rights advocates who were combatting a legacy of impunity.[49] The following provides detail on the Court's review of emergency declarations and citizen petitions regarding the unconstitutionality of certain provisions within the Military Criminal Code.

Judicial Review: The Constitutional Court's Rulings on the Emergency Institution

The Constitutional Court is tasked with automatically reviewing all emergency declarations and decrees, within one day of their announcement by the executive.[50] This is significant in that though judicial review of emergency decrees was in place prior to this moment (via the Supreme Court), it was not in the hands of an independent body armed with a progressive Constitution and a mandate of upholding rights that were more reflective of human rights norms than ever before. The ability for the Constitutional Court to automatically review declarations of emergency, and the resulting decrees, resulted in transformative changes to the emergency institution. Early on, the Court ruled that its duty was to not only formally assess the executive's desire to obtain increased powers during a crisis but also examine whether the crisis warranted such a declaration.[51] This activism on the part of the Court led to a fairly rapid shift away from a permanent state of emergency in Colombia to a milieu in which governments would have to go to greater lengths to establish the legitimacy of the decrees or refrain from declaring states of emergency altogether. For example, between 1984 and 1991, the Supreme Court declared only 9% of the state of siege decrees void, while between 1992 and 1996, the Constitutional Court voided 34% of the same decrees.[52]

In addition to the decline of emergency rule in Colombia during this time, nullification of emergency laws by the Court eroded the executive's ability to seamlessly legislate on legal reforms, including the contents of the Military Criminal Code. Prior to 1991, battles over jurisdiction concerning human rights cases were largely in the hands of a body sympathetic to Colombia's security apparatus, the Disciplinary Tribunal. Through Article 256, the 1991 Constitution created a new body, the CSJ, to arbitrate on these matters. At first, the CSJ followed the path paved by the Disciplinary Tribunal. Given the Constitution's sanctioning of military jurisdiction for all military and police offenses during war, this is not necessarily surprising. However, a few years into its operation, in response to citizen petitions, the Constitutional Court began a steady and consistent challenge to key elements of the Military Criminal Code, specifically the nature of criminal offenses and jurisdiction concerning serious acts of violence. The Court determined its decisions upon consideration of the arguments made by a citizen in his/her initial petition, as well as statements in support or opposition of the petition from the Procurador General, statements from interested citizens, and statements from leaders within the armed forces, the Ministry of Defense, and other state bodies.

In 1995, the Constitutional Court took one of the first steps toward altering the emergency institution by directly challenging the Military Criminal Code. On March 29, the Constitutional Court issued judgment C-141, ruling that there is a conflict of interest when the military is heavily engaged in violence as a party to the conflict and then also sits in judgment of the excesses of war. Specifically, the ruling states that the pre-constitutional norm that empowers active-duty officers to perform as prosecutors or judges in military courts does not comport with the constitutional guarantees of an autonomous and impartial judge.[53] It thus ruled that only civilians and retired military officers could sit on courts martial.[54] A citizen, Nelson Rafael Cotes Corvacho, submitted this petition to the Court. Congress responded to this ruling by passing an amendment to Article 221 of the Constitution, which provides that active-duty military officers *can* serve in courts martial. As a result, the Military Criminal Code remained unaltered.

That same year, in judgment C-578/95, the Constitutional Court provided its first assessment of the term *orden del servicio*, or orders of service, within the Military Criminal Code. The petition was submitted by the Defensor del Pueblo at the time, Jaime Córdoba Triviño. Córdoba made the argument that Article 15 of Decreto Ley 85 de 1989 (an emergency decree) was unconstitutional. This decree, enacted by the president in 1989, amended existing disciplinary regulations within the Military Criminal Code. Article 15 specifically states that when a subordinate is given orders from his/her superior that involves the commission of a crime, the subordinate should expose this information and his/her superior; however, if the superior continues to insist that the order be executed, the subordinate must comply.[55] In his charge, Córdoba argued that the use of the term "all" in reference to orders given by a superior, violates several articles of the Constitution, including Articles 1, 2, 6, 18, 91, and 95, in its promotion of a principle of blind obedience to authorities. Córdoba draws on the language of human rights, enshrined in Article 95 of the Constitution, to support his claim that subordinates as well as superiors within the armed forces are committed, as part of their public duties, to respect the rights of others and defend human rights as a foundation of peaceful coexistence.[56] In its response to Córdoba's petition, the Court concluded that a service order is an order that seeks to carry out the objectives of the military institution; an order that goes against the interests of the public or violates the objectives of the military institution, can therefore not be conceived as an act of service.[57] The Court specifically references sexual assault and torture in its statement that any military order that includes the commission of these crimes may under no circumstances qualify as a service order. Additionally, the Court cites international humanitarian law and Article 93 of the Constitution, the *bloque de constitucionalidad*, to argue that when military personnel engage in a clear violation of international humanitarian law, the international treaty must always be treated as superior to domestic statutes.[58]

A month later, the Court again ruled on military jurisdiction. As stipulated in Article 241, para 8 of the Constitution, the Court automatically considers the constitutionality of proposed statutory bills. In June 1995, the president of the Senate, Juan Guiermello Angel Mejia, presented Law No. 58/94 and 264/95 Cámara, the Statutory Administration of Justice, to the Court. Several citizens and state bodies weighed in on the proposed bill. In the end, the Constitutional Court delivered judgment C-037, which rules some elements of the bill constitutional and others unconstitutional. Regarding military justice specifically, the Court concluded that given military examining magistrates were employed by the executive, they could not be regarded as independent or impartial.[59]

The rulings from the Constitutional Court are binding on all other judicial authorities in the country. However, reports from local organizations and the Inter-American Commission of Human Rights (IACHR) indicate that initially other courts did not comply with the rulings on military courts, particularly the CSJ. Through the 1991 Constitution, the CSJ was appointed as the mediator on jurisdictional battles between courts. Up until 1997, the Fiscalía and the military justice system did not come to agreement on jurisdiction for human rights cases. As a consequence, the Fiscalía would often petition to have serious human rights cases transferred from the military jurisdiction to the ordinary courts. The military, in turn, would petition to have the ordinary courts transfer certain human rights cases to their courts. If the petition from either jurisdiction was denied, the jurisdictional conflict would move up to the CSJ.[60] Because the CSJ rarely ruled in favor of ordinary courts, human rights prosecutions remained at a relatively low level during the years 1991–1997 (see Graph 5.1 below).

Yet, the Constitutional Court's rulings in 1995 and 1996 were, in a sense, building a case for what transpired in the following few years. In 1997, the Constitutional Court issued its strongest challenge to military jurisdiction and the operation of military courts. The petition was submitted by citizen Jaime Enrique Lozano, who had experience as a clerk in the judicial system. The National Police and the Public Ministry submitted statements defending the constitutionality of the Code. The CCJ contributed statements supporting the petitioner. Several of the arguments made by the CCJ were incorporated into the Court's final ruling.[61] The Court's judgment C-358/97, issued on August 5, ruled that key sections of the Military Criminal Code were unconstitutional. Specifically, the Court ruled that the broad jurisdiction granted to military courts regarding acts related to "service" had violated Article 221 of the Constitution. "Service" was argued to not include crimes against humanity because such crimes violated the central objectives of the security forces, namely the security of the civilian population. Additionally, the Court ruled that military jurisdiction must be regarded as exceptional, and where there is any doubt about jurisdiction, the default should be the ordinary courts, save for cases where it is demonstrated that the case in question is an exception.[62] The 1997 ruling was significant in its explicit referral to violations of international human rights law, specifically crimes against humanity. It made the strongest and clearest argument for why military jurisdiction over serious cases of human rights violations was unconstitutional.

Building on the 1997 ruling, the Court again ruled in 1998 that several articles within the Military Criminal Code were unconstitutional. The petitioner in this case, Rafael Barrios Mendevil, an attorney affiliated with Colectivo de Abogados, directly cites the American Convention on Human Rights and the International Covenant on Civil and Political Rights in his argument that the state is obliged to assure everyone the right to an effective remedy to repair the damages caused by a violation.[63] The CCJ contributed statements in support of the petitioner's arguments. In its ruling, C-145/98, the Court declared several articles within the Code to be unconstitutional, and it specifically argued that the inclusion of active members of the armed forces on oral courts martial was incompatible with the rights to due process and access to justice.[64]

The effects of these rulings by the Court were not immediate. The CSJ continued to send the majority of human rights cases to military courts in violation of the Court's 1997 ruling. The IACHR reported in 1999 that though the Ministry of Defense reported that close to 180 cases had been transferred from military courts to ordinary courts, the commission found that most of the cases cited by the Ministry were not human rights cases.[65] However, only a month after the 1997 Court ruling, President Samper's administration sent a draft of a new military criminal code to the legislature. This draft sought to incorporate much of what the Constitutional Court had recommended through its rulings on military jurisdiction and human rights from 1995 to 1997. In 1999, Congress passed a new Military Criminal Code (Law No. 522 of 1999). Key articles in the 1999 Military Criminal Code reflect previous Court rulings. For example, Article 214 in the new code states security force members cannot simultaneously be in a command position while they are an investigator, prosecutor, or judge in a military court; Article 3 removes torture, genocide, and forced disappearance from consideration under military jurisdiction; and Article 305 establishes the right of victims to be civil parties before a military court (though they cannot seek compensation through this court).[66]

The main criticism of the new code was the omission of human rights violations allegedly committed most often by security forces up until this point in the war: extra-judicial killing, rape, and aiding and abetting atrocities carried out by paramilitary groups. Despite these weaknesses, the new Code was important in that one of the key legal reforms to result from emergency legislation had been fundamentally altered to incorporate citizen demands for human rights prosecutions. The 1999 Military Criminal Code is a product of a high level of contestation between the Court, the state, and citizens. Through a series of rulings at the Constitutional Court over a period of six years, the emergency institution was gradually displaced.

Trends in the Transfer of Human Rights Cases to Military Courts and Civilian Courts[67]

In addition to the increase in human rights prosecutions after 1997, there is an upward trend after 2000 in the number of human rights cases CSJ awards to civilian courts, and the number of cases, following petitions from the Fiscalía, the military authorities transfer to civilian courts. The CSJ was relatively unwilling at first to adhere to the 1997 Constitutional Court judgment on jurisdiction, but its rulings on jurisdiction for human rights cases noticeably shift after Congress passes the 1999 Military Criminal Code. The most striking illustration of this change is the CSJ's decision in the Nydia Bautista case. On June 29, 2000, the Constitutional

Court instructed the CSJ to reconsider its 1996 decision in which it referred a case of forced disappearance, torture, and death of a member of the M-19 guerrilla group, Nydia Bautista, to military courts. After reviewing the case, the CSJ reversed itself and assigned jurisdiction to the civilian courts invoking the 1997 Constitutional Court ruling and arguing that the criminal acts in question were not related directly to military service.[68] In the end, the accused in the investigation, retired General Alvaro Velandia Hurtado, was not prosecuted because the Fiscalía closed the case in 2004.[69]

Between 2000 and 2014, there is a shift in the number of human rights cases transferred out of military courts and placed in civilian courts. At times, the CSJ transferred these cases, at other moments the military courts moved the cases themselves, and, finally, in recent years, cases were moved following decisions made by review committees at the Ministry of Defense. In 2000, the CSJ transferred 80 cases from military courts to civilian courts and the majority of these cases involved serious human rights violations. Between 2001 and 2002, the CSJ continued to award a higher number of human rights cases to civilian courts compared with military courts: in 2001, 20 cases went to the civilian courts while 11 cases were awarded to military courts; in 2002, CSJ sent 12 cases to the civilian courts and 6 to the military court jurisdiction.[70] Between 2002 and 2003, the Superior Military Tribunal sent 72 cases to the civilian courts, 26 of which included serious human rights violations.[71] Then, between 2005 and 2008, as a result of a review conducted by a Ministry of Defense senior level committee on extra-judicial killings, 600 human rights cases were transferred from military courts to civilian courts. In 2009, the number of transferred cases remained relatively high, at 250.

In 2010, both the military courts and the CSJ transferred a number of cases to civilian courts; the former sent 140 cases while the latter awarded 91 cases. In recent years, cases were moved as a result of an agreement, referred to as *Mesa Tecnica*, between the Ministry of Defense, the Procurador General, and the Fiscalía, to resolve jurisdictional conflicts in cases of extra-judicial killings.[72] In 2011, 170 cases were transferred from the military courts to civilian courts and 101 cases were transferred in 2012. In 2013 and 2014, however, CSJ begins to slowly increase the number of cases awarded to military courts. This subtle shift may be partially explained by new strategies employed by the military to regain control over human rights cases. The following discusses this recent change.

A Change in the Military's Discourse

Though the picture of human rights prosecutions shifts after 1997, contestation over jurisdiction was far from over. Graph 5.1 illustrates that the military was forced to relinquish increasing numbers of human rights cases, but the fight to win back control of these cases was renewed by the military in 2010 and it continues today.[73] What is noteworthy about the military's efforts on this front is that after losing several times to the Constitutional Court, which consistently ruled that several aspects of the Military Criminal Code were unconstitutional, the military employed a strategy in which they seek to alter the discourse on human rights cases and military jurisdiction. On December 10, 2003, Congress passed a government-proposed reform to the Constitution, Legislative Act 02 of 2003. This act allowed armed forces personnel to perform as judicial police officers, arrest civilians, interrogate them, collect evidence, and carry out other activities influencing the direction and outcomes of trials.[74] The Court received a petition challenging this law from Gustavo Gallón, director of the CCJ, along with other citizens.[75] The Constitutional Court declared this act unconstitutional in August 2004, arguing it violated the fundamental rights of citizens.

In 2010, the Military Criminal Code was altered through Law 1407, which was passed by Congress. Law 1407 extended the list of violations excluded from military jurisdiction. The excluded violations would therefore include not only torture, genocide, and forced disappearance but also crimes against humanity, international humanitarian law, violations and other acts construed as unrelated to service.[76] While this move was heralded as a significant step in the ability of ordinary courts to prosecute a backlog of serious human rights violations, a law passed only a few years later in 2012 largely nullified its influence. Legislative Act 02 of 2012 proposed a reform to the constitution that would establish military criminal courts as the sole jurisdiction for criminal proceedings related to all military operations.[77] Congress passed the law in 2012. However, after several citizens, including Gustavo Gallón, director of the CCJ, collectively brought an action for unconstitutionality against the law, the Constitutional Court agreed and struck it down in October 2013.[78]

The military continued to contest jurisdiction in 2013, and this time the effort was marked by what some within the human rights community described as a dangerously "elegant" strategy.[79] Senate Bill 85 of 2013 sought to establish new parameters for military jurisdiction. Specifically, the bill mandates that all homicides committed by military personnel be tried in military courts, though it excludes from military jurisdiction crimes such as extra-judicial killing and sexual violence. The controversy over false positives (discussed further below) is relevant here in that most of those cases were categorized as homicide and thus, this may have been an attempt to keep false positive cases within the military courts.[80] Additionally, because extra-judicial killing and sexual violence are not crimes codified in Colombia's criminal code, it is possible that these and other human rights violations could still land in the hands of military court personnel.

Lastly, and most pertinent to the evolving discourse employed by the security apparatus concerning jurisdiction, Senate Bill 85 attempts to establish, for the first time, that international humanitarian law should be the framework applied in military courts. Though Senate Bill 85 was reformed in April 2015 with language that all human rights cases would remain in ordinary courts, as of June 2015, Congress had passed an amendment to Article 221 of the Constitution, which stipulates that ordinary and military courts must apply international humanitarian law when investigating and prosecuting cases related to the conduct of the armed forces.[81] The military's recent employment of the international humanitarian law framework is noteworthy in that as opposed to rejecting outright the notion that ordinary courts should handle all human rights cases, the military seeks to establish parameters for its jurisdiction that could appear agreeable to those on the Constitutional Court or agreeable to some within the human rights community.

Gustavo Gallón, director of the CCJ and a former judge on the Constitutional Court, argues the military's recent strategy is based on several inaccuracies. Gallón asserts that when the military argues that international humanitarian law authorizes actions taken in war and thus these laws apply to the conduct of their personnel, the military (and its lawyers) have an incorrect understanding of the laws of war; the laws of war *prohibit* actions that security forces can take (e.g., violence against civilians); they do not authorize actions.[82] The appeal to international humanitarian law as the framework for military jurisdiction is a sophisticated argument that reflects the military's will to gain back control over all offenses performed by its personnel. Between 2012 and 2013, there is a sudden spike in the number of human rights cases transferred to military courts by the CSJ and this illustrates the effects of short-lived laws supporting military jurisdiction.[83] Significantly, in February 2016, through Sentencia C-084, the

Constitutional Court ruled that the amendment to Article 221 passed by Congress in 2015 was constitutional as long as international human rights law serves as the framework for evaluating crimes committed by members of the armed forces. Specifically, the Court ruled that any application of international humanitarian law as a framework for violations committed by the armed forces during conflict cannot disregard the convergent and complementary application of international human rights law.[84] This marks a key moment in which the Court has pushed back on the military's attempt to control jurisdiction of human rights cases. The ruling also indicates that future battles over jurisdiction are likely on the horizon.

The judges on the Constitutional Court have evolved since the early 2000s and judicial activism may be waning as a result of a more conservative composition.[85] These shifts, and the military's recent employment of the laws of war argument, will undoubtedly have an impact on the trend in human rights prosecutions going forward.

Human Rights Prosecution Data

The civil war years prior to 1991 are characterized by widespread impunity initiated and reinforced by standards within military criminal codes. Though the war in Colombia continued and the violence against civilians increased during the 1990s and 2000s, human rights prosecutions emerged for the first time during this period and there was a general upward trend in the number of military and police officials held to account. The following provides detail on human rights prosecution data gathered on Colombia between 1976 and 2014. It also includes a discussion of emblematic cases to illustrate how gradual displacement produced change within Colombia's emergency institution, leading to improvements in human rights prosecutions.

In Colombia, between 1976 and 2014, 210 human rights prosecutions were held involving 1073 state actors.[86] Of them, 94% of defendants were convicted in the initial trial, through an appeal, or when the Supreme Court upheld a conviction after a defendant's appeal. The conviction rate over time is high in Colombia compared with other cases in this book and this outcome is a by-product of the increasing number of cases that were heard in ordinary courts as opposed to military courts. The majority of cases involve extra-judicial killings and forced disappearances of civilians and most of the defendants are members of the armed forces or police. These prosecutions investigated 4358 of the 19,437 civilian deaths caused by state actors, a prosecution rate of 22.4%.[87] The prosecution rate makes evident that impunity remained a serious problem throughout the conflict. There is complexity, however, to the story of accountability in Colombia. Investigations and prosecutions of human rights cases within the judicial system were generally inadequate as a result of barriers in access to justice, the administration of justice and continued threats and violence against those working in the legal sector. However, as the prior section outlined, the emergency institution that facilitated this outcome was not static. Gradual displacement of the military criminal code, and the creation of a new code, produced a shift in the number of human rights prosecutions conducted in ordinary courts by the late 1990s.

The prosecutions in Colombia can be broken down into two distinct phases: 1991–2005 and 2006–2014 (see Graph 5.1). The first phase depicts the undeniable shift from a prior era of impunity to increasing levels of human rights prosecutions. The second period of prosecutions consists of a few different types of cases. Some cases resulted from the 2005 Justice and Peace Law (JPL), which established an alternative justice system within the Fiscalía to administer investigations and prosecutions of demobilized paramilitary members for serious human rights violations. These years, particularly 2009–2011, are also marked by trials related to the false positive cases, many of which emanated from the JPL paramilitary confessions. The remaining prosecutions include the conclusion of lengthy trials initiated several years earlier.

Human Rights Prosecutions: 1991–2005

The military courts had a virtual monopoly on human rights cases as a result of the 1958 Code of Military Criminal Justice, and thus, the only prosecutions between 1976 and 1988 include a handful of convictions in a few police torture cases in 1985 and acquittals of military personnel for the murder of a suspected M-19 member in 1980 (see Graph 5.2). The most noticeable spike in human rights prosecutions occurs after 1997 but the upward trend is gradual at first. The CSJ did not automatically award human rights cases to ordinary courts, even after the Constitutional Court ruling on jurisdiction in 1997. But, by 2001 the number of cases the CSJ awards to the ordinary courts increases dramatically. Additionally, the Constitutional Court takes an active role in a few key cases during this time period to challenge the CSJ's intransigence. This shift in jurisdiction, which had a large impact on the rate of prosecutions in Colombia, is best illustrated through a discussion of three important cases.

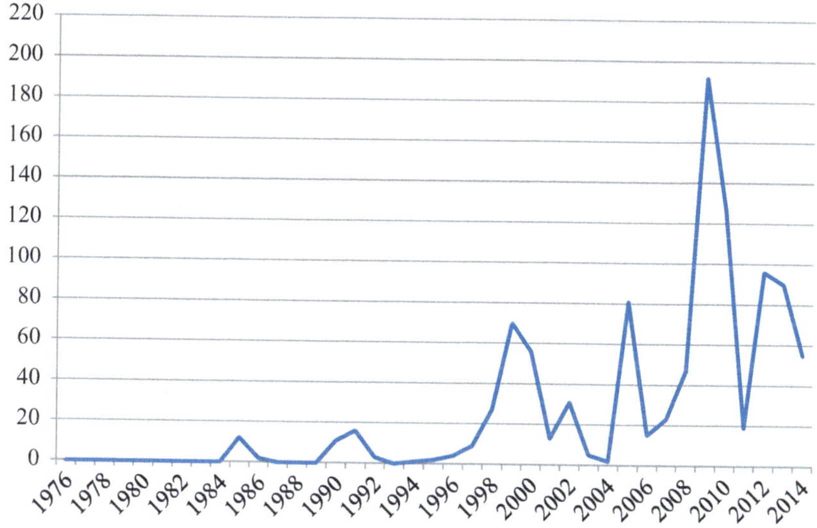

Graph 5.2 Convictions of state actors in Colombia

In one well-known case, later referred to as the "19 Merchants" case, a high ranking military officer, General Farouk Yanine Díaz, was accused of paying paramilitary members to locate and kill 19 men in 1987. Though the Human Rights Unit within the Fiscalía launched an investigation of General Yanine in 1995 leading to an arrest warrant, the military filed a *colisión de competencia*, requesting a transfer of the case to the military courts.[88] The CSJ awarded the Yanine case to the military courts, and in 1997, General José Bonett acquitted General Yanine and three of his military colleagues of homicide and kidnapping charges.[89] In 1996, a year before the verdict, the CCJ filed a petition on behalf of victims' families with the Inter-American Commission for Human Rights concerning this case. The Commission referred the case to the Inter-American Court of Human Rights in 2001, and in 2004, the Court ruled that the Colombian government must provide reparations to the victims' families.[90]

The CSJ awarded military jurisdiction during this time in another prominent case involving a high-ranking officer. In May 1999, Brigadier General Jaime Uscátegui was arrested on charges he was connected to the July 1997 massacre of dozens of civilians in Mapiripán. A few months later, the CSJ transferred the case from the ordinary courts to the military courts. In 2001, a military court convicted Uscátegui and sentenced him to 40 months of imprisonment for failure to prevent the massacre carried out by the AUC paramilitary faction in Mapiripán. The court also convicted Lieutenant Colonel Hernan Orozco, who was sentenced to 38 months in prison.[91] Uscátegui's sentence was reduced for work performed and he was released in July 2001. A few months after the CSJ awarded this case to the military courts in 1999, Nory Giraldo de Jaramillo, the common law spouse of one of the victims of Mapiripàn, initiated an *acción de tutela* at the Constitutional Court against the Disciplinary Tribunal of the CSJ.[92] Nory Giraldo de Jaramillo, represented by Luis Guillermo Pérez Casas, argued in the *tutela* that the CSJ's decision to award this case to military courts violated the preamble and Articles 1, 2, 3, 13, 29, 229, and 235. Specifically, the applicant argues that the CSJ's decision violates the Constitutional Court's 1997 decision on jurisdiction and it fails to consider the Colombian state's obligations to international human rights law.[93] In response to the *tutela*, the Constitutional Court issued a ruling in November 2001 that mandated that the Mapiripán case be returned to the ordinary courts. In essence, the Court overturned the CSJ's decision to award this case to the military courts.[94] In this ruling, the Constitutional Court concluded the following regarding General Uscátegui's actions in the Mapiripán case:

> The military forces have an absolute obligation to prevent ignorance of international humanitarian law ([which is] an absolute constraint, even under a state of emergency, according to the provisions of article 214 of the Constitution) and the rights, which, under the international treaties ratified by Colombia, cannot be suspended during such periods [...]. To allow them to occur, either because they are actively involved in them or because they have neglected their state duty to protect the rights of citizens, constitutes a flagrant violation of their position as guarantor of the minimum basic conditions of social organization and they can therefore never be considered to be service-related acts.[95]

The Fiscalía indicted Uscátegui in 2003 and in 2007 an ordinary court acquitted the General and convicted Lieutenant Colonel Hernan Orozco, sentencing him to 40 years of imprisonment.[96] The Fiscalía immediately appealed the lower court's decision to acquit General Uscátegui, and in 2009 the Superior Tribunal of Bogotá sentenced him to 40 years of imprisonment.[97] Though Uscátegui appealed his 2009 conviction, the Supreme Court upheld it in 2014, ruling the general was responsible as an author of a crime by omission for the massacre in Mapiripán. The Supreme Court ruled that he was complicit in the violence by deliberately failing to prevent paramilitary groups from carrying out the murders of innocent civilians.[98] This conviction is the most severe sentence in Colombia's history for an officer of this rank and, notably, the sequence of events would not have been possible if the Mapiripán case had remained in the military's jurisdiction.

In addition to the *acción de tutela* submitted by a victim's family member in 1999 on the Mapiripán case, in the same year, Colectivo de Abogados and the Center for Justice and International Law (based in Washington D.C.) submitted a petition to the Inter-American Commission of Human Rights. On September 15, 2005, the Inter-American Court of Human rights ruled the Colombian State "internationally responsible" for the crimes that took place in Mapiripán. In 2003, long before his final conviction and sentence by the Supreme Court, General Uscátegui filed his own petition at the IACHR alleging that the Colombian State had failed to protect fair trial rights and there had been unwarranted delay in criminal proceedings against him concerning the case of Mapiripàn. The IACHR ruled his petition admissible in November 2014 and the final ruling on the case is yet to be decided.[99]

In a final example, the CSJ reversed its decision to initially award a case to the military courts in 2004. The case involved the murder of five family members, including a minor and an infant, by armed forces. The murder occurred on April 10, 2004, in Cajamarca, Tolima, and the armed forces immediately identified the deaths as "military errors" performed in a counter-insurgency operation. The CSJ initially awarded jurisdiction to the military courts in June on the grounds that the violence constituted an act of service.[100] Then, after the Procuraduría initiated its own disciplinary investigation of the deaths and ruled that statements by the soldiers involved were suspicious given ballistics and medical evidence its office had gathered, the CSJ reversed its decision in November 2004 and transferred the case to the ordinary courts. In 2009, the Third Criminal Court of Ibague convicted five soldiers of murder in the Cajamarca case and issued sentences ranging from 35 to 40 years.[101]

Prosecutions Under the Justice and Peace Law: 2006–2014

In addition to the human rights cases prosecuted in civilian courts, the years 2006–2014 are marked by the emergence of a new set of cases resulting from the 2005 JPL. The JPL established a separate criminal accountability process in an effort to demobilize paramilitary factions and award reduced sentences in exchange for confessions.[102] After complaints about the law were issued by local and international human rights organizations, the Constitutional Court ruled the law constitutional in 2006 with stipulations on the need for cooperation from the defendants and respect for victims' rights.[103] The Colombian government then issued Decree 3391 in November 2006, which adopted some of the conditions from the Court's ruling and contradicted others. The judicial outcomes resulting from the JPL process were abysmal. Of the 31,670 people who demobilized between November 2003 and mid-2006, only 2695 declared their interest in applying for the benefits of the JPL.[104] As of 2013, the JPL courts had only convicted 14 paramilitary members for serious human rights violations.[105] The conviction rate under the JPL process is particularly stark considering that since 2006, the Justice and Peace Unit gathered information through paramilitary confessions on approximately 39,546 acts of violence involving 51,906 victims.[106] The JPL has received extensive criticism, including the problem of high-ranking paramilitary members' extradition to the United States for drug trafficking charges, excessive delays, and limitations on victims' participation rights. One of the most significant gaps involves the government's refusal to assist in the provision of reparations where a demobilized person's resources are insufficient. Through the aforementioned Decree 3391 of 2006, the government abdicated itself from responsibility of utilizing funds from the national budget to compensate victims involved in the JPL process.[107]

Despite the meager number of prosecutions resulting from the JPL, the paramilitary confessions made several subsequent prosecutions of security personnel possible. The prosecution data indicate that between 2009 and 2011, seven prosecutions were held involving 46 members of the armed forces for explicitly engaging in what is termed *falsos positivos* (false positives) cases. All 46 defendants were convicted in ordinary courts. The false positives cases involve incidents in which military personnel falsely presented civilians, who were extra-judicially executed, as "killed in combat." Several confessions provided by paramilitary members during the JPL proceedings resulted in evidence that this practice had become fairly widespread among the armed forces, often in collaboration with paramilitary factions, and as a means to meet government expectations concerning the defeat of the guerillas.

These prosecutions are largely unrelated to the gradual displacement of the military criminal code. The JPL was the beginning of a new era and a set of policies on the part of the government concerning justice in the midst of a transition to peace. The prosecutions of paramilitary members under the JPL transpired in an alternative justice system within the Fiscalía. There were no investigations led by the Human Rights Unit nor were they subject to questions of jurisdictional competency. The JPL outlined its own parameters for investigation and prosecution, separate from the Military Criminal Code.

The complexity that lies behind the landscape of human rights prosecutions in Colombia illustrates that the barriers to judicial accountability are numerous in a democracy at war, but the milieu is far from static. The protection of security personnel and the sanctioning of all actions performed "in service," otherwise understood as the core logic of impunity within the military criminal code, underwent gradual displacement. As a result of citizen petitions and rulings from a court willing to challenge the will of the executive and scrutinize the emergency institution, one of the main restrictions on human rights prosecutions, military jurisdiction over state crimes, was eroded. Gradual displacement of the military criminal code produced an increase in the number of human rights prosecutions for close to 20 years.

Afterword: Transitional Justice Laws and the Peace Accord

In recent years, human rights prosecutions were shaped by a growing number of transitional justice laws in Colombia. For example, Law 1424 of 2010 established parameters for establishing non-judicial mechanisms for the creation of truth and historical memory and it placed limits on the information gathered through these proceedings that could be later used in a criminal proceeding. The Legal Framework for Peace (Legislative Act 01 of 2012) initiated a system of selectivity and case prioritization so that patterns of violations could be identified and the persons most responsible for grave violations would be held to account.[108] When peace negotiations between the government and the FARC commenced in 2012, early on, the government appeared to be showing its hand concerning how justice would be considered in a peace accord. The sentiment within the peace talks on matters of justice was largely compromise, negotiation, inclusion, and stability. In September 23, 2015, an agreement issued by the FARC and the Santos government, established five to eight-year penalties (not to include prison time) for those who confessed to serious violent crimes.[109]

The Colombian government and the FARC finalized a peace agreement in the fall of 2016, and following a narrowly defeated referendum on the accord, Congress passed a revised agreement in November 2016. Peace talks between the government and the ELN have experienced fits and starts, but they remain ongoing. Despite the comprehensiveness of the 2016 agreement and extensive demobilization efforts since the accord was brokered, grave violations continue in Colombia. Targeted violence against indigenous and Afro-descendant communities has been particularly high and several activists have been killed. As transitional justice theories and empirics on post-conflict transitions demonstrate, the future of judicial accountability in Colombia will be significantly shaped by the terms of the peace accord. Point five of the peace accord outlines provisions for a truth, justice, reparation, and non-repetition system, which includes a Special Peace Jurisdiction as the main judicial mechanism. In November 2017, a law to implement the Special Peace Jurisdiction was passed by Congress. Within this system, 3491 ex-guerillas and 1714 current and former members of the security forces have indicated their willingness to be tried.[110] The extent to which state violations will be adequately handled by this court, however, has been called into question. For example, the implementing law does not yet specify the sanctions war criminals will receive, and the already identified leniency and flexibility of the five to eight-year penalties for the most serious crimes has created tremendous controversy. Additionally, the dilution of the command responsibility definition in the Special Peace Jurisdiction Law may allow several leaders of the armed forces to evade judicial accountability. This may incite interference from the International Criminal Court, which would act if this provision in the law is seen to violate language in the Rome Statute. Finally, the status of false positive cases in the Jurisdiction remains unclear and third-party civilians, including landowners, politicians, or members of organized crime groups, may not be compelled to appear in this court, despite the fact that the JPL confessions produced information on approximately 13,000 non-combatants who aided and abetted serious human rights violations.[111]

The findings in this chapter illuminate a few key factors when considering the future of judicial accountability in Colombia. First, emergency institutions do not necessarily fade after peace is brokered. Sri Lanka and Northern Ireland illustrate this reality in that criminal justice processes in both cases continue to be affected by crisis laws and the powers these laws afford security personnel. If the military criminal code remains unchanged from its current form, its legacy may continue to weigh heavily on both citizens' perceptions of government accountability and future judicial proceedings in the ordinary criminal justice system. Second, the pushback from the security apparatus on the extent to which their own senior officers will be held to account continues in the design and implementation of the Special Jurisdiction for Peace. Weakened language on command responsibility, and its relationship to requirements within the Rome Statute, resulted from pressure on the part of members of the security apparatus during the final phases of the peace accord.[112] Thus, it is likely that human rights prosecutions in the ordinary criminal justice system and in the Special Jurisdiction for Peace will continue to be shaped by the emergency institution. Historical conceptions of government culpability and accountability, and subsequent iterations within the military criminal code, reverberate in justice processes today.

Notes

1. Interview with Eduardo Carreña Wilches, Bogotá, Colombia, May 2015.
2. Interview 27, Bogotá, Colombia, June 2015.
3. Interview 30 (Phone), August 2015.
4. Tate, Winifred. *Counting the Dead: The Culture and Politics of Human Rights Activism in Colombia*. Berkeley: University of California Press (2007), 37–38.
5. Dix, Robert H. *The Politics of Colombia*. New York: Praeger Publishers (1987), 39–40.
6. Dix, 95.
7. Dix, 49.
8. Tate, 40.
9. Tate, 51–52.
10. Gallón, Gustavo. Human Rights: A Path to Democracy and Peace in Colombia, in Christopher Welna and Gustavo Gallón, eds., *Peace, Democracy and Human Rights in Colombia*. Notre Dame, IN: University of Notre Dame Press (2007), 362.
11. Inter-American Commission on Human Rights (1999). Colombia Country Report, Chapter V, Administration of Justice and Rule of Law, para 68.
12. Gallón (2007, 364).
13. Guembe, Maria José and Helena Olea. No justice, no peace: Discussion of a legal framework regarding the demobilization of non-state armed groups in Colombia, in Naomi Roht-Arriaza and Javier Mariezcurrena, eds., *Transitional Justice in the Twenty-First Century*. New York: Cambridge University Press (2006), 124.

14. Osterling, Jorge Pablo. *Democracy in Colombia: Clientelist Politics and Guerilla Warfare.* New Brunswick: Transaction Publishers (1989), 56–57.
15. Uprimny, Rodrigo. The Constitutional Court and Control of Presidential Extraordinary Powers in Colombia, in Siri Gloppen, Roberto Gargarella and Elin Skaar, eds., *Democratization and the Judiciary: The Accountability Function of Courts in New Democracies.* London: Frank Cass Publishers (2004), 62.
16. Pahl, Michael R. Wanted: Criminal Justice – Colombia's Adoption of a Prosecutorial System of Criminal Procedure, *Fordham International Law Journal* 16(3) (1992), 618.
17. Pahl, 628.
18. Pahl (1992).
19. Pahl (1992).
20. Uprimny (2004, 51).
21. See discussion of Decreto 007 in Gustavo Gallón, *Quince Años de Estado de Sitio en Colombia, 1958–1978.* Bogotá: Libreria y Editorial American Latina (1979).
22. Andreu-Guzmán, Federico. 2006. Military Jurisdiction and International Law: Military Courts and Gross Human Rights Violations (Vol. 1). International Commission of Jurists/Colombian Commission of Jurists, 222.
23. Andreu-Guzmán, 223.
24. See discussion below on key rulings by the Constitutional Court that sought to establish certain offenses, namely serious human rights violations, as unrelated to "service."
25. Andreu-Guzmán, 223.
26. Andreu-Guzmán, 223.
27. Umaña Luna, Eduardo. 1962. Factores Socio-Jurídicos de la Impunidad, in Germán Guzmán, Orlando Fals Borda, Eduardo Umaña Luna, eds., *La Violencia en Colombia: Estudio de un Proceso Social (Tomo I)*, 383–384.
28. Andreu-Guzmán, 230.
29. Scheuerman, William E. "Emergency Powers." *Annual Review of Law and Social Science* 2 (2006): 257–277.
30. Uprimny (2004, 54).
31. Uprimny (2004, 55).
32. Andreu-Guzmán, 241.
33. Andreu-Guzmán, 242.
34. Procuraduría General de la Nación (1993–1994), cited in Andreu-Guzmán, 231.

35. Cepeda, Manuel José. Democracy, State and Society in the 1991 Constitution: The Role of the Constitutional Court, in Eduardo Posada-Carbó, ed., *Colombia: The Politics of Reforming the State*. New York: St. Martin's Press (1998), 72.
36. Constitución de 1991 (Colombia).
37. Inter-American Commission on Human Rights (1999, para 74).
38. Constitución de (1991).
39. Pizarro, Eduardo and Ana María Bejarano. Political Reform After 1991: What Still Needs to Be Reformed? in Christopher Welna and Gustavo Gallón, eds., *Peace, Democracy and Human Rights in Colombia*. Notre Dame, IN: University of Notre Dame Press (2007), 182–183.
40. Dix, 177–178; Posada-Carbó, Eduardo, ed. *Colombia: The Politics of Reforming the State*. New York: St. Martin's Press (1998), 54–55.
41. Posada-Carbó, 59.
42. Constitución de (1991).
43. Posada-Carbó, 61.
44. Uprimny (2004, 61).
45. Constitución de (1991).
46. See Article 242, paras 1 and 2 of the Constitución.
47. A 1995 petition was submitted by the Defensor del Pueblo, or Defender of the People. The Defensor is an independent Ombudsperson who is tasked with advocating for citizen rights. See further discussion of this petition below.
48. Tate, 118.
49. Simmons, Beth. *Mobilizing for Human Rights: International Law in Domestic Politics*. New York: Cambridge University Press (2009), 119.
50. See Article 214, para 6, Constitucíon de (1991).
51. Uprimny (2004, 55).
52. García-Villegas, cited in Uprimny (2004, 55).
53. Sentencia C-141/95. The Constitutional Court of Colombia, 1.
54. Inter-American Commission on Human Rights (1999), Ch V, para 21; Andreu-Guzmán, 232.
55. Sentencia C-578/95. The Constitutional Court of Colombia, 5.
56. Sentencia C-578/95, 6–7.
57. Andreu-Guzman, 245.
58. Sentencia C-578/95, 1.
59. Andreu-Guzmán, 234.
60. Inter-American Commission on Human Rights (1999), Chapter V, paras 38–39.
61. Sentencia C-358/97. The Constitutional Court of Colombia.
62. Inter-American Commission on Human Rights (2013). Colombia Country Report, 167; Andreu-Guzmán, 246.

63. Sentencia C-145/98. The Constitutional Court of Colombia, 6.
64. Andreu-Guzmàn, 234.
65. Inter-American Commission on Human Rights (1999), Chapter V, para 43.
66. Andreu-Guzmán, 239–240.
67. The discussion on CSJ rulings and transfers from the military courts to ordinary courts is based on data included in U.S. State Department Human Rights Reports from 2000 to 2014.
68. Annual Human Rights Reports Submitted to Congress by the U.S. Department of State: Colombia. 2000.
69. Andrea Torres (Bautista's niece), a lawyer, put together an action for review of the Nydia Bautista case in 2015 and she is attempting to have the case reopened. See: http://pbicolombia.org/2015/01/28/andrea-torres-bautista-is-the-legal-coordinator-for-nydia-erika-bautista-foundation-in-the-coming-months-andrea-will-travel-to-spain-to-tell-the-foundations-story-and-the-story-of-how-her/
70. Annual Human Rights Reports Submitted to Congress by the U.S. Department of State: Colombia. 2000; 2001; 2002.
71. Annual Human Rights Reports Submitted to Congress by the U.S. Department of State: Colombia. 2003.
72. Inter-American Commission on Human Rights (2013, 169).
73. Some of the human rights prosecutions that transpired in the mid-2000s result from the accumulation of rulings on military vs. ordinary jurisdiction, while others emanate from the 2005 Justice and Peace Law. The latter conditions are discussed in the section on human rights prosecution data.
74. Gallón (2007, 387).
75. Sentencia C-816/04.
76. Human Rights Watch. "Colombia: Withdraw Military Jurisdiction Expansion Bill" (July 8, 2014).
77. Inter-American Commission on Human Rights (2013, 171).
78. Sentencia C-754/13; Inter-American Commission on Human Rights (2013, 184).
79. Interview 27, Bogotá, Colombia, June 2015; Interview 29 (Phone), June 2015.
80. Human Rights Watch (2014).
81. Amnesty International. Public Statement. AMR 23/1854/2015 (June 12, 2015). Colombia: Reform of Article 221 of the Political Constitution on jurisdiction of military courts threatens to exacerbate impunity.
82. Interview with Gustavo Gallón, Bogotá, Colombia, June 2015.
83. For example, the Office of the High Commission of Human Rights reported in 2013 that several false positive cases were transferred to the military courts by the CSJ while Legislative Act 02 of 2012 was in effect. This Act was in effect for less than a year.

84. Colombian Commission of Jurists. Sentencia sobre fuero penal militar: un compromiso irrestricto de la Corte Constitucional con los derechos humanos. February 2016.
85. Int. Gallón (2015).
86. Prosecution data is based on annual U.S. State Department Country Reports on Human Rights from 1976 to 2014, and additional case details are drawn from local newspaper articles, Fiscalía reports and reports from Colombian and international organizations.
87. The prosecution rate is calculated by dividing the number of civilian deaths investigated through human rights prosecutions by the total number of civilian deaths caused by the state. The number of civilian deaths caused by the state is based on the data from the Basta Ya! Colombia Report (2013). The total includes 11,302 civilian deaths due to selective assassination by armed forces and paramilitary factions, and 8135 civilian deaths due to massacres by armed forces and paramilitary factions occurring between 1981 and 2012. See statistics compiled by this report at: http://www.centrodememoriahistorica.gov.co/micrositios/informeGeneral/estadisticas.html
88. Human Rights Watch World Report. 1997. Colombia.
89. Annual Human Rights Reports Submitted to Congress by the U.S. Department of State: Colombia. 2006.
90. See the July 5, 2004, ruling in the *"19 Merchants" (Alvaro Lobo Pacheco and others v. Republic of Colombia)* case: http://www.corteidh.or.cr/cf/Jurisprudencia2/busqueda_casos_contenciosos.cfm?lang=en
91. Annual Human Rights Reports Submitted to Congress by the U.S. Department of State: Colombia. 2001.
92. Sentencia SU-1184/01. The Constitutional Court of Colombia.
93. Sentencia SU-1184/01, 3–4.
94. Sentencia SU-1184/01; Andreu-Guzmàn, 247.
95. Andreu-Guzmán, 247.
96. Annual Human Rights Reports Submitted to Congress by the U.S. Department of State: Colombia. 2007.
97. Annual Human Rights Reports Submitted to Congress by the U.S. Department of State: Colombia. 2009.
98. Annual Human Rights Reports Submitted to Congress by the U.S. Department of State: Colombia. 2014
99. Inter-American Commission on Human Rights, Report No. 94/14, Petition 623–03. Admissibility. Jaime Humberto Uscátegui Ramírez and family members. Colombia. November 6, 2014.
100. Colombian Commission of Jurists. 2004. En contravía de las recomendaciones internacionales: "Seguridad democrática," derechos humanos y derechos humanitario en Colombia: Agosto de 2002 a Agosto de 2004.
101. Annual Human Rights Reports Submitted to Congress by the U.S. Department of State: Colombia. 2009.

102. Guembe and Olea, 127–130.
103. Inter-American Commission on Human Rights (2013, 130).
104. Inter-American Commission on Human Rights (2013, 132).
105. Annual Human Rights Reports Submitted to Congress by the U.S. Department of State: Colombia. 2005–2011.
106. Inter-American Commission on Human Rights (2013, 134).
107. Inter-American Commission on Human Rights (2013, 141).
108. Inter-American Commission on Human Rights (2013, 148–149).
109. Human Rights Watch. "Colombia: Dealing Away Justice, Government, FARC Agree to No Prison Time for Atrocities" (September 28, 2015).
110. Isacson, Adam. "Rescuing Colombia's Post-Conflict Transitional Justice System." Washington Office on Latin America. November 29, 2017.
111. Isacson, Adam (2017).
112. Isacson, Adam (2017).

Bibliography

Amnesty International. Public Statement. AMR 23/1854/2015. 2015. Colombia: Reform of Article 221 of the Political Constitution on Jurisdiction of Military Courts Threatens to Exacerbate Impunity, June 12.

Andreu-Guzmán, Federico. 2006. *Military Jurisdiction and International Law: Military Courts and Gross Human Rights Violations*. Vol. 1. Geneva: International Commission of Jurists/Colombian Commission of Jurists.

Annual Human Rights Reports Submitted to Congress by the U.S. Department of State: Colombia. 2000.

Annual Human Rights Reports Submitted to Congress by the U.S. Department of State: Colombia. 2001.

Annual Human Rights Reports Submitted to Congress by the U.S. Department of State: Colombia. 2002.

Annual Human Rights Reports Submitted to Congress by the U.S. Department of State: Colombia. 2003.

Annual Human Rights Reports Submitted to Congress by the U.S. Department of State: Colombia. 2006.

Annual Human Rights Reports Submitted to Congress by the U.S. Department of State: Colombia. 2007.

Basta Ya! Colombia: Memorias de Guerra y Dignidad. 2013. Grupo de Memoria Histórica.

Cepeda, Manuel José. 1998. Democracy, State and Society in the 1991 Constitution: The Role of the Constitutional Court. In *Colombia: The Politics of Reforming the State*, ed. Eduardo Posada-Carbó. New York: St. Martin's Press.

Colombian Commission of Jurists. 2004. En contravía de las recomendaciones internacionales: "Seguridad democrática," derechos humanos y derechos humanitario en Colombia: Agosto de 2002 a Agosto de 2004.

———. 2016. Sentencia sobre fuero penal militar: un compromiso irrestricto de la Corte Constitucional con los derechos humanos, February.

Constitución de. 1991. English Translation. Available at: https://constituteproject.org/

Dix, Robert H. 1987. *The Politics of Colombia*. New York: Praeger Publishers.

Gallón, Gustavo. 2007. Human Rights: A Path to Democracy and Peace in Colombia. In *Peace, Democracy and Human Rights in Colombia*, ed. Christopher Welna and Gustavo Gallón. Notre Dame: University of Notre Dame Press.

Guembe, Maria José, and Helena Olea. 2006. No Justice, No Peace: Discussion of a Legal Framework Regarding the Demobilization of Non-state Armed Groups in Colombia. In *Transitional Justice in the Twenty-First Century*, ed. Naomi Roht-Arriaza and Javier Mariezcurrena. New York: Cambridge University Press.

Human Rights Watch. 2014. Colombia: Withdraw Military Jurisdiction Expansion Bill, July 8.

———. 2015. Colombia: Dealing Away Justice, Government, FARC Agree to No Prison Time for Atrocities, September 28.

Human Rights Watch World Report. 1997. Colombia.

Inter-American Commission on Human Rights. 1999. Colombia Country Report, Chapter V, Administration of Justice and Rule of Law.

Inter-American Commission on Human Rights. 2013. Colombia Country Report.

Inter-American Commission on Human Rights, Report No. 94/14, Petition 623-03. Admissibility. Jaime Humberto Uscátegui Ramírez and family members. Colombia. November 6, 2014.

Interview 27, Bogotá, Colombia, June 2015.

Interview 29 (Phone), June 2015.

Interview 30 (Phone), August 2015.

Interview with Eduardo Carreña Wilches, Bogotá, Colombia, May 2015.

Interview with Gustavo Gallón, Bogotá, Colombia, June 2015.

Isacson, Adam. 2017. Rescuing Colombia's Post-Conflict Transitional Justice System. Washington Office on Latin America, November 29. Available: https://www.wola.org/analysis/colombias-post-conflict-justice-framework-remains-vague-becoming-less-fair/

Osterling, Jorge Pablo. 1989. *Democracy in Colombia: Clientelist Politics and Guerilla Warfare*. New Brunswick: Transaction Publishers.

Pahl, Michael R. 1992. Wanted: Criminal Justice – Colombia's Adoption of a Prosecutorial System of Criminal Procedure. *Fordham International Law Journal* 16 (3): 608–634.

Pizarro, Eduardo, and Ana Maríae Bejarano. 2007. Political Reform After 1991: What Still Needs to Be Reformed? In *Peace, Democracy and Human Rights in Colombia*, ed. Christopher Welna and Gustavo Gallón. Notre Dame: University of Notre Dame Press.

Posada-Carbó, Eduardo, ed. 1998. *Colombia: The Politics of Reforming the State.* New York: St. Martin's Press.

Sentencia C-141/95. The Constitutional Court of Colombia.

Sentencia C-145/98. The Constitutional Court of Colombia.

Sentencia C-358/97. The Constitutional Court of Colombia.

Sentencia C-578/95. The Constitutional Court of Colombia.

Sentencia C-754/13. The Constitutional Court of Colombia.

Sentencia C-816/04. The Constitutional Court of Colombia.

Sentencia SU-1184/01. The Constitutional Court of Colombia.

Simmons, Beth. 2009. *Mobilizing for Human Rights: International Law in Domestic Politics.* New York: Cambridge University Press.

Tate, Winifred. 2007. *Counting the Dead: The Culture and Politics of Human Rights Activism in Colombia.* Berkeley: University of California Press.

Umaña Luna, Eduardo. 1962. Factores Socio-Jurídicos de la Impunidad, in Germán Guzmán, Orlando Fals Borda, Eduardo Umaña Luna, *La Violencia en Colombia: Estudio de un Proceso Social (Tomo I).*

Uprimny, Rodrigo. 2004. The Constitutional Court and Control of Presidential Extraordinary Powers in Colombia. In *Democratization and the Judiciary: The Accountability Function of Courts in New Democracies*, ed. Siri Gloppen, Roberto Gargarella, and Elin Skaar. London: Frank Cass Publishers.

CHAPTER 6

Human Rights Prosecutions and Democracies at War in Comparative Perspective

On July 19, 2014, the *New York Times* published an article detailing the horrific rape and murder in 2004 of a young woman, Thangjam Manorama, in Manipur State, India. Though members of the Indian military were allegedly responsible, ten years after the crime, no one had been charged. Community members, activists, and lawyers argued that this was the result of one single factor: "a colonial-era law in effect in India's periphery that gives blanket immunity from prosecution in civilian courts to Indian soldiers for all crimes, including rape."[1] This crime, and many others like it, occurred within one of the oldest democracies in the world, where there is no shortage of human rights institutions. And yet, the law cited by these citizens, known as the Armed Forces Special Powers Act, remains in place today. This book demonstrates that the incident in India is not anomalous. Human rights prosecutions in democracies at war are intimately connected to the creation, oversight, and enforcement of emergency institutions. Any hope for prosecutions was dependent on the extent to which the core logic of impunity was challenged, altered, or removed, by agents of change. Though emergency laws have been identified as central in fostering human rights abuses during conflicts, there has been little comparative investigation of how these laws protect state actors and produce acts of resistance by those who suffer under them.

The possibility for state actors to be held accountable through human rights prosecutions in democracies at war is shaped by the extent to which

M. Lynch, *Human Rights Prosecutions in Democracies at War*,
Human Rights Interventions,
https://doi.org/10.1007/978-3-319-96908-4_6

agents of change, including citizens, human rights NGOs, and political actors, were able to challenge, alter, or eliminate the emergency institution. Challenges to the emergency institution were made possible through four specific factors: independent oversight of executive emergency powers, judicial review of emergency laws, judicial independence, and access to regional human rights courts. Three forms of institutional change resulted from these conditions: layering, conversion, and gradual displacement. Institutional continuity in Sri Lanka emerged because there were few avenues for citizens or other actors to challenge the logic of impunity in the emergency and anti-terrorism laws. In Northern Ireland, while layering challenged the logic of impunity, it did not eliminate it altogether from the emergency institution and the conversion of inquest laws into ordinary legislation precluded hundreds of human rights investigations. Conversion placed a greater number of restrictions on human rights prosecutions in Spain. As opposed to one part of the emergency institution (inquest clauses in Northern Ireland), all of the incommunicado provisions in the anti-terrorism laws were folded into ordinary legislation in the early years of Spanish democracy. Colombia experienced the highest prosecution rate compared to the other cases as a result of gradual displacement of the military criminal code, which has limited state violation cases to military courts.

The following is a discussion of the theoretical and substantive implications of the book's findings. This chapter not only presents evidence-based conclusions about the patterns of human rights prosecutions in these cases, it also provides essential guidance for future research on countries that are experiencing both an emergency institution and citizen demands for judicial accountability.

Legal Mobilization to Challenge the Emergency Institution

Citizens pursued human rights prosecutions in all four cases. The findings of this book demonstrate, however, that this was not the only strategy employed to challenge impunity. In the two cases where rates of prosecution were highest, Northern Ireland and Colombia, citizens also pursued legal challenges to the apparatus promoting impunity: the emergency institution. This form of legal mobilization is significant in that it created openings for justice that were not available in Sri Lanka and Spain. Two key factors enabled citizens to engage in this form of litigation: the Constitutional Court in Colombia had a mandate to review challenges to emergency laws and, in the absence of local judicial review mechanisms, citizens in Northern Ireland went to the European Court of Human Rights. In both cases, levels of human rights prosecutions were raised because litigation was not solely pursued to secure a conviction in a court of law. It was also used as a political strategy, "with the power to inspire rule revision."[2] Various actors challenged the logic of impunity within the emergency institution at the courts as a means to amend or abolish the rules. Legal mobilization to challenge the emergency institutions in Northern Ireland and Colombia was strengthened by the fact that citizens not only had the capabilities to pursue these forms of legal challenge, they also had access to international human rights law in making their claims. Human rights treaties have the potential to raise the expectation among mobilizing citizens that their efforts will be successful because if international human rights law can be cited in a legal case against the state, victims and their families may have more leverage than they would have relying on domestic criminal law alone.[3] Though the European Convention on Human Rights was not accessible to citizens in local courts in Northern Ireland, key clauses within the convention strengthened arguments that citizens made at Strasbourg concerning abuse of emergency powers. In Colombia, citizens and leaders of human rights organizations cited international human rights law in their petitions to the Constitutional Court concerning unconstitutional aspects of the military criminal code. This persuaded the Court to strike down clauses in several cases.

The opportunity for citizens to challenge the emergency institution in Northern Ireland and Colombia provided them with an additional strategy for holding state actors accountable. A comparison of citizen capabilities in these two countries reveals that, while access to the European Court of Human Rights was important for citizens in Northern Ireland, regional human rights courts remain limited in the impact they can have on domestic level accountability outcomes.

The Impact of Regional Human Rights Courts on Domestic Prosecutions

Why did regional human rights courts not play as significant of a role in challenges to the emergency institution in Spain and Colombia? The Northern Ireland case is notable in that citizens brought cases concerning state violations quite early in the Court's life span and in the first few years of the conflict. We might expect that Spain would display a similar pattern, but this is not the case. A small number of cases were brought to Strasbourg concerning human rights violations related to the Basque conflict, but most of these were heard in the 2000s. Thus, pressure from European Court cases on the Spanish government to "clean up" investigations or to revise clauses in anti-terrorism laws does not figure here as it did in the Northern Ireland case. A few key factors are important. In part, Spain's later entry to the Council of Europe (1977) and ratification of the European Convention on Human Rights (1979) provides some clarification. Ratification of the European Convention on Human Rights (ECHR) placed Spain within the jurisdiction of the Court when its democratic constitution was only one year old. Spain's status as a young democracy and new to the Court is significant because it meant that the democratic legal culture in the country was relatively immature, particularly when compared to the United Kingdom. The United Kingdom had been in the Court's jurisdiction for two decades by the time the conflict in Northern Ireland erupted. Thus, as one human rights attorney explained to me, many Spaniards obtaining a law degree in the 1980s or before did not have training in the European Convention on Human Rights or the Court in Strasbourg.[4] The fact that the Court only uses French and English was an additional barrier for Spanish citizens.[5] There is evidence in recent years that Basques, in particular, view the European Court as an additional tool for challenging the Spanish state. The number of torture cases has gradually risen and in most of the cases the Court has ruled in favor of the applicants. Given the historical challenges of seeking accountability for ill-treatment and torture cases in domestic courts, the Court is now seen as an essential resource.

In Colombia, the Inter-American Commission on Human Rights has played a very active role in critiquing Colombia's judicial system, specifically, the issue of military jurisdiction over human rights cases, and the Court has considered several individual cases of serious violence. Colombia ratified the Inter-American Convention on Human Rights in 1973 and recognized the Court in 1985. Yet, the first ruling on state violence was not issued until ten years later in 1995. While several cases involving high levels of state violence followed this moment and continue today, the Court's investigation prompted a domestic trial or a reopening of an investigation in only a handful of instances. For example, after the Court ruled in 2007 that the state was responsible for human rights violations that occurred in the massacre at La Rochela in 1989, the Fiscalía reopened the case for investigation in 2009. Similarly, in 2004, the Court ruled that paramilitaries were responsible for a 1987 massacre (known as the "19 Merchants" case) and that the state had colluded with the paramilitary actors in the commission of the crime as well as obstructing justice. After this ruling, the Uribe government asked the Supreme Court in 2005 to review its decision on the case.[6]

Many of the cases of state violence heard by the Court were extremely drawn out at the Inter-American Court of Human Rights. While in theory the Court's investigation of a case may have prompted judicial action in local courts, the actual rulings can have more force in that they may explicitly demand that the government continue ongoing judicial proceedings on the matter, start new proceedings, or work to ensure an impartial trial process. Thus, while the Court was important in shaping the trajectory of a few human rights cases in local courts, it did not wield influence in the majority of domestic prosecution efforts. Additionally, unlike the role of the European Court in the Northern Ireland case, the Court did not receive legal challenges to the emergency institution because a strong local judicial review mechanism, the Constitutional Court, was in place.

Judicial Review Is Not Enough: The Role of Positive and Negative Judicial Independence

Colombia's experience of gradual displacement signals the impact of local judicial review mechanisms on prosecution patterns. Citizens are empowered, through constitutional clauses, to petition a court regarding a powerful legal apparatus. But, gradual displacement of the military criminal code would not have been possible without the presence of positive and negative judicial independence. The Constitutional Court was empowered to be autonomous through constitutional provisions, but unless judges exhibited positive judicial independence, or the consistent willingness to generate rulings that countered the executive's will, it is unlikely that the emergency institution would have been seriously challenged. It is the combination of both forms of judicial independence that made it possible for the judicial sector to scrutinize the logic of impunity within the emergency institution over a period of time. Notably, Colombia's record of positive and negative judicial independence is variable. Prior to the creation of the Constitutional Court in 1991, the Supreme Court appeared fairly unwilling, with the exception of a few cases, to challenge the military's jurisdictional control over human rights cases. The Constitutional Court's first ten years display a remarkable departure from this legacy and much of this can be explained by who was appointed to the Court and the fact that the Court was armed with upholding a new set of progressive rights. But politics is not completely absent from the Court's performance. Since 2000, increasing numbers of judges that were less willing to challenge the government on military jurisdiction were appointed to the bench. This is reflected in Court rulings that display a bit more reticence. In some rulings, the Court accepted the military's shift in discourse, specifically the employment of international humanitarian law as a framework, and in other rulings, it qualified the military's arguments. Though citizens retain the right to challenge emergency laws, judicial interpretations of their petitions will likely continue to be somewhat unpredictable.

The legal reforms created during the democratic transition in Spain facilitated high levels of judicial independence. If incommunicado detention had not been increasingly normalized in ordinary law, and it had remained within crisis laws, it is possible that this practice would have been subject to greater judicial scrutiny. Conversion, in effect, created a stranglehold on existing judicial review procedures. The absence of judicial independence was most deeply felt in Northern Ireland and Sri Lanka. In the former, some judges were clearly attempting to consider the implications of a shoot to kill policy on citizens' rights. The legacy of the emergency institution and the largely Protestant composition of the local courts, however, proved too powerful. In Sri Lanka, control of the judiciary by the executive was much more direct. Though the 1978 Constitution stipulated that emergency regulations could not violate constitutional rights, which prompted a few significant cases in the 1980s and 1990s, the tide turned when, beginning in 1999, the Supreme Court was led by a Chief Justice intent on stifling dissent and removing any judge that disagreed with the executive.

Institutional Change and Human Rights Prosecutions

The empirical evidence demonstrates that gradual displacement produced the highest levels of human rights prosecutions. Gradual displacement of the emergency institution in Colombia illuminates that local judicial review mechanisms and high levels of judicial independence are more powerful than independent oversight of the executive alone. Even where oversight procedures are put in place through constitutional or other legal provisions, rubberstamping is common and indeed it was a barrier in all four cases concerning the creation and passage of emergency legislation.

Layering was the most common form of institutional change across the cases for the simple reason that crisis laws are often subject to debate and revision via parliamentary rules and judicial review mechanisms. Layering produced relatively low levels of human rights prosecutions because rule revision failed to eliminate the logic of impunity. In both Northern Ireland and Spain, rubberstamping via parliamentary oversight procedures made it difficult for significant alterations to occur. Additionally, though emergency laws considered at the European Court of Human Rights produced key moments of layering in the Northern Ireland case, the Court placed a tremendous amount of confidence in the British government during the conflict years. As a result, revisions to the logic of impunity were often shallow.

Evidence of conversion in democracies at war reveals a few significant findings about the relationship between emergency laws and human rights prosecutions. Change agents are not only those who aim to eliminate the emergency institution. Governments can also engage in institutional change to defend the status quo and deflect judicial scrutiny. Converting emergency legislation into ordinary laws was a strategic weapon for political actors in Northern Ireland and Spain. This finding, in particular, has import for conclusions about models of emergency law.

Models of Emergency Law

Models of emergency rule provide frameworks for how to consider government accountability when an executive possesses emergency powers and is at risk of abusing them. Constitutional relativism, the extralegal model, common law emergency oversight, and legal formalism each fall short in explaining democracies at war in that they miss several key elements of the diverse political contexts in which these frameworks tend to operate. There is also a tendency to consider these models in isolation from one another. The empirical findings from Sri Lanka, Northern Ireland, Spain, and Colombia, and the comparative findings discussed above, provide several key insights on the conditions that fostered prosecutions and how features across the models worked in tandem to create openings for justice.

First, the emphasis on judicial review within the common law emergency oversight model suffers from a narrow understanding of what judges are capable of in a volatile conflict environment and the limits of constitutional design. While judicial oversight of emergency legislation by Colombia's Constitutional Court was a central condition for improving the likelihood that human rights cases would be heard in civilian courts as opposed to military courts, in Sri Lanka, judicial actors were disempowered by the constitution to consider serious violations. Though Supreme Court judges in Sri Lanka could, for a time, rule on aspects of emergency legislation, they were limited in that they could only consider rights enshrined in the constitution; the right to life and a right to a judicial remedy are not included in the constitution. The model's assumption that judges are often protected from political pressures in common law regimes and can therefore engage with controversial decisions with little fear or concern[7] also does not hold up in the Sri Lankan case. Presidents regularly stacked the courts with their allies and when a few judges went against the grain, they were swiftly transferred off the Supreme Court. In contrast, in Colombia, the 1991 Constitution granted a highly progressive mandate to judges on the Constitutional Court. Additionally, because emergency laws had been subject to judicial review in the past (via the Supreme Court), scrutiny was normalized and encouraged when the Constitutional Court was newly tasked with this mandate.

The common law model also does not account for how judicial bodies may be disempowered or heavily pressured at some moments during a crisis and at other times quite activist. This can produce inconsistent records of judicial review over time, which, in turn, means irregular checks on government abuse. For example, in Colombia, the Supreme Court was fairly lenient toward the executive in its review of emergency laws during the 1980s. This changed after the 1991 Constitution when the Constitutional Court was tasked with a progressive agenda and a new set of rights to uphold. The empirical findings from the cases indicate that, given some of the limitations of judicial review, both positive and negative judicial independence must also be present in order for oversight to be effective and sustainable.

Second, the common law emergency oversight model misses the reality that if judicial actors are largely only able to engage in ex post facto review of emergency legislation, the disastrous impacts on accountability will have long since passed. The Northern Ireland case exemplifies this point. In a context in which victims and their families had no recourse to a local judicial review mechanism, the European Court of Human Rights emerged as the central arena for debates and rulings on emergency law and its impact on accountability. The pace of proceedings at a regional human rights court is painfully slow and the Northern Ireland chapter demonstrates how some cases involving emergency rule in the 1980s were not considered by the Court until the mid-2000s. As a result, there was little immediate change to the logic of impunity stemming from European Court rulings.

Third, empirical evidence from the four cases lends support to the legal formalist model, which argues for the creation of ex ante guidelines within constitutional provisions to constrain executive power during an emergency. In Colombia, key provisions within the 1991 Constitution enabled judicial review to be a strong force for human rights prosecutions. The Constitutional Court was granted the power to review every state of emergency declaration and subsequent emergency decrees within one day of their announcement by the executive. It could nullify the declaration and it did on several occasions. This prevented the possibility that the Court would only be reviewing emergency measures several years after the fact. Further, the Colombian Constitution gave the Court the power to review and challenge past emergency measures, and though this was ex post facto review, it produced some of the most significant changes to the military criminal code. Finally, as the Colombian chapter makes evident, the constitutional right for citizens to bring petitions challenging emergency laws to the Constitutional Court, was an essential component to the judicial review process that was not present in the other cases, either because citizens did not have access to such rights within their country's constitutions (Spain and Sri Lanka), or because there were simply no constitutional rights to access (Northern Ireland). Notably, in the early years of Spain's democracy, when it became evident that public prosecutors were not going to investigate police use of ill-treatment and torture against suspected Euskadi Ta Askatasuna (ETA) detainees, Basque citizens largely drew on a constitutional right to a private prosecutor to make claims against the state. Though Spanish citizens were not empowered to challenge the emergency institution to combat impunity in torture cases, they drew on other constitutional rights to achieve this goal.

One of the most consistent findings across the four cases was the problem of strong veto power in the hands of those who created and/or benefited from the emergency institution. Even where the executive was required to seek approval from parliament for emergency legislation, parliaments often acted as a rubberstamp for the laws. Ex ante constitutional provisions may in theory attend to this problem by requiring increasing majorities as emergency decrees are extended over time or by mandating the involvement of minority parties in oversight procedures.[8] The latter possibility, while potentially fruitful in some cases, would likely not have mattered in a case like Northern Ireland. The process of regular oversight meant that emergency laws were subject to fiercer scrutiny than traditional parliamentary debates. The Labour Party contributed lengthy recommendations each time oversight committees conducted a review of emergency laws. In the end, however, the reports tended to be quite restrained in their recommendations and they often deferred to the executive's (Conservative) belief that emergency laws were warranted and lawful. Additionally, though in some instances leaders of the oversight committees suggested significant reforms concerning impunity, as in the case of the Colville report, parliamentary debate transcripts demonstrate that arguments from the party in power tended to rule the day. Ex ante constitutional provisions that establish a stricter system of checks and balances by empowering judicial bodies to engage in review procedures beyond ex post facto mechanisms might assist in curbing the effects of rubberstamping.

Finally, the ways in which governments engaged in conversion signals the need for explicit ex ante restrictions on a government's ability to fold crisis laws into ordinary law at any time during or after the crisis period. Conversion was a central barrier in Spain and Northern Ireland because once this occurred, measures that had an enormous impact on human rights prosecutions, namely incommunicado detention and controls on the inquest process, were no longer subject to the same level of scrutiny reserved for crisis laws. Once crisis provisions became "ordinary," they became normalized and legitimized. Conversion reveals an important finding about emergency institutions in democracies at war: routine scrutiny, both internal and external, and the need to meet fairly high levels of legitimacy in governance, prompts governments to move their illegal actions further from the public's view, and to design legal protections for state actors. When emergency regulations on inquests received negative attention in Northern Ireland, similar provisions for controlling the process were transferred into ordinary legislation and they remained there for decades. In Spain, when incommunicado detention was folded into the Penal Code, ill-treatment of detainees became normalized and police treatment of detainees was no longer subject to judicial reviews.

Implications of the Findings for Democracies at War

The Colombian case provides essential insight for interpreting how ex ante constitutional provisions can enhance the prospects of human rights prosecutions in democracies engaged in war. However, it is by no means the book's conclusion that the rate of human rights prosecutions in Colombia is a mark of success. Though the ex ante constitutional guidelines empowered both citizens and the Constitutional Court to turn the tide on the matter of military jurisdiction, in the end, the battle between the military, the Court, the government and citizens, continues today. Thus, as opposed to presenting Colombia as a model to be emulated, the findings in this case illustrate that a higher number of human rights prosecutions may be achieved as a result of particular components of constitutional design. Empirical evidence from each of the cases demonstrate that the logic of impunity within emergency institutions can be challenged and even abolished if ex ante constitutional provisions include the following measures: judicial review mechanisms to evaluate emergency declarations and emergency and anti-terrorism laws put in place during a crisis; the right for citizens to petition the judicial review body; provisions ensuring both positive and negative forms of judicial independence; prohibitions on transferring emergency laws into ordinary legislation.

The landscape of human rights prosecutions in democracies at war is unique from other conflict cases. Given their standing in the international community and their multiple obligations to international human rights laws, the governments in these countries are participants in highly visible and closely monitored conflicts. This produces a climate in which democratic governments go to great lengths to design and implement protection mechanisms in emergency and ordinary laws that shield state actors from judicial scrutiny. These strategies, and the agents of change that seek to challenge them, have not yet been recognized in a comparative sense as a common thread across democracies at war.

The findings in this book provide a road map for interpreting and analyzing similar cases. Both Israel and India have strong emergency institutions and legacies of impunity. It would therefore be fruitful to trace to what extent constitutional rights matter to prosecution efforts; whether there are ex ante constitutional provisions constraining the executive in times of emergency and supporting judicial independence; and whether there is evidence that administrations have incorporated emergency provisions into ordinary law as a means to avoid human rights prosecutions.

The conflicts in democracies at war are well documented; the patterns of human rights prosecutions are not. This book demonstrates why the story of judicial accountability in these cases must be amplified—if not only for those for whom it matters most, then also for what it reveals to us about the pursuit of justice in a violent democratic state.

Notes

1. Harris, Gardiner. "In Remote Corners of India, Immunity for Soldiers Who Kill and Rape Civilians," *The New York Times*, July 20, 2014.
2. Simmons, Beth. *Mobilizing for Human Rights: International Law in Domestic Politics.* New York: Cambridge University Press (2009), 114.
3. Simmons, 119.
4. Interview 18, Bilbao, Spain, 2010.
5. Yllera, Ignacio Sánchez. "La irrelevancia de la prueba ilícita en la jurisprudencia del Tribunal Europeo de Derechos Humanos." Paper presented at the Training Seminar for Public Prosecutors, Madrid, Spain, April 2012 (manuscript on file with the author).
6. Hillebrecht, Courtney. The Domestic Mechanisms of Compliance with International Human Rights Law: Case Studies from the Inter-American Human Rights System, *Human Rights Quarterly* 34(4) (2012): 959–985.
7. Scheuerman, William E. Emergency Powers. *Annual Review of Law and Social Science* 2 (2006), 267.
8. Scheuerman, 272.

Bibliography

Harris, Gardiner. 2014. In Remote Corners of India, Immunity for Soldiers Who Kill and Rape Civilians. *The New York Times*, July 20.

Hillebrecht, Courtney. 2012. The Domestic Mechanisms of Compliance with International Human Rights Law: Case Studies from the Inter-American Human Rights System. *Human Rights Quarterly* 34 (4): 959–985.

Interview 18, Bilbao, Spain 2010.

Scheuerman, William E. 2006. Emergency Powers. *Annual Review of Law and Social Science* 2: 257–277.

Simmons, Beth. 2009. *Mobilizing for Human Rights: International Law in Domestic Politics.* New York: Cambridge University Press.

Yllera, Ignacio Sánchez. 2012. *La irrelevancia de la prueba ilícita en la jurisprudencia del Tribunal Europeo de Derechos Humanos.* Paper Presented at the Training Seminar for Public Prosecutors, Madrid, April 2012 (Manuscript on File with the Author).

Index[1]

[1] Note: Page numbers followed by 'n' refer to notes.

M. Lynch, *Human Rights Prosecutions in Democracies at War*, Human Rights Interventions,
https://doi.org/10.1007/978-3-319-96908-4

The manufacturer's authorised representative in the EU is Springer Nature Customer Service Centre GmbH, Europaplatz 3, 69115 Heidelberg, Germany. If you have any concerns regarding our products, please contact ProductSafety@springernature.com

Printed and bound by CPI Group (UK) Ltd, Croydon, CR0 4YY
23/09/2026
02221545-0001